AN ILLUSTRATED HISTORY OF INTERIOR DECORATION

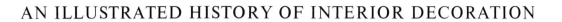

MARIO PRAZ

AN ILLUSTRATED HISTORY OF INTERIOR DECORATION

from Pompeii to Art Nouveau

THAMES AND HUDSON

Translated from the Italian *La filosofia dell'arredamento* by William Weaver

First published in Great Britain in hardcover in 1964
by Thames and Hudson Ltd, London
Reprinted 1982 and 1983

Published in hardcover in the United States of America in 1982
by Thames and Hudson Inc., 500 Fifth Avenue, New York, New York 10110

First paperback edition 1994

Library of Congress Catalog Card Card Number 94–61063

British Library Cataloguing-in-Publication Data

A catalogue record for this book is available from the British Library

ISBN 0-500-27815-6

Printed and bound in Italy

TABLE OF CONTENTS

TABLE OF CONTENTS

TABLE OF CONTENTS

for Goldi

Introduction

Our forefathers in the past (and in the present century, a few idlers in provincial cities, before war violated even the most remote places) used to spend their hours of leisure in pastimes as delightful as they were useless; and among these self-imposed tasks none perhaps was ever so singularly vain and pompous as the practice of writing didactic verses.

Many years ago I happened to be spending some torrid July days in the old library of a labyrinthine palazzo in Fano, setting in order the books collected by the great-grandfather of a relative of mine. The library had been formed around 1830, and the many volumes of theology, belles-lettres and art—among which Cicognara's *History of Sculpture* stood out—made a fine showing with their old tooled bindings in classical or Neo-Rococo style, on shelves surmounted by casts of statues in a plaster so fine that if you picked one up by the neck, the head came off in your hand and the rest crumbled to powder on the floor. At that time I happened upon a *Collection of Didactic Poems* in several volumes; from the very Proem, the reader was plunged into that profoundly bland atmosphere which, as I said above, continued to exist within the sleepy walls of our provincial cities until the blare of trumpets announced the recent Apocalypse. Among other things the Proem said: "Our Italy, to whom no one can deny first place in Epic and Lyric Poetry, has far surpassed all other Nations also in the quantity and the exquisite quality of those poetic compositions belonging to the Didactic school . . . Just as even the most austere Philosophy has never refused to join hands at times with the Muses, who instill in the heart an affectionate inclination towards the severity and purity of its disciplines, so the Epic, Tragic, and Lyric Poets have constantly, in all ages, treated every kind of argument, and have contributed to the perfecting of the philosophizing art . . . Truly in the Didactic Poem, the Philosopher finds food to nourish his thoughts and his inclinations, and the Scholar finds satisfying nourishment for his application. The Man-of-Letters can wander among beloved images, and even Young Men of good breeding and Ladies of culture in pleasant moments of leisure encounter, in the diversity of subjects, a congenial pastime thanks to the elegance of these verses." These poems sang of bees, the farm, gastronomy, the cultivation of rice and the immortality of the soul, syphilis and the solar system, gold, pearls, glass, coral, the silkworm and the art of war, electricity, the pneumatic machine and the education of the heart, chess and earthquakes, the pleasures of the imagination and the training of hunting dogs, wet-nurses, canaries, mirages, good taste, how to bring up chaffinches, and the dictates of fashion.[1]

The composition of these poems went on for a number of years; in some cases it was the hobby of a whole lifetime, a daily concern like the poet's regular meals and the healthy exercise of his limbs; and he wrote with even more gusto in the idleness of his country house, where the constant flow of hendecasyllables was measured by the slow tolling of the hours from the village bell-tower. It was, in short, a willingly assumed task, and *The Task*, in fact, was the title of a little didactic poem not included among the elegant verses in that *Collection*, though its theme interested me even more than the immortality of the soul, for the original intention of the poem was to narrate, cloaked in the graces of poetry, the evolution of a piece of furniture: the sofa. "*I sing the Sofa,*" began William Cowper . . .

> "*I, who lately sang*
> *Truth, Hope, and Charity, and touch'd with awe*
> *The solemn chords, and with a trembling hand,*
> *Escaped with pain from that adventurous flight,*
> *Now seek repose upon a humbler theme;*
> *The theme, though humble, yet august and proud*
> *The occasion—for the Fair commands the song.*"

After the first verses the poet digressed, and that sofa of his had to wait almost half a century before anyone occupied it. "The proprietor lies asleep on a sofa—the weather is cool—the time is near midnight: we will make a sketch of the room during his slumber." The sofa had been abandoned by one madman, and now another retrieved it; his name was Edgar Allan Poe.

But not even the description of the romantic interior in Poe's essay, *Philosophy of Furniture*, fulfills our expectations; only a Brillat-Savarin could have satisfied them with a systematic series of meditations on transcendental furnishing. And for that matter, Poe invoked no poetic Muse. Perhaps the last attempt to sing of furniture was that of a certain Count Gherardo Prosperi who, in his little poem on *Fashion* written in

about the middle of the last century, described that curious S-shaped *canapé* known as a *vis-à-vis* or *confident*.

> "*Two half-moons form the seat, in inverse pose,*
> *So that one half's right end is there invited*
> *To touch the other's left, in union close,*
> *And thus in sigmoid form are they united.*
> *Both tall and ample are the backs conceived*
> *So heads, as well as shoulders, there may rest,*
> *One near the other, from all fatigue relieved.*
> *And, too, th' industrious Goddess thought it best*
> *To raise supports at either end, a pair,*
> *Extending them, below, to left and right,*
> *So arms could seek, when tired, a refuge there;*
> *But at the centre no bound'ry did indite*
> *The Goddess, but open left the coupl'd seat.*
> *So Love decreed, for lovers' froward hands*
> *Must there be free, to clasp, in gestures sweet,*
> *The neighb'ring limb; nor hindrance stands*
> *To check the mutual touch, and Love may guide*
> *The movements then of mistress and of wight.*
> *All hail this chair, the saucy Cupid cried,*
> *The boon of boldest youths and ladies bright.*"

Would it be possible to resume *The Sofa* today at the point where Cowper left it, and to sing for example: "But who first invented the curvèd back" for chairs and so adopted their line to the comfort of the human body in repose? Or perhaps not in verses, but in a prose as neat and precise as that of Gladys Burlton in her book which teaches shop clerks their art (*Retail Selling*)? Can a modern man-of-letters "wander among beloved images", and a philosopher seek "food to

nourish his thoughts and his inclinations" in a theme apparently so worldly as that of the furnishing of houses?

Houses! How many epithets can be attached to the word "house". At the end of the second World War, the most frequent adjective in Europe was "destroyed". In Rome, thank God, this destruction wasn't an omnipresent reality, but it was enough to go out of the city, one only had to leave Rome for Viterbo, as I did in those days. You crossed the Milvian Bridge, guarded by its stone saints; just as when you left the city in the old days, your imagination ran ahead of you, by habit looking forward to the villas with their gardens and to Viterbo itself, that ancient Italian city with its churches and its medieval quarter. You knew that the city had been badly hit, but your eyes had still not seen it; and

the bullet-riddled houses along the road, the twisted carcasses of tanks and trucks were lost in the vast background of the stark Latium landscape with its severe and solemn lines, much as you had fixed it forever in your mind one remote day when, returning from Viterbo for the first time, the countryside at sunset presented an enchanted vision, as if created, modulated by the faint, insistent notes of a shepherd's simple pipe. If you looked closer now, you saw that flocks were rarer, the cultivation of the fields scarce; it was as though the waters of the Flood had only recently receded, leaving the corpses of dinosaurs at the sides of the road. You passed beneath the walls of Sutri, apparently still intact, and you already dared hope that what you had heard was an exaggeration, that the destruction of Viterbo might be much less

Figure 1: Karl Beckmann.
Drawing Room of Prince Wilhelm of Prussia
in the Palace at Berlin, watercolor, c. 1840.
COLLECTION CHARLOTTENBURG PALACE,
BERLIN.

serious than people had told you. At Vetralla came the first, vivid image of ruin; but you saw, up on the mountain, San Martino al Cimino unharmed, with its Gothic church, and with the memory of a summer in the shade of those chestnuts (only four years before!), when from time to time people would go to the gay medieval city (and in those days it seemed an enormous sacrifice to have to stand, head bent, in the old and rickety bus). That memory returned, smiling, for the last time. For at Viterbo's Roman Gate, the magic screen of memory was brutally torn away, and your mind was gripped by rubble, destruction, and horror. The visitor couldn't proceed, or had to force his way forward over an uncertain, despoiled terrain, crossed by the impotent track of a little narrow-gauge railroad. "There are still four hundred victims under here," you were told at the Florentine Gate, and wherever you looked, you could see only shattered, ruined buildings, the hollow orbits of windows, and fragments of walls, houses split in two, with the pathetic sight of some still furnished corner, dangling above the rubble, surrounded by ruin: pictures hanging on broken walls, a kitchen with the pots still on the stove and there, in what must once have been a drawing-room, a sofa.

Like a *collage* by Max Ernst, a bed in a boudoir is grazed by the furious waves of a stormy sea; or an abyss yawns at the foot of the most ordinary middle-class dining room; so reality had decided to make the surrealist's mad fantasy come true.

A sofa. *I sing the Sofa.* Among the many themes that Cowper touches on in his poem is the cataclysm of the day, the Sicilian earthquake: "Man rendered obnoxious to these calamities by sin; God the agent in them."

"Alas for Sicily! rude fragments now
Lie scatter'd, where the shapely column stood.
Her palaces are dust. In all her streets
The voice of singing and the sprightly chord
Are silent. Revelry, and dance, and show,
Suffer a syncope and solemn pause:
While God performs upon the trembling stage
Of his own works his dreadful part alone ...
Such evils Sin hath wrought ..."

But the matter isn't so simple, and the evangelical Cowper knew it. For if we choose to see a precise

intention behind such immense disasters, by what tragic irony, in the most devastated square of Civitavecchia, where there wasn't enough wall left for a dog to pee against (*non remansit canis mingens ad parietem*), was there left untouched a mediocre statue of Saint Francis with the words: *Peace and Goodness?* Tragic irony? Or paradoxical statement, that in the midst of the most desolate of horrors, what really matters, what is normal is still peace and goodness, the house and not the ruin, life and not death?

The houses will rise again, and men will furnish houses as long as there is breath in them. Just as our primitive ancestor built a shapeless chair with hastily-chopped branches, so the last man will save from the rubble a stool or a tree stump on which to rest from his labors; and if his spirit is freed for a while from his woes, he will linger another moment and decorate his room. Who can choose to believe, with the Marquis de Sade, that Nature's only aim is destruction, that destruction and death are the norm, that the mouth of our ancient Earth is red from devouring the fruit of her womb?

*   *   *

As in every other field, so in the field of decoration, men can be divided into two categories, indeed divided into two races, as Charles Lamb would say. There are the beautiful and the ugly, the good and the bad, the static and the dynamic, the gay and the melan-

Figure 3: F. W. Klose.
Queen Elizabeth of Prussia's Apartments
in the Charlottenburg Palace, watercolor.
COLLECTION CHARLOTTENBURG PALACE,
BERLIN.

choly, the loquacious and the taciturn, the generous and the miserly, with infinite intermediary states and the most peculiar combinations of opposites. For Lamb all the most varied classifications could be reduced to the basic difference between "the men who borrow and the men who lend." I would venture to suggest an even more fundamental distinction: men who care about their house, and men who care not at all about it. Here too, of course, there are the usual intermediary states: men who care a little, or a fair amount, or only at certain periods in their life; there are men who show some interest in furniture only when they are setting up a house for marrying, and once that terrible expense is made, they forget about it (perhaps these men—though the thought is horrifying—are in the majority). There are some who are completely insensitive to what surrounds them, others who adapt themselves and perhaps even enjoy living in surroundings that most people would consider intolerable. I confess that it is extremely difficult for me to understand the spirit of men who care nothing for possessions or for their house. Each of us sees his colleagues from some personal point of view; and a carpenter will be closer to another carpenter, a doctor to another doctor, even though they come from different nations, than a carpenter to a doctor and vice versa. Every day I come in contact with those who are in many respects my similars, but who care nothing for what surrounds them; and I must say that any affection I feel for them is put to a severe test when I discover this failing in them. "He doesn't care about houses," is in my lexicon a statement as serious and final as, in the lexicon of a moralist, an essential lack of ethical sense would be, if discovered in a colleague. If they say to me: "Watch out, that man cheats at cards," I don't turn a hair; but occasionally I have paled at seeing some friend I have known for years in his home for the first time. It was like turning over one of those ivory figurines carved by the German artificers of the Renaissance, which show a lovely woman on one side and a worm-ridden corpse on the other. The man who has no sense of the house and who is not moved by the harmony of handsome furnishings is for me, as for Shakespeare, the man who "hath no music in himself, a man fit for treasons, stratagems and spoils. The motions of his spirit are dull as night, and his affections dark as Erebus. Let no such man be trusted!"

A venerated master of mine at the University of Florence used to say, from his lectern, many learned things about the Provençal poets. I hung on his every word. But it was a grim day when I first crossed the threshold of his house. As soon as the door was opened, I was confronted by a loathsome oleograph of a Neapolitan shepherdess (that same oleograph used to turn up often in the shops where unclaimed objects from the state pawnshop, the Monte di Pietà, are sold). The shepherdess, shading her eyes with her hand, affected a simpering smile, while Vesuvius smoked in the background. The illumination was entrusted to an electric bulb enclosed in a little iron cage, so that it wouldn't be broken as it was moved back and forth along the shelves of books. It's curious, the squalor, the unnecessary and even deliberate squalor in which people who profess a sensitivity to the fine arts choose to live, or manage to adapt themselves.

I am suspicious of the taste of a professor of Italian literature who can dwell under the same roof with a living room "suite" in the most rickety Liberty style.[2]

I imagine that he must feel toward Petrarch the same indifference that allows him to tolerate such a desecration. An art historian can live in a house crammed with pictures from the floor to the ceiling, pictures collected by some relative and stuffed into the house as a ragpicker stuffs his sack with rags: terrible, mediocre pictures, others not bad or even good, discards from sacristies, "local color" pictures of little, late-19th century masters, even framed colored post cards. Along with these are bric-a-brac of every kind: authentic porcelain pieces, "lucky" dwarfs, catacomb lamps, brass oil-lamps, ancient fragments piled on shelves, in corner-cupboards, china-cabinets, all covered by a magnanimous veil of pitying dust, a fundamental and systematic ugliness, fruit of that dead relative's infallible instinct for every deviation from taste. The bedroom of this same relative, shut up, kept just as he left it, with an enormous bedstead in *Umbertino*[3] baroque, forms the nucleus, the internal tumor of the apartment. The Venetian blinds are stuffed with old, yellowing newspapers between the slats. And yet this art historian seems to be a refined man, an enthusiastic scholar: but to me, his mind is as impenetrable as that of some Polynesian savage. If he is aware of the nightmarish squalor in which he lives, what power of abstraction must he not have? That of a saint who sings during his martyrdom? Or does he accept the house as a hairshirt that secretly and pleasurably makes his thighs bleed? Or is it merely that his spirit is divided into water-tight compartments with areas which the esthetic sense never refreshes, and what for a normal organism would be poisonous is harmless for him after such long familiarity? But in that case, this dark corner of his soul frightens me just as, in his

house, I am frightened by the closed and darkened room of the dead relative. I give up trying to understand men of his type. I feel much closer to that wife of Zachariah whom Hale White describes in *Revolution in Tanner's Lane:* "She could not sit still if one ornament on the mantelpiece looked one way and the other another way, and she would have risen from her deathbed, if she could have done so, to put a chair straight."

In a number of cases I may be wrong, I may not take into sufficient account an elusive sentimental factor, the association value that humble or even ugly objects have for many people. The late critic and scholar Arrigo Cajumi, for example, was unable to rid himself of a rickety little writing desk, carved in the manner of the fake "antiques" made in the Italian town of Cascina. It reminded him of his adolescence and his first steps in an art in which he was to become, alas all too briefly, a master. And Antonio Bueno, a painter so meticulously subtle and orderly, can allow in his living room a sofa and two vast, shapeless, sprawling armchairs, covered with a threadbare brown velvet embossed in pretentious arabesques. These pieces and the little low table in their midst, with its curved legs and its glass top covering what might be the cane seat of some Viennese stool, remind me of cheap English boarding-houses where the stale odor of cabbage mingles with the smell of an old, fat dog whose failing health deprives him of the comfort of a good bath. Bueno not only tolerates this furniture, he loves it, because it belonged to his parents and has survived times and removals which Bueno's spirit cannot dismiss. (For that matter I don't believe Bueno cares much about order and neatness, except in his paintings, which he paints in a studio so full of rubbish, empty tubes, and all sorts of ramshackle odds and ends that to compare it to a garbage-heap would be an understatement. Both studio and living room look out towards the hill of Fiesole, and Bueno probably doesn't feel the contrast between those interiors and that exterior any more than Benedetto Croce was disturbed in his meditations by the enchanting view from his windows when he was a refugee at Sorrento, a view to which he said habit made him indifferent).

There are probably those who agree with Thoreau, who wrote in *Walden:* "I had three pieces of limestone on my desk, but I was terrified to find that they required to be dusted daily, when the furniture of my mind was all undusted still, and I threw them out the window in disgust. How, then, could I have a furnished house?"

Many people may reproach me for judging my fellow-man in this way, by a trifling and external criterion, and they will remind me that clothes do not make the man, and therefore the house does not describe the man who lives in it. But I would prefer to apply another famous saying: *Le style est l'homme même.* The house is the man: *tel le logis, tel le maître,* or if you prefer "tell me how your house looks and I'll tell you who you are." The house is the man, even when you can hardly call it a house, and now I am thinking of those who live for years in hotels or in furnished, rented rooms, who do not change, though they could, but settle with absolute indifference into the place where "fortune flings them" (Dante, *Inferno* 13, 98). The way a man reacts to his surroundings is, for me, a far surer indication than the suit he wears (though for that matter one might also question the accuracy of the old Italian proverb: "The habit doesn't make the monk"). For a man may realize the impossibility of giving any

grace or elegance to his external appearance, even with the aid of the most expert tailor, and he may therefore give up dressing with care; but he can always, even if he is deformed, project about himself his ideal of harmony and beauty so that his spirit may be constantly reflected in it.

I spoke just now of the house of a painter; he was fortunate in not having among his critics Félix Fénéon, the critic of Neo-Impressionism who, in speaking of painters, wanted to consider not only their technique but also "some very precise information on their income, their epistolary activities and their furniture." Dickens and Gogol have written about the capacity that objects have for expressing their owner. Podsnap's silver (in *Our Mutual Friend,* chapter eleven) was characterized by a "hideous solidity". "Everything was made to look as heavy as it could, and to take up as much room as possible." Twenty years before, in *Dead Souls,* Gogol described Sobakevich's house: "Tchitchikov looked round at the room again and everything in it, everything was solid and clumsy to the last degree and had a strange resemblance to the master of the house. In a corner of the room stood a paunchy walnut bureau on four very absurd legs looking exactly like a bear. The table, the armchairs, the chairs were all of the heaviest and most uncomfortable shape; in short, every chair, every object seemed to be saying, 'I am a Sobakevitch too!' or 'I too am very like Sobakevitch!' "

This is the house in its deepest essence: a projection of the ego. And furnishing is nothing but an indirect form of ego-worship. The contemplative kind of man who is a lover of the beautiful house may properly be defined as a narcissist. To some extent this narcissism is common to all men, for only a few limit their house to the strictly utilitarian, without trying to adorn it. But when care for the house becomes a veritable cult, then the narcissism is patent, gross. And it is surprising that Edmond de Goncourt, that subtle analyst and narcissist, seems unaware of this when he prefaces his *La maison d'artiste,* that poem of interior decoration, by observations in which an interest for furniture and objects is considered a surrogate of love for woman: "On leaving his love, the focus of a man's reflections is in large part the pretty inanimate objects which his passion has invested with a little of the nature and character of his love." A narcissist *par excellence,* Robert de Montesquiou, said, an apartment is "a mood." He might have said, "My furniture is my feeling," thus adapting a famous passage from Byron: "and to me / High mountains are a feeling . . . and with the sky, the peak, the heaving plain / Of ocean, or the stars . . ."[4]

This passage from Byron, which is frequently quoted to illustrate how man's soul is resolved in his natural surroundings, makes me wonder if this pantheistic feeling isn't a natural phenomenon basically akin to the narcissism of the lover of furnishing. Examining this feeling in Gabriele D'Annunzio, the critic Alfredo Gargiulo made a distinction between the authentic pantheism of the religious poet which involves complete disinterest in any seductive aspect of the universe and the conviction that the universe is One and is Spirit, and the pseudo-pantheism of a sensual and visual poet like D'Annunzio, who "loves the individual aspects of the universe and doesn't go back to the single source, lingering on each one of them, plunging deeper, living in its individuality, drawing pleasure from it, praising it (as in *Le Laudi!*), without any moral and

religious elevation, that is to say, without considering a principle in which he and his individual object must be fused." The proof of the truth of Gargiulo's analysis is found in the identification of that pantheistic sentiment, in the last phase of D'Annunzio's life, with his self-indulgence in the furnishings of the Vittoriale, the "folly" where he spent the latter part of his life. For the poet of the *Laudi,* the decoration of his earlier, Tuscan villa, La Capponcina, had represented an accessory to his living among those great furnishings of Nature, *magnalia Naturae,* which are the sea, the mountains, the pinewoods; but then this plenitude was dissipated, the pantheistic horizon was narrowed to the sculptures, the marble columns, the stuffs, and the rubbish (yes, rubbish; for D'Annunzio's taste was anything but reliable) of the Vittoriale.

I am not speaking of what you might call the state rooms at the Vittoriale conceived by the architect Maroni. These are pure madness and don't reflect D'Annunzio's taste, which one mustn't wrong by identifying it with the red and blue panels and the vulgar gilt decorations of the dining room or the absurd Michelangelesque travesties of the other formal rooms all designed by Maroni. I am talking, rather, about the poet's private rooms, stifling with their deep divans groaning under great piles of cushions, with their draperies, their *boiseries,* and the objects of two continents and various religions mated in a sense of devout profanation which at times involuntarily approaches Surrealism (at the base of a predella, before the ciborium, there is the broken wheel of a motorboat). These apartments, which suggest the stuffy odor of *papier d'Arménie* and the music of *Tristan und Isolde,* which if played here would justify the qualification "pornographic" given it by D. H. Lawrence, represent

the tragic involution of the pantheistic sentiment of their owner.

First the mountains and the waves, then furnishings were his feelings: two aspects, only apparently different, of the same narcissism. And if one wanted to make a list of the great narcissists of history, I dare say one would discover that all of them liked the most sumptuous and elegant in decoration. Need I mention Nero's *Domus Aurea?* I omit the long and obvious line from Heliogabalus to Gilles de Rais, to William Beckford and Ludwig II of Bavaria, all of it material for a Dantesque canto. (And while I'm on the subject, I leave to the Dante scholars the question of deciding to what region of hell Minos would have condemned the excessive worshipers of furnishing. Personally I feel that Purgatory would be enough. After all, where is their sin, beyond a disproportionate and over-vigorous love? For that matter, as we shall see, the love of furnishings must have been a fairly infrequent affair in the days of Alighieri.)

It has been said that just as the body—according to the Swedenborgian philosophy—is nothing but a projection, an expansion of the soul, so for the soul, the house where it lives is nothing but an expansion of its own body. For a soul that loves order and cherishes experience, numerous delicate affinities are established between itself and the things of its outward abode, so that finally there is no longer any distinction between the outward and inward. The surrounding aspects (like the light which at a particular hour creeps to a par-

Figure 4: Fernand Pelez.
Interior of a Bedroom, watercolor.
COLLECTION MARIO PRAZ,
ROME.

ticular picture or space upon the wall, the scent of the flowers that is wafted beside a particular window) become for the soul not merely so many apprehended objects, as themselves powers of apprehension and doorways to things beyond, "seeds or rudiments of new faculties, by which it, dimly yet surely, apprehends a matter lying beyond its actually attained capacity of sense and spirit." So the surroundings become something more than a mirror of the soul. They are, indeed, a reinforcement of the soul, or to return to the mirror-image, they are a play of many mirrors which open infinite perspectives, depths of identical, multiplied reflections. "Cette pièce où des glaces se faisaient écho et se renvoyaient à perte de vue,

dans les murs, des enfilades de boudoirs roses . . ."[5]

The surroundings become a museum of the soul, an archive of its experiences; it reads in them its own history, and is perennially conscious of itself; the surroundings are the resonance chamber where its strings render their authentic vibration. And just as many pieces of furniture are like moulds of the human body, empty forms waiting to receive it (the chair and the sofa are its pedestals, the bed a sheath, the mirror a mask that awaits the human face in order to come to life, and even in those pieces where the integration with a human counterpart is less evident, like the wardrobe or the chest of drawers, a symmetry similar to that of the human body still dominates, for handles and knobs

*Figure 5: The Columned Salon
in the Residence of the Wittgenstein
Family at Ivanovskij, watercolor.*
COLLECTION DON AGOSTINO CHIGI,
ROME.

are aligned like eyes and ears on the head) so finally the whole room or apartment becomes a mould of the spirit, the case without which the soul would feel like a snail without its shell. The anthropomorphic and theriomorphic forms so frequent in furniture are only indications, reminders of how furniture shares in man's life. The time-hallowed lion's paw on an antique piece still retains some vestige of its primitive, ritual significance, which was to transmit its nobility and strength into the person who sat on a chair that was thus supported. The ultimate meaning of a harmoniously decorated house is, as we have hinted, to mirror man, but to mirror him in his ideal being; it is an exaltation of the self.

For this reason, perhaps even more than painting or sculpture, perhaps even more than architecture itself, furniture reveals the spirit of an age. And there is nothing like a retrospective exhibition of furnished rooms in chronological sequence to declare to us, at first glance, the varying personalities of the rooms' occupants.[6]

Far less revealing of the owners' character, for example, are the minutely conceived, crowded, phantasmagorical rooms of the bourgeois 19th century. Walter Benjamin[7] sees the reason for this exaggeration in the contrast between the surroundings of a man's work, his office, where a flat prosaic atmosphere dominates, and the surroundings of his comfort and his leisure, the home, which must propitiate his dreams and illusions; the world of business is opposed to the world of the heart. "The interior represents the universe for the private individual. He collects there whatever is distant, whatever is of the past. His living room is a box in the theatre of the world."

The consummation of this cult of the interior takes place, according to Benjamin, at the end of the century with *Art Nouveau*. "Its aim is revealed as the apotheosis of the individual. Its theory is individualism. With Vandervelde the house is the expression of the personality. Ornament is for this house what the signature is for a painting . . . *Art Nouveau* . . . represents the last attempt at escape by an art besieged by technology in its ivory tower. It mobilizes all its reserves of intimacy. They find their expression in the mediumistic language of lines, of the flower as symbol of naked, vegetative nature, opposed to the surrounding world, armed with technology. The new elements of construction in iron, the bearing structures, embarrass *Art Nouveau*. In the ornamentation it tries to bring these forms back to art. Reinforced concrete reveals new possibilities of plastic conformation in architecture. In this period the true centre of gravity of living space is moved into the office. What is destitute of reality finds its place in the home. Solness, the Master Builder, sums up *Art Nouveau*: the attempt of the individual to overcome technology on the basis of his own inwardness leads him to ruin."

The furnishing of a house can also indicate a lack of personality. I don't know what our grandchildren will think when they see our "Twentieth Century" houses, if any of them should survive for posterity. I, however, do know what to think of the monotonous series of drawing rooms in many a Roman *palazzo*, decorated with mediocre if not downright bad carvings, stuccowork, baroque paintings, and gilt chairs in *Umbertino* baroque—often with the family arms—lined up against the wall, not for anyone to sit on but to function only as mute, liveried servants, asserting a pretentious and empty pomp. The consoles, the sofas of these living rooms are to true furniture what limbs afflicted and made helpless by elephantiasis are·to healthy arms and legs. We were once summoned to such an apartment for the honor of being presented to a Royal Highness. The best pictures had been taken from the walls as a precaution against air-raids, and the bereaved frames gaped like hollow eyesockets. At the moment when the lofty personage arrived, all the shutters were closed by a servant, though it was still day, and in the grim, artificial light of the dusty chandeliers, all that lifeless display offered a perfectly appropriate background for a vacillating monarchy.

These Roman drawing rooms, to tell the truth, are no more civilized than an *izba* in the steppes; worse, for in such rooms civilized forms have decayed into threadbare formulas intended only to impress the vulgar and the superficial. Of the many pleasures that furnishings can give their owners, such rooms can give only the ugliest: the pleasure of possession.

It's self-evident, of course, inherent in the fundamental narcissism of furnishing, that possession plays an integral part. The inscription that one reads over the façade of Rossini's house in Bologna, *Non domo dominus, sed domino domus* (Not the master for the house, but the house for the master), suggests an antithesis that for the true lover of the house doesn't exist. The house for the master, and the master for the house; this synthesis isn't found in philosophical treatises, because philosophers in general belong to the race of men who don't care about houses. Since the house is an expression, an expansion of the ego, being not only an articulated system of comforts, but also that private world in which the ego likes to be daily mirrored, possession, as first corollary, must logically follow.

The house is the sphere of influence, the vital space, the fief, the domain, the allodium, or whatever other expression that lawgivers and politicians may be pleased to coin, to signify what, in the child's primitive language, is expressed with a petulant: "That's mine!" I know of nothing sillier or more irritating than the inscription to be read over a certain Spanish house: *Por comodidad de sus amigos patrón* (For the comfort of his friends). This nobleman who, with such an inflated gesture, proclaims he is not master of his house, that it exists instead for the comfort of his friends, as if he were merely the guardian and manager of a vague cooperative, this vain boaster who bows at the door and exclaims with a smile: "It is yours"—we know how he would act if put to the test, if his friends really behaved in his house as in a tavern. No, at the threshold of one's house even Communism stops, and the blow of the knocker or the ring of the bell which asks admission is an action no less solemn than one's stopping at a frontier.

As grotesque as this Spanish nobleman, it seems to me, was that English gentleman, a certain Warter, who once when he was abroad (in Spain, as it happens) learned, during a game of chess, that a fire back in England had destroyed all of his furniture, whereupon he phlegmatically said to his opponent: "Your turn."[8]

Love of the house cannot be satisfied by the furnishings of others. The most sumptuous of surroundings does not satisfy that need, for one who feels it, if he knows that the things about him are not his, that he is no more than a passing guest. *Parva sed apta mihi.* By a subtle and inevitable process, the man who cares for his house can easily become a collector.

"The interior," Walter Benjamin writes,[9] "is the refuge of art. The true inhabitant of the interior is the

Figure 6: F.-E. Villeret.
Boudoir of the Princess Barjatinskij
in Paris, watercolor, November 1842.
COLLECTION DON AGOSTINO CHIGI,
ROME.

collector. He takes it upon himself to transfigure things. He assumes a Sisyphus-like task: to remove from objects, by possessing them, their quality of merchandise. But he gives them only an amateur's value, not the value of use. The collector not only transports himself, as in a dream, to a distant or past world, but also to a better world, in which men are not provided with the things they need any more than in the everyday world, but things themselves are freed from the servitude of having to be useful.

"The interior is not only the universe, but also the sheath of the private man. To inhabit means to leave traces. In the interior these traces are accentuated. Coverings and protective shields, all sorts of cases and covers are invented, in which the traces of objects in daily use are disguised. In the interior even the traces of the inhabitant are covered. The detective novel is born, which sets out to search for these traces. The *Philosophy of Furniture* and his mystery stories show in Poe the first physiognomist of the interior. The

Figure 7: Giuseppe Naudin.
A Room in the Palazzo Ducale
at Parma, watercolor, c. 1832.
COLLECTION MUSEO GLAUCO LOMBARDI,
PARMA.

guilty parties in the first detective novels are not gentlemen, nor *apaches*, but bourgeois private citizens."

Collecting is no more than a development, a degeneration of the need to project an atmosphere around oneself. It can be only a pleasant distension, a not reprehensible plumpness, but it can also be a tumor and, alas, a cancer. Among the masters of decoration themselves, we find martyrs of this cancer. The greatest French cabinet-maker of the 17th century, André Charles Boulle, in addition to being a creator of furnishings, "le plus habile de Paris dans son métier," was also a passionate collector. He suffered from this disease to such a degree that, despite his immense earnings, he was plunged into debt, and neither lawsuits nor the threats of Louis XIV's minister Louvois could restrain him from this dangerous downward path. At eighty, he saw his collection of drawings and paintings by great masters sold at auction, along with some furniture made by his own hand, inlaid with metal or tortoise shell or colored woods, his own creatures with which he evidently had been unable to part. The expansion of his own person in sumptuous surroundings was here favored by the art that he himself exercised.

Charles Cressent, the great cabinet-maker of the Regency, was also above all the decorator of his own rooms, and he loved to feast his eyes on furniture from his own workshop as well as on treasures of the past, paintings by Dürer, Holbein, Rembrandt, Rubens, bronzes by Giovanni Bologna, porcelain from China and Saxony. His sumptuous furnishings were scattered in the various auction sales which saddened the last years of his life. By imperceptible degrees the taste for furnishings grew to a mania. It is Narcissus who bends lower and lower over the fatal pool and as he

"... admires
All things for which he himself is admired; ...
As the yellow wax melts before a gentle heat,
As hoar frost melts before the warm morning sun,
So he, wasted with love, is consumed by its hidden flame.[10]

Like every love, the love of furnishings wants to be fed, and it can be fed only with daily worship, with what Henry James[11] has happily defined "the mysteries of ministration to rare pieces." It is not merely a question of contemplating and conserving; the impulse to perfect and increase is irresistible. And cast to the winds are warnings like Cicero's:[12] "In a house, the slaves who take care of the paintings, the statues, the vases of chased silver, the Corinthian bronzes, who clean them and rub them and set them in their places, are scorned by their companions; and thus, in a nation, the men who abandon themselves to the passion for these objects are at the lowest level of slavery.... When I see you contemplating a painting of Echion, a statue of Polyclitus, admiring, emitting cries, I say that you are the slave of nonsense. Are these not magnificent things? I admit they are, for we too have the eye of an expert. But I beseech you: these beautiful things must not be fetters for men, but playthings for children ... If Mummius could see with what passion such people handle a Corinthian vase, he who disdained the whole of Corinth, would he take them for distinguished citizens or for diligent servants?" On those enamored of furnishings is also wasted the condemnation of Seneca, who deplored the passion "for objects, material burdens to which a pure soul, mindful of its origin, would not become attached;" and in vain La Bruyère presents the grotesque description of the owner of handsome apartments:[13] "A bourgeois likes buildings; he has a palace built, so beautiful, so rich, and so adorned that it is uninhabitable; the owner, ashamed to live in it himself, perhaps unable to make up his mind to rent it out to a prince or a business man, retires to the garret where he ends his days, while the suite of rooms and the mosaic floors are the prey of the English and the Germans who go there from the Palais-Royal, from the Palais Lesdiguières and from the Luxembourg. They never stop knocking at that handsome door: all of them ask to see the house, no one to see its master.''

La Bruyère's satire, for that matter, misses the mark, for the owner he describes is a parvenu, afraid of spoiling ''the good drawing room,'' rather than an enthusiast of fine furnishings, who creates them in · order to live in their midst, unable to live anywhere else, in fact. La Bruyère has seen only the most vulgar aspects of collecting, the snobbish desire for what is rare or fashionable, luxury practiced to dazzle others, not the innate need to create a mirror of perfection around one's own person. The true lover of furnishings does not maintain his home for the comfort of his friends, nor even for their amazement. It is only reluctantly and with some annoyance that he agrees to make a *tour de propriétaire* for visitors. It is erroneous to believe that he lives only for this. He doesn't make his house beautiful to receive others in it, or to inflate his ego with their admiration. Narcissus wants none of the nymphs' admiration. He is a solitary, and rather melancholy contemplator.[14]

Perhaps this is why many of the most famous owners of sumptuously furnished houses were exhausted potentates and financiers, neurotic, refined, sad people for whom furnishings were indeed an expansion, but above all an escape, and by this token deserving of all respect, for as Hale White observes:[15] ''. . . men should not be too curious in analyzing and condemning any

means which nature devises to save them from themselves, whether it be coins, old books, curiosities, butterflies, or fossils.''

We have no way of guessing what was in the soul of Duc Jean de Berry, of the Archduke Ferdinand of the Tyrol, or of the Emperor Rudolph II, pioneers in the field of collecting rather than furnishers, fond of gaily illuminated books of the hours, of coconuts bound in gold, of works of art and automatons, of mummies of strange beasts, of bezoar-stones, of objects made of shells and hummingbird feathers, mandrakes, musical and scientific instruments, and of every rare or amazing object, which they piled up in the *Schatz-* and *Wunderkammern* of their palaces and castles. Judging from his portrait by Holbein, Jean de Berry looked like a stocky bourgeois, one might even say a bourgeois mindful of peasant origins. Rudolph II is perhaps not personally responsible for one exquisite and decadent detail which has come down from him to us: a very rich cabinet encrusted with medallions, enamels, shells, coral, with all the drawers empty except for a secret compartment containing a lock of a woman's blonde hair, ''only a woman's hair,'' in Swift's phrase. And we cannot reconcile the love of furnishings with the other crude, barbaric aspects of the character of that lunatic Paul I of Russia who ordered Kotzebue to describe minutely the castle of Saint Michael which he had built.[16]

None of these sovereigns perhaps strolled through the artificial paradises of their collections with any secret melancholy; none of them had anything akin to the mad, lonely spirit of Ludwig II of Bavaria, who mobilized an army of German professors so that he could live in the false scenery of a *Roi Soleil;*[17] but we can be sure that fictional creatures like Walter Pater's

Carl of Rosenmold and Huysmans's des Esseintes must have had any number of foreshadowings and prototypes in history. From past generations the moderns have inherited two things, as Hugo von Hofmannsthal observed:[18] fine antique furniture and hypersensitive nerves. "In furniture there is all the fascination that draws us towards the past, and in our nerves, the drama of the present's doubts." Hypersensitive nerves and love for furniture are indeed connected phenomena.

In general patricians who inherit splendid furnishings from ancestors move among them naturally and, even if they care for their inheritance, they never hesitate to mix the modern and the antique, odd chairs and signed pieces, with an aloofness that Baldassare Castiglione, author of *The Courtier*, would have approved. But the true enthusiast of furnishing is like the herbalist who selects each flower, gathers, assorts,

Figure 8: J. S. Decker.
Bedroom of the Archduchess Sofie
in the Palace at Laxenburg, watercolor.
COLLECTION SANSSOUCI,
POTSDAM.

harmonizes, and never tires of seeking perfection. It was not the Rothschilds, the Goldschmidts, and the Camondos who at the end of the last century first revived a taste for the furniture and objects of the French 18th century; but once they had learned this lesson from the Goncourts, the pupils became more methodical even than their masters, and in their homes they created the most flawless Regency and Louis XVI décors that we know. And certainly Leopoldskron, the castle of the bishops of Salzburg, can never have been so systematically furnished in Rococo style as it was when Max Reinhardt made it his home.

It cannot be said of all these lovers of furnishings that they assembled themselves their surroundings, piece by piece. But it can be said of Count Moïse de Camondo who, in his fixation to create for himself a house absolutely like that of a refined gentleman of the second half of the 18th century, patiently traced for years the pieces later to find their ideal place in his house. He waited for them to come up at sales, and when they eluded him, he overtook them elsewhere and made them his. A little lacquer cabinet signed by Pierre Garnier was brought back from England to stand beside its twin, which had already adorned Count de Camondo's house for twenty years, and there is a similar story about a pair of *meubles d'appui* by Leleu, reunited after many years in a room of his *hôtel* near Parc Monceau in Paris, thanks to the tireless passion of the collector, who for the twin gave a Paris collector some magnificent 18th century gouaches in exchange. And we can be sure that no reunion of twins in classic comedies, from Plautus to Shakespeare, was ever accompanied by such joy as must have been Moïse de Camondo's after these triumphs.

Unlike so many other collections lovingly assembled, this one was not scattered. When Moïse died in 1935 he left it to the State in memory of his son Nissim, killed in the war in November 1917, with the condition that the furnishings remain in the arrangement that he had established. Théophile Gautier (in an essay included later in his *History of Romanticism*) deplored the sale of Victor Hugo's furniture in 1852. There are those, however, who are pleased when, at the death of an owner, his beloved possessions are scattered so that they may find others who love them as much, or almost, or even more, so that the objects may glow in the warmth of another person and, so to speak, become grafted into his life. And no one can deny the fascination in the history of certain pieces of furniture, their passage through illustrious or fatal hands. If a certain piece once stood for a while in the rooms of Marie Antoinette, it can now make a sensitive person shudder, and even stir the coarser spirit of a parvenu. The mere description in a catalogue of such a piece, with all the technical terminology, the name of the cabinet-maker, and the circumstances of its creation, will make an initiate's head swim, just as the most arid description of a coat-of-arms intoxicates an enthusiast of heraldry. How can one resist, for example, the persuasive opulence of this description of an inlaid piece by Boulle, from a Royal inventory of 1685? "An ebony bureau inlaid with flowers of different color woods. On the top is depicted a vase of flowers posed on the end of a table with birds and butterflies and at the four corners the crowned monogram of the king. A frieze of the same inlay encloses this design on all sides. At the corners of the frieze is a *fleur de lys,* and at the middle of each side of the frieze is a shell between two bands of lavender wood and thin ribbons in white. There are three large drawers which close with a key. The plaques of the locks and the ring-shaped pulls are of gilded bronze. Posed on five balls of blackened wood, each decorated in the center with a bronze shell."

Others feel it only just that masterworks of patience and taste, such as the décor of certain rooms, be conserved like museums, after the spirit which gave them life has fled. After all, a house is not like the garden in Shelley's *The Sensitive Plant* which, when the lovely lady who cared for it died,

"became cold and foul,
Like the corpse of her who had been its soul . . ."

If the original function of a décor ceases to be the resonance chamber for certain strings, still other strings may vibrate in it. Among the many indifferent or idle or vulgar visitors, there will also be the sensitive spirit who, even if only for a moment, will feel the warmth which once animated all the lovely furnishings. A wide-spread prejudice invariably associates coldness with the very nature of a museum. Where things are listed in a catalogue, given numbers, fixed to walls or protected by velvet ropes so that no ill-disposed visitor may rob or deface, there—in common opinion—all is death and graveyard. Classified in glass cases, similar objects set in a row, lovely as they may be, all fragrance vanishes, all enchantment departs: the rational order suppresses their imaginative aura. Whence the modern tendency to present museums like furnished, decorated apartments, and the curious inventions of Wilhelm Valentiner, consultant of American collectors, who tried to enliven museum rooms with picturesque vistas, allowing a masterpiece to be glimpsed through cur-

tains, sipped like an apéritif, or garnishing a picture with appetizing side-dishes of rare stuffs and ornamental plants. These expedients have a bric-a-brac flavor; indeed, they are the ultimate product of that taste for bric-a-brac which was so strong toward the end of the 19th century.

Quite different from such spurious décors are those furnished houses which subsequently have become museums, like the house of Count de Camondo, in fact. But even though this house is now officially a museum, I still found it far from easy to visit. Perhaps it was this difficulty which cast for me a heavenly halo over the harmonious rooms which I had seen reproduced in the pages of *L'Illustration*. Three times I tried to cross that house's threshold, and three times the surly doorman sent me away, the first time protesting that the museum was closed for the summer (and it was that summer of 1937 when Europe was for the last time united and festive at Paris for the last of those international exhibitions which from 1851 on had fostered the delusion that all nations were prosperous and agreed on peaceful good works, dancing in the lights of the pavilions, as in a garish Pageant of Progress). The second time, in the late autumn of 1938, I was told that the museum's *objets d'art* had been packed away for safekeeping because the war seemed imminent. The third and final attempt at entry was in July of 1939, the day after the great Bastille Day parade, when the streets were cluttered with marching troops, the skies with roaring airplanes, and the air with defiance and threats, when soon a hail of iron and fire was to fall on all houses, whether hovels or palaces, like the one in which, at a corner of the park, the sumptuous furnishings of Moïse de Camondo had lovingly been assembled. The furniture of mahogany, rosewood, ebony, cedar, the pieces by Leleu, Topino, Weisweiler, Riesener, Martin Carlin, those pieces whose patina was created by time and by the caress of loving hands; the rugs of Savonnerie and Aubusson, whose stylized leaves and flowers had been the soft, artificial meadow for footsteps as cautious as those of priests in a temple; the China porcelains with their mounts of gilded bronze; the pictures by Vigée-Lebrun, Hubert Robert, Drouais, and Guardi; the bronzes of Gouthière and of Thomire; the tapestries with subjects taken from Boucher; the panels painted by Huët—all were now sleeping in some vault, waiting for a storm-cloud far grimmer than the one that had gathered over their heads a century and a half earlier. The trees of the park no longer formed a natural curtain at the windows of the graceful rooms, diffusing a sylvan tone, a flavor of Arcadia, in settings of a sensuality that was too much a quintessence, an unendurable exquisiteness. In the rooms emptied of their treasures, there could no longer be heard, at intervals, like birdcalls in the forests, the silvery trill of the carillon-clocks. The visitor to the empty rooms would not hear even these clocks. He would be less fortunate than a similar visitor who wandered through desolate Versailles the day after the Revolution and listened, in the room of Marie Antoinette, to the soft flutes and harps, the dying tones of the clock which impassively, with its musical sounds, had sung all the hours of the Revolution in that royal dwelling deprived of all its guests.[19] Thus the carillon of the Cathedral of Saints Peter and Paul in St. Petersburg, for several months after the Russian Revolution, was to sound every day at noon the notes of the anthem: *God Save the Tsar!*[20]

"She comes! she comes! the sable Throne behold
Of Night *primaeval and of* Chaos *old!*
Before her, Fancy's *gilded clouds decay,*
And all its varying rainbows die away.
Wit *shoots in vain its momentary fires,*
The meteor drops, and in a flash expires.
As one by one, at dread Medea's strain,
The sick'ning stars fade off th' ethereal plain;
As Argus's eyes by Hermes' wand opprest,
Clos'd one by one to everlasting rest;
Thus at her felt approach, and secret might,
Art *after* Art *goes out, and all is Night.*
See skulking Truth *to her old cavern fled,*
Mountains of Casuistry heap'd o'er her head!
Philosophy, *that lean'd on Heav'n before,*
Shrinks to her second cause, and is no more.
Physic *of* Metaphysic *begs defence,*
And Metaphysic *calls for aid on* Sense!
See Mystery *to* Mathematics *fly!*
In vain! they gaze, turn giddy, rave, and die.
Religion *blushing veils her sacred fires,*
And unawares Morality *expires.*
For public Flame, *nor private, dares to shine;*
Nor human Spark *is left, nor* Glimpse *divine!*
Lo! thy dread Empire, CHAOS! *is restor'd;*
Light dies before thy uncreating word;
Thy hand, great Anarch! lets the curtain fall,
And universal Darkness buries All."
—Pope, *The Dunciad,* Book VI, 629–56

Of the many apartments I visited in former times, how many can still be traced today? At the end of the second World War I wondered if the classic house of Sir John Soane still stood in a vast, grey London

Figure 11: K. A. Beine.
*Room in the Villa Dackenhausen
at Castellammare, watercolor, July 1842.*
COLLECTION DON AGOSTINO CHIGI,
ROME.

square, with its melancholy, fenced-in garden. That house as still as a tomb, at the bottom of a sea of fog, with its funereal Egyptian motifs wed to the less severe Greek and Roman ones, that house which has the air of a museum and of a catacomb, with busts, sarcophagi, urns, bas-reliefs, red and black Greek vases, furniture of dark mahogany, smoky ceiling paintings and, in the heart of the house, that cruel lay sermon, that profane *via crucis,* Hogarth's pictures which illustrate the progress of the young rake from orgy to gallows. But another Egyptian-inspired apartment has been destroyed, the drawing room of the Residenz at Cassel with its walls and divans of yellow silk amid the black of the woodwork and the black marble of the great stove, and with reflections of black and yellow in the gilded bronze palmettos of the vast circular mirror which opened in the fresh azure of the ceiling.

Why, among the apartments I once visited, do I recall the most sequestered and funereal? Is it perhaps because they seem most in key with the ruin that has menaced or engulfed them? And yet I have seen gay apartments, their gaiety, of course, tempered and veiled, for the fragrance of the past everywhere links the beautiful to the sad.

Whenever I pass through a city, I never fail to visit whatever illustrious furnished houses are open to outsiders. Galleries, churches, famous views, landscapes made immortal by the poets, yes, all of these find me far from indifferent; but for houses I have a special weakness. It's not only that I find myself more in touch with the past: the very arrangement of the furnishings acts on me like a spell. The odor of the furniture, of the wax on the floors, of the ancient rooms is as pleasing to me—or even more pleasing—than the

scent of meadows in spring; and among my own furniture I was once especially fond of a little Restoration *toilette* of aromatic cedar which, in the silence of the room, gave off its subtle fragrance in rare gusts, which one had to seek out, standing in just the right place, as one does to look at a picture.

I have a weakness for watercolors of interiors, too, especially the kind that were painted in the first half of the 19th century, the patient work of minor artists or amateurs, which reproduce every piece of furniture, every object, every detail of the carpets and the curtains, the sense of the lights and shadows in the room. That same sense of light and shadow that Giuseppe Tomasi di Lampedusa evokes in "Places of My Infancy," describing his family's house in Palermo:[21] "A door with green hangings gave onto the antechamber . . . And from there the eye fell on a perspective of drawing rooms extending one after the other the length of the façade. Here for me began the magic of light, which in a city with so intense a sun as Palermo is concentrated or variegated according to the weather even in narrow streets. This light was sometimes diluted by the silk curtains hanging before balconies, or heightened by beating on some gilt frame or yellow damask chair which reflected it back. Sometimes, particularly in summer, these rooms were dark, yet through the closed blinds filtered a sense of the luminous power that was outside; or sometimes at certain hours a single ray would penetrate straight and clear as that of Sinai, populated with myriads of dust particles and going on to vivify the colors of carpets, uniformly ruby red throughout all the drawing rooms: a real sorcery of illumination and color which entranced my mind forever. Sometimes I rediscover this

Figure 12: Ciuli.
*Room in the Palazzo Caramanico
in Naples, watercolor, April 1842.*
COLLECTION DON AGOSTINO CHIGI,
ROME.

luminous quality in some old palace or church . . ."

I never tire of looking at a series of color reproductions of paintings of interiors from the watercolor collection of King Friedrich Wilhelm IV of Prussia (the originals were in the palace of Berlin and are now, in part, at Sanssouci and the Charlottenburg palace). Those great halls, those rooms, depicted just as they were when they were inhabited by the people whose taste they reflect, seem to me vibrant with expectation, still animated by human warmth, like a bed only recently abandoned by the man who slept in it. The flights of rooms and corridors, glimpsed through the doors, and the walls thick with paintings, the knick-knacks, the busts, the statuettes and porcelains, the flowers under glass bells, breathe an intimacy that you never find in the rooms which serve as backgrounds for the official portraits. It is the absence of the human form, or its presence only as a mere figure or mannikin or as a framed painting on a wall which turns the furniture and the objects into the true *dramatis personae*. The patterns of the carpets, the stuffs, the wall-papers, the grain of the woods (the watercolorists are so scrupulous), the embroidery of the firescreens and the footstools, the framed petit-point, the overweening majolica stoves, each item freely makes its voice heard. If the view of a lake or a mountain's wooded slope is seen amid the heavily-draped curtains at the windows, the atmosphere of the rooms becomes more hushed; if one could stretch out a hand into the strip of light that falls on the floor, one could feel its warmth. These watercolors so accurately preserve the taste of that age that you would almost say the doors and windows depicted in them have never been opened since then, and that we breathe the spirit still enclosed there — the comparison is perhaps overworked, but it is certainly appropriate here — the scent of perfume that lingers in an ancient phial.

Many aristocratic families possess similar watercolors. Sometimes they are of little interest to the descendants and become scattered, and this is how I was able to buy some of them. In the same way I was also able to buy a little oil painting which shows Queen Isabella of Naples in her apartment at Capodimonte (*Fig.* 189), sold not long ago at an auction in Rome along with other objects which formerly belonged to the Del Drago family. Other families have kept these small and unappreciated treasures (one such album, made for the Comte de Chambord, is at Katchine castle near Prague, dating from about 1835, and has been published by Hardvillier; another, of the apartments of Francis I of Austria in the Hofburg in Vienna, with watercolors by J. Decker, was executed in 1826 for Marie d'Orléans, daughter of Louis-Philippe, and is now at the Metropolitan Museum in New York) and I am indebted to the courtesy of Don Agostino Chigi, who allowed me to reproduce in this book some watercolors from an album of a kind once perhaps frequent, though I had never encountered it before (*Figs.* 5, 6, 9, 11, 12, 14, 15, 19, 20, 282–302).

This album comes from the Wittgenstein family, who are related to the Chigis; it was assembled around the middle of the last century by Ludwig von Wittgenstein, son of General Wittgenstein who distinguished himself in the campaigns against Napoleon. He had married a Barjatinskij, Leonilla, whose family owned lands in Russia·and in the Rhine country, and the album commemorates the houses they lived in, their own and those they inhabited when they went abroad, to France, Germany, Italy, Switzerland, England. With views of the various countries and of interiors of the houses, the album is a documentation both of the life of a great family of the last century and of their taste in decoration. Some leaves of the album are missing. They were given by descendants to Russian relatives and were lost during the revolution. Perhaps one day they'll turn up in some Soviet museum.

Of the life of the Wittgenstein princes and of their similars in 19th century Europe, where despite the French Revolution the aristocracy still retained much prestige and had a monopoly on pleasures and pastimes (that today in a reduced and popularized form, are shared by almost everyone), certain of these watercolors give us such a restful, idyllic picture that I defy even the most hardened supporter of the present not to feel a twinge of nostalgia for the past. In one picture, the Wittgensteins with their little court (some Russians, others foreigners, the children's tutors) are sitting at a table in the garden of Zausze, on a July day in 1839 (*Fig.* 15). There are eight of them, being offered foods and wines by four servants, the group set against a tall hedge of a very delicate green, the same green of the lawn before the low pink-roofed wooden house. In the silence of that hour and place, the people and the flowering plants (roses and hollyhocks) seem to possess the same dreamy quality of things that, set apart, waft their sweetness on the solitary air. In another watercolor (*Fig.* 14) the same artist (a certain Hess, or perhaps Hesse, difficult to identify among the many of that name, but perhaps Ludwig Ferdinand Hesse) paints, in the shade of the poplars and delicate foliaged birches, the French tutor Monsieur Marillac, dressed in white and grey almost as if he wanted to be camouflaged by the surrounding birch trunks, sitting on a bench beside little Peter. On the lawn opposite, Marie

Figure 14: Hess or Hesse.
Members of the Wittgenstein Family
at the Farm of Macha in Zausze,
watercolor, July 1839.
COLLECTION DON AGOSTINO CHIGI,
ROME.

is playing with a white kid, and Tony is in the arm of her wetnurse, dressed in red. This watercolor bears the name of the place, *La Ferme de Macha à Zausze,* and the date, July 22, 1839. The work vaguely recalls the ingenuous spell of the Douanier Rousseau. Other watercolors of this album show the family dining in the garden in Paris, one of them signed by Villeret in May, 1837, the other by Girard in May, 1843. In a watercolor by Ciuli of June, 1842, there is only the table, all laid, under a blue-and-white striped awning on the terrace of the Villa Dackenhausen at Castellam-mare, and a tall, intensely green vine dominates the scene. It is so life-like that we could almost take seats ourselves at that table, were we not restrained by our respect for the princes Wittgenstein who, any moment, will come out of the door of the villa, through which we can catch a glimpse of the interior. The interior is given us in another watercolor by Karl Andrejevich Beine (*Fig.* 11). And in this one, as in the one by Ciuli of Palazzo Carmanico in Naples (*Fig.* 12) and in the one of Palazzo Parisani in Rome, we see the same portrait of a lady with a child in her arms, in the same frame: a portrait which the Wittgenstein family evidently carried with them from one dwelling-place to another, to create a home-like atmosphere.

Thus there is a continuity in these pictures, and there is also a continuity in the taste of the furnishings and in the background of the various countries, the annual pilgrimage or progress of the noble family from the Russian countryside in summer and fall, to the winters in Rome, spring in Paris or Baden, and the summers on the Isle of Wight or in Switzerland, with Naples reserved for late spring. And there is also an international continuity which led to intimacy and intermarriage

with other noble families of Europe, creating in a restricted, congenial circle that European community which today's statesmen still cannot carry out on a democratic plane. There was a united Europe of royal and noble families and, as in all families, there were arguments which they called wars; but they spoke the same language and in the end they always came to an agreement—at the people's expense, historians may say. Then the steam engine came, and brought industry, capitalism, the urban movement, the masses, and the Iron Curtain and space travel. The world, though it becomes standardized and infinitely contracted and smaller, has gotten out of control. It is no longer possible for anyone to sum it up in an album like that of the Chigis, with a miniature by Migliara inserted in the binding, depicting a quiet and shady cloistered corner; an album which shows us the mighty as they enjoyed the delights of handsome apartments, elegant dinners, balls, and conversations, or witnessed—as a change—the rustic pastimes of the humble, while they classified under a general denomination of "pictur-esque" the daily toil of the *mujik.* As you leaf through this album, you can almost hear that carillon of the impassive clock at Versailles which went on playing after Marie Antoinette had appeared to the populace for the last time on the scaffold of the guillotine, or the carillon of the Cathedral of Saints Peter and Paul playing "God Save the Tsar!" when the Russian revolution had swept away Tsar and Wittgensteins and Barjatinskij as well as those few water-colored leaves of sumptuous houses, removed from the Chigis' album and presented to their Russian kinfolk.

In 1955 in Vienna I happened to buy ten or so watercolors of interiors, some of them signed by Pieter

Figure 15: Hess or Hesse.
The Wittgenstein Family in the Garden
at Zausze, watercolor, July 1839.
COLLECTION DON AGOSTINO CHIGI,
ROME.

Francis Peters, others by Wilhelm Dünckel, and still others—of a later date—by Fernand Pelez, Senior (*Fig.* 4);[22] but I have no idea who lived in those rooms. Much more vivid is the story of two little pictures representing rooms of the royal palace in Naples at the time of Murat. Now hanging in my house, they seem to extend it magically, and those miniature rooms which I enter only in my fantasy are no less real to me than my own rooms. It's as if I opened a secret door in my living room, to enter a wing of an abandoned palace, a kind of second house of mine, with shadowy coffered ceilings where human voices no longer resound.

Of those little paintings, one—an oil (*Fig.* 16)—is a replica, obviously by the same hand, of a watercolor (*Fig.* 164) of an interior of the palace at Naples which the Conte G. B. Spalletti reproduced in his *Souvenirs d'enfance de la Comtesse Rasponi fille de Joachim Murat* (1929).[23] A passage from these memoirs enlightens us on the subject of the painting: "These little receptions took place in the billiard room or in the room known as the *grand cabinet* of the Queen [Queen Carolina, Caroline Murat]. Nothing could be more enchanting than the arrangement of the latter. The little picture painted by Monsieur Clarac, which is in my bedroom, is quite a faithful representation of it, but still gives only an imperfect idea. The end of the room, where my mother's writing desk stood, was all of mirrors and opened onto the famous terrace which, along with the view of the bay, was reflected infinitely on those crystal walls. The Queen gave audiences in this room, but despite the charm of the view, did not stay there as a rule."

Clarac who, before becoming famous as curator of antiquities at the Louvre, was the tutor of Murat's children from 1808 to 1813, has painted the Queen seated at her writing desk; looking up from the book which she is holding, half-shut, in her right hand, she turns her back to us to look at her four children playing on the terrace. Dressed in white, with a bonnet in the watercolor (*Fig.* 164) or bareheaded in the oil (*Fig.* 16), the Queen is sitting at the great window, which a white curtain separates from the rest of the room which is in shadow. Beyond the terrace, with its balustrade and its decorative pots, the mountains of the Sorrento peninsula and Capri stand out in a rosy light against the sea, which is of a delicate blue dotted by two white sails. On a chair in the room, near the curtain of the door to the left, a strangely-designed military hat, the *czapska*, is lying; it belongs to one of Murat's little sons whom we see running on the terrace. To the right, on the blue and white striped wall in the shadow, half of a painting appears; we recognize it as Correggio's *Education of Cupid*.

The Correggio painting, reproduced with painstaking accuracy, adorns also the right wall of the room depicted in the second of the little paintings, a watercolor which has come into my hands (*Fig.* 17). Although the room in the Royal Palace at Naples depicted in this work is analogous in form and has the same view of the bay, it is quite different from my small oil painting (*Fig.* 16) in the rest of its decoration. One presumes that in the interval between the two pictures a change in the arrangement of the furnishings took place. Elie Honoré Montagny, painter of Queen Carolina, who in 1811 made this watercolor, precise as a miniature, has reproduced every tiny detail of the room, the reflections of the white satin draperies which adorn it all around, above the wine red dado, the Pompeiian arabesques of

Figure 16: Comte de Clarac.
 Caroline Murat in the Royal Palace,
Naples, oil painting.
 COLLECTION MARIO PRAZ,
 ROME.

the ceiling, the little cups, the coffee pots, the porcelain vases which clutter the two marble tables at the side walls, which have antique supports, one a Cupid holding a goose in his hands and the other a kneeling Persian with a Phrygian cap on his head. In the window at the end there is a sofa and a table covered with a green rug, and to the left, at an angle, another window, which makes one believe that this corner room was the last in that wing of the palace opening onto the great terrace. At the end wall, above a console made from fragments of a Roman table, filled with vases and plates, and flanked by two tall tripods, hangs Correggio's *Ecce Homo*. In the center of a large carpet, all of vines on a maroon ground, there is a porphyry cup on a base of monopode lions. Artificial flowers in bouquets and fan-like arrangements are scattered about the room: in a great Apulian amphora set on the ground, in vases on the tables and tripods, and beneath a glass bell placed under the console.

Crystalline in its clarity, this room awaiting its inhabitants is eloquent and moving; the more so because we possess the text of the drama that unfolded there, reported to us by contemporaries: the Duchesse d'Abrantès, and the biographers of Madame Récamier. "The Queen lived in Naples in the most enchanting of residences. From her bedchamber she could see the whole bay. The room was furnished in exquisite taste; it was draped in white satin, and the folds of the soft, silken stuff were wonderfully in harmony with the pink and white coloring of the Sovereign." One day in January, 1814, Juliette Récamier was introduced into this apartment and was struck by the pallor and the agitation of Murat and Caroline. To keep his throne, Murat had made an alliance with the enemies of Napoleon. The dramatic encounter as reported to us cannot be accepted word for word; we wouldn't swear that Murat really said: "They'll call me a traitor! They'll call me Murat the Traitor!" And we don't know whether, when led to that window, Madame Récamier advised him to remain loyal to France or whether, showing her the English ships in the harbor, Murat then said, in a changed voice: "You see, all is over!", as Ballanche reports the scene; or in a voice choked with tears: "There is the reason why France will hail me with the name of traitor!" as the Duchesse d'Abrantès narrates it; or simply: "So I am a traitor," as Madame Lenormant quotes him. It is enough for us to catch the rhythm of that scene, without trying to make out the exact words; it is enough to follow the excited movements of the characters, to linger over certain gestures which, precisely because at first glance they seem insignificant, the narrators have never elaborated with their imaginations: the gesture of Carolina who takes a glass from a table and fills it with water of orange blossoms so that Murat will drink it and calm himself, and Murat's movement as he goes off beyond "the numerous, swaying folds of the satin that draped the entrance to the room in Oriental fashion."

In this watercolor by Montagny, the room's draperies are composed and motionless; on the tables with their elegant supports are lined up the cups, the knick-knacks, the vases; from the window the enchanting bay smiles. It is a scene of eternal Elysium. And this is how the painter chose to immortalize it for us, with loving care. The inhabitants of that room have long since gone to their deaths: one of them died violently, under the bullets of a firing squad. Next to the door of the room the key is still hanging, as if the master had only left it there a moment ago, and the bell-rope is waiting for a hand to pull it. But in vain. Of the magnificent furnishings nothing is left today within those walls. On July 12, 1823, the former Queen of Naples, calling herself by an anagram, the Contessa di Lipona, sold at an auction at Christie's in London thirteen valuable paintings, including Correggio's *Ecce Homo* and *The Education of Cupid*. They were bought for two hundred eighty thousand five hundred francs by the Marquis of Londonderry, and from him, in 1834, they passed to the National Gallery. The statue of Cupid with the goose became part of the collection of the Prince of Salerno, made a fleeting appearance at the Museo Borbonico, then came to rest at Chantilly. The kneeling Persian, originally from the Farnese Gardens, can be seen today at the Museo Nazionale in Naples. His face and his hands are black, of that marble known as "paragone"; surprisingly, in the watercolor this young man's face is pink and white. Of the other, less illustrious art objects I do not know the fate, but the miniaturist has been so precise in painting them that if I came upon them today in a museum, in a private collection, or at a dealer's, I would recognize them.

Doesn't all this furnish an inspiring suggestion for some fancier? Some collectors have devoted their whole lives to the search for objects that once decorated a given room and were later dispersed. Such men occupy, among lovers of furnishings, something like the place that translators occupy in the field of the arts: they recreate according to a set guide, they furnish a room as if following an obligatory rhyme scheme, they put together a puzzle where some pieces are inevitably beyond finding. Such an enterprise of reconstructing the past is only possible when the objects can be identified through descriptions in archives or catalogues, by well-documented changes of hands, or—as with the Naples palace—by precise paintings of the rooms.

The assistance which these paintings of interiors can offer became clear to me in the case of the portrait of a Spanish lady made at the beginning of the 19th century. This portrait, of small dimensions, shows a blond, plump lady, dressed in the classic Spanish *manola* costume, garnished with braided cords on the shoulders and hems of the dress, with a carnation in her hair and a white lace mantilla which covers her head and is crossed at her breast, falling in two long white strips almost to her knees; her right hand, hanging by her side, is holding a fan; her left presses one end of the mantilla to her breast; the park in which she is depicted has well-defined groups of trees, and in the background a little mound surmounted by an equestrian monument whose profile suggests that of Pietro Tacca's Philip IV in the garden of the Royal Palace of Madrid. The sky, which is pink at the horizon, darkens to a deep blue in the upper part of the picture, as if to bring the head of the lady into sharper relief. The portrait came from a noble Neapolitan family and is quite similar to other small paintings belonging to Prince Massimo, of the same dimensions and by the same artist, the Spanish court painter José Pablo Lacoma (1784-1849). As to the identification of the subject, I suspected that she was the daughter of Carlos IV, Maria Isabella, Queen of the Two Sicilies, who married Francesco I of Naples in 1802.

My surprise can be imagined when, as I was examining under a magnifying glass the reproduction of a watercolor by Garnerey of the drawing room of the Duchesse de Berry in the Pavillon de Marsan, I saw on the wall, matching a male portrait on the opposite side of a round mirror, a picture which seemed to correspond in every detail to my portrait of the Spanish lady. The same arrangement of light and shadow in the background, the characteristic two ends of the mantilla falling to the knee, and if, instead of having only a black and white reproduction before me, I could have examined the original with my glass, I'm sure that the identification would have been confirmed. Now Maria Carolina, Duchesse de Berry, was the daughter of Francesco I of Naples, and the stepdaughter of Maria Isabella, and it can be imagined that the two portraits flanking the mirror in her drawing room were, in fact, those of her parents, the two sovereigns.[24]

The original of Garnerey's watercolor (*Fig.* 168) is in the castle of Brunnsee in Austria, property of Conte Lodovico Lucchesi-Palli, descendant of the Duca della Grazia, second husband of the Duchesse de Berry. What better proof could be found of what the Duchesse d'Abrantès wrote of Garnerey, that "he painted a room with such enchantment in the details that every supporting-rod of the chairs of the apartment could be identified, and yet nothing was finicky, everything was fascinating in those very details."[25] He is the painter of eight views of the park and hothouses of Malmaison which commemorate the Empress Josephine's love for flowers and exotic plants. Collected in a binding of red morocco, these views were once a part of the Empress's library, then they passed to that of the Dukes of Leuchtenberg, through Eugène de Beauharnais, and were sold in the auction in Zürich

in 1935 when that library was dispersed. From there they found their way back to their first home, Malmaison.

The precision of the miniaturists of interiors, like Garnerey, has something disturbing about it. For who, in ordinary life, ever observes with such minute attention the decoration of a room? Who doesn't limit himself to embracing the whole with a general glance, deriving vague and sometimes quite illusory impressions from it? If the owners themselves (unless they are amateurs of furnishing) can often not exactly remember all the details of the rooms they live in, how can we expect more of casual visitors or occasional guests? So it is not surprising that describers of the same room at times contradict one another, as eyewitnesses of any kind tend to do. The impression that an ordinary person retains of a room, especially if he is unfamiliar with styles, is quite rudimentary. Thus those veristic novelists who went to such pains to give almost an inventory of the objects in a room which served as the background of their characters' actions were really taking unnecessary trouble. We can be certain that none of those characters ever gave the things around them more than an idle glance, that the fact of the existence of a given piece of furniture or item of décor had no importance in the development of the story, and that finally those descriptions, meant to establish for the reader a certain local color, are neither more nor less than the literary counterpart of the watercolors of interiors by Garnerey and his colleagues.

However inferior in evocative power written descriptions may be to painted images, they are not read without some pleasure. These descriptions, like the

little pictures of interiors, also allow us to penetrate the privacy of other people's houses without moving from our own easy chair. I don't mean to consider such purely fantastic descriptions as that of the *petite* *Maison-Surprise*, "masterpiece of erotic architecture," which the Marquis de Sade gives us in *Zoloé*,[26] with such a dose of superlatives that it becomes, as is usual with this author, boring; or the deliberately absurd

Figure 17: Elie-Honoré Montagny.
Room in the Royal Palace,
Naples, watercolor, 1811.

COLLECTION MARIO PRAZ,
ROME.[26a]

43

description of the apartment of an exquisite contained in that parody of Disraeli, Thackeray's *Codlingsby*. Fantastic also is the description of Paquita's boudoir in *La Fille aux yeux d'or* of Balzac intended, like Sade's, to "warm the coldest of beings." Still we find there considerations on the effects of certain colors (white, red, gold) disposing the spirit to voluptuousness, which could be set beside others of Baudelaire in *La Fanfarlo* on the necessity of smallness and softness in rooms propitious to love-making. Both descriptions have a mannered flavor, and there is also something mannered about the similar conclusion of the two passages, which are best quoted in the original, to make their affinity more evident:

Balzac: "Ce fut au milieu d'une vapoureuse atmosphère chargée de parfums exquis que Paquita, vêtue d'un peignoir blanc, les pieds nus, des fleurs d'oranger dans les cheveux noirs, apparut à Henri agenouillée devant lui, l'adorant comme le dieu de ce temple où il avait daigné venir."

Baudelaire: "C'est au fond de ce ravissant taudis, qui tenait à la fois du mauvais lieu et du sanctuaire, que Samuel vit s'avancer vers lui la nouvelle déesse de son coeur, dans la splendeur radieuse et sacrée de sa nudité."

Such vague descriptions, which aim not so much at giving the details of an atmosphere as its effect on the spirit of him who enters it, leave no trace in the memory of the reader as descriptions. But one does remember those descriptions prompted less by the imagination than by the precise observation of the taste of the period. From certain minor works of Balzac we remember, to tell the truth, only pages like those in *Un début dans la vie*, where the pavilion of Madame Moreau is described:

"Moving her living quarters to the first floor, Madame Moreau had been able to transform the former bedroom into a little living room. The main drawing room and this smaller one, richly decorated with handsome pieces chosen from the old furnishings of the château, would certainly not have been unworthy of the house of a lady of fashion. Hung with white and blue damask, formerly the stuff of a huge state bed, this room, whose furniture of gilded wood was upholstered in the same stuff, offered to the visitor's gaze curtains and portieres which were very full and lined with white taffeta. Pictures which came from old, destroyed *trumeaux*, jardinières, some charming modern pieces, as well as an antique crystal chandelier gave this room an aspect of grandeur. The smaller living room, entirely modern and in Madame Moreau's taste, imitated the form of a tent, with its sofas of blue silk against a lilac-colored background. There was the classic divan with its cushions and its footstools. Finally the jardinières of which the head gardener was in charge, rejoiced the eye with their pyramids of flowers...."

Balzac's inventory is nonetheless lacking in that precision which alone can make things tangible. Furniture of gilded wood, classic divan—nothing is told us of their precise shape; and if we manage to visualize the room in the form of a tent, it is because we recall the similar one of Josephine's which really exists at Malmaison. Not that minute descriptions are necessary to give the atmosphere of a room. Hale White, in *The Autobiography of Mark Rutherford*, says only a few words about the house of the Arbour sisters, who were: "suffering much from ill-health, but perfectly resigned, and with a kind of tempered cheerfulness always apparent on their faces, like the cheerfulness of a white sky with a sun veiled by light and lofty clouds." He says only that, in their house: "Everything was at rest; books, pictures, furniture, all breathed the same peace. Nothing in the house was new, but everything had been preserved with such care that nothing looked old."

It's odd, but we see much more clearly this vaguely-mentioned house than we do the pavilion of Madame Moreau, described at such length and enriched by those rather vulgar observations: "would not have been unworthy of the house of a lady of fashion" and "the jardinières of which the head gardener was in charge." In the same book by Hale White we find a more detailed description, that of the little living room in Mardon's house, and here too every detail strikes home, and we have before our eyes a clear little Biedermeier picture, with its Windsor chairs, a niche on either side of the fireplace, one with the tea-caddy, a work-box, glasses and a carafe filled with water, the other niche converted into bookshelves, and the portraits of Bacon and Voltaire and Dürer's *Saint Jerome* on the walls, and half a dozen plants on the window-sill (aspidistras no doubt) acting as a screen.

What is it that Balzac's description lacks which is found so naturally in the descriptions of Hale White? There is only one word to describe it, a Northern word, as the sentiment it expresses is Northern in origin: *Stimmung*. That sentiment, that sense of the interior was born in times relatively close to our own. The love of precious objects is something else; that has always existed, reaching that apex of refinement which worried Cicero, as we have seen. And it is also another

matter to take pride, as the rich man of whom Horace speaks, in a house gleaming with ivory, with gold coffered ceilings and architraves of Hymettus marble set on columns cut in farthest Africa. Such taste for sumptuous décor is something different from a sense of the house's intimacy, the house conceived as a mirror of the spirit. This is a modern discovery, as is landscape, in the sense that we conceive it today, which is certainly not as it was conceived in Horace's time. For Horace the delights of rustic life lay in rural occupations accompanied by, if by anything, a sense of religiosity, which Walter Pater has tried to interpret for us in his *Marius the Epicurean*, though the gentleman-farmer he describes is probably closer to the Victorian Englishman than to the ancient Roman.[27] Just as the love of the country in Roman times always had a background of practicality: the care of plants and flocks and bees, the gathering of fruit, the harvesting of crops; so the cult of the house always had a practical basis: there was the chaste wife, the innocent children, the household gods. The only moment, in the famous ode of that distinguished *ruris amator* Horace, *Beatus ille*, which approaches contemplation (to lie in the shade of an ancient ilex, or on the soft grass, to listen to the murmur of the waters and the song of the birds) is also resolved in a practical consideration: all these things are good because they help a man sleep.

What the owners of the houses in Herculaneum and Pompeii may have felt, beyond the repose of their peristyles adorned and murmuring with waters, we have no way of knowing: a sense of the house, of home, must surely always have been there, in however rudimentary a form, but still tangled in a net of

merely physical sensations. No painter or writer has left us any documentation of it, unless we want to give great weight to certain charming Pompeiian decorative motifs, which show appreciation of the elegance of a basket of flowers or fruit, of a group of amphorae and vases—in a word, showing a detached satisfaction in lovely decorations.[28] And the existence of a love for furniture is proved, beyond the passage from Cicero, by the high degree of technical achievement attained in furniture-making in antiquity, by the refinements which—according to the historians of furniture—are not found again until the 18th century. With the opening of the tomb of Tutankhamen objects came to light which show how Empire cabinet-makers, after thousands of years, were not far off the mark in their imitations of Egyptian furniture derived by indirect and often conjectural methods. But no cabinet-maker has ever been able to reproduce the simple per-

fection of the Greek chair, whose profile of graceful curves underlines the elegant position of the human body when seated. This profile of *klismós* is rhythmically carved on sepulchral steles, and demonstrates the relationship between this object designed to support man and the living creature that man uses for transportation: the horse. This relationship is, from primitive times, indicated in theriomorphic legs and, in the Greek chair, is typified by the elastic, equine elegance of the profile. Furniture is, in origin, of two species: furniture that supports and furniture that contains; the former suggests animal forms; the second, architectonic; the chair is inspired by the horse; the linen chest, like the coffin for that matter, is inspired by the house. Now if that Greek chair's profile, a model of functional elegance to arouse the envy of our century which talks so much of functionalism, recurs in the steles and Greek vase paintings as a charming motif,

Figure 19: Haase.
Bedroom and Dressing Room in
the Wittgenstein Residence at Kamenka,
watercolor, November 1837.

it is clear that those ancients must have felt the grace of the object and have loved it, loving also those arrangements of pieces, sober though they were, which formed the decoration of their rooms. Roman furnishing, more varied than the Greek, contained in essence all the types that later centuries were to rediscover or develop; but as I have said, a taste for furniture is not necessarily accompanied by a taste for the interior. The pieces of furniture had a physical perfection, but they still lacked a soul; one could, in other words, repeat here what has often been said in comparing a Greek statue with a Christian one.

Walter Scott, in a page of *Ivanhoe*, attempted to evoke a medieval interior, the apartment of Lady Rowena. "The walls were covered with embroidered hangings, of which different-coloured silks, interwoven with gold and silver threads, had been em-

ployed, with all the art of which the age was capable, to represent the sports of hunting and hawking. The bed was adorned with the same rich tapestry, and surrounded with curtains dyed with purple. The seats had also their stained coverings, and one, which was higher than the rest, was accommodated with a footstool of ivory, curiously carved. No fewer than four silver candelabras, holding great waxen torches, served to illuminate this apartment. Yet let not modern beauty envy the magnificence of a Saxon princess. The walls of the apartment were so ill finished and so full of crevices, that the rich hangings shook to the night blast, and, in despite of a sort of screen intended to protect them from the wind, the flame of the torches streamed sideways into the air, like the unfurled pennon of a chieftain. Magnificence there was, with some rude attempt at taste; but of comfort there was

Figure 20: E. Gärtner.
Bedroom of the Wittgenstein Residence
in Berlin, watercolor, April 1836.
COLLECTION DON AGOSTINO CHIGI,
ROME.

little, and, being unknown, it was unmissed."

We'd better not check too carefully the furnishings of this room, since Scott himself admits to having fused the customs of two or three centuries, introducing into the reign of Richard I (twelfth century) circumstances of considerably earlier or considerably later periods. Thus the decorations with hunting themes are characteristic of the 14th and 15th centuries;[29] the bed with purple hangings which Scott mentions, for that matter, would seem to be the very bed of Réné d'Anjou in a famous miniature of 1470, now in the National Library, Vienna. Scott is, however, correct in his impression that there were few pieces of furniture and many stuffs, for it was in stuffs that the Middle Ages concentrated all luxury. The focal point of the room was the fireplace; the universal piece of furniture the cassone; there was no symmetrical arrangement of furnishings, no play of light and shadow, for the light that filtered through the small windows was dim, and the windows were made even more opaque by stained glass or small leaded bull's-eye panes. And yet it is precisely in these Nordic, apparently gloomy surroundings that Stimmung, the sense of intimacy, was first born.

The medieval idea of beauty and of security was always something segregated, removed from the world: the cloister, the castle, the walled city, the closed garden, the orchard. In the 15th century the French, with the help of tapestries, transformed their rooms into exquisite, shady artificial orchards, where the life of the woods, the fields, and the hunt were faintly reflected like a light filtered through deep water. This medieval use of tapestries was quite different in concept from the simple landscape decoration of an-cient Egyptian floors or from the mechanical "opening out" on the world which was attempted in the so-called "second style" at Pompeii.

The still atmosphere of an aquarium reigns in the first paintings of interiors in the modern sense of the word: interiors that are not merely rooms but mirrors of the soul. In the miniature of the Birth of Saint John, in the famous Heures de Milan of 1416, attributed to Jan Van Eyck and assistants (Fig. 35), a door in the background, surmounted by a shelf laden with dishes and kettles, allows us to glimpse other rooms, streaked with calm shafts of light, and every object in that background is as painstakingly portrayed as the objects on the chest and table in the foreground. The picture breathes a sense of order, of neatness which dominates even the characters themselves and is the soul of the picture. There is a similar harmonious peace in the portrait of the merchant Arnolfini and his wife painted by Jan Van Eyck in 1434, where the couple, as rigid as wax statues, are in harmony with the immobile life of the things surrounding them: the bed and the big chair covered with red stuff, the brass lamp, the slippers, the elegant pair of red shoes, the oranges on the coffer under the window. Here too the Stimmung is determined above all by the sense of the apartment, given by the door opened to the other rooms. The open door is here presented in rather a sly way: it is seen reflected in a mirror which hangs upon the inner wall.

The Northern artists have often rendered this sense of intimacy in paintings of saints and humanists in their studies. Dürer painted Saint Jerome sitting in the sun's warmth near the window of his cluttered room, between his cardinal's hat and a gourd with elegant trailing tendrils (*Fig.* 55). The Neapolitan painter of the mid 15th century, Colantonio, whose style was so steeped in the Flemish spirit that his painting was once attributed to Hubert Van Eyck, painted Saint Jerome as the loving doctor of his lion (*Fig.* 56), from whose paw he extracts a thorn: the saint and lion are seen in a little alcove of shelves piled high with books, boxes, vases, bottles, letters, all executed with a scrupulous zeal found again only centuries later in the watercolors of Biedermeier interiors. Quentyn Matsys depicted Erasmus of Rotterdam fenced in, almost shrouded in the wood paneling of the walls, with a pair of scissors hanging from the shelves of books. This sense of intimacy is not found in the interiors painted by the Italian Renaissance artists, where—if you look for example at Ghirlandaio's *Nativity of the Virgin* (*Fig.* 52)—the architecture lends a solemn and staid note. One painter is an exception, Carpaccio, who learned from the Northerners the magic of a door that allows a glimpse of other rooms, as in his *Nativity of the Virgin* (*Fig.* 51), in the Accademia Carrara at Bergamo, and above all in his *Dream of Saint Ursula* (*Fig.* 50), which gives us all the poetry of a Renaissance room made of airy spaces and delicate strength. In this painting the aspiration of the vertical lines of the slender columns of the bed, the slim statuettes above the doors, the little altarpiece on the wall with its lamp and its holy-water stoup, the slender plants in graceful pots on the windowsill, and the upward tapering back of the chair, are repeated in the figure of the angel who enters with a flutter of sharply pointed wings. Likewise the immense peace of the horizontals of the paneling of walls and ceiling, and the outline of the canopy of the bed, find a counterpart in Saint Ursula lying on the bed in perfect serenity. The sense of vastness and of emptiness that prevents us from feeling any *Stimmung* in the interiors of a Ghirlandaio or an Andrea del Sarto is completely absent in the *Dream of Saint Ursula*. This painting is the documentation, rare south of the Alps, of a way of feeling that was already widespread in the North.

Indeed today, with pictures and furniture of the Renaissance, even though the former are often of supreme quality and the latter are full of dignity and cheer, it is very difficult to create a room that has anything intimate about it. We have seen dozens of those rooms in villas and museums, with white walls on which altarpieces and terracottas, often famous ones, are hung, frequently presented against some rich brocade or velvet. At cleverly spaced intervals are seat-chests and arm chairs, Savonarola chairs and little cupboards lined up with some Gubbio or Castel Durante majolica. Everything is beautiful, noble, and yet cold, sterile, as if the air had been sucked out of the room, as if every object were wearing a cellophane protective cover, like rare bindings. In every corner you feel that a shaft of electric light is lying in ambush, and that, at the right moment, it will give the object a tricky appearance, while the tormented soul of Dossena, the celebrated creator of fakes, wanders about doing eternal penance and, like the dice-players in Dante's *Purgatorio,* he "repeating the throws . . . sadly learns."

Perhaps it is the predominance of the architectonic element which prevents intimacy in Renaissance rooms[30] as in the interior scenes painted by Renaissance artists, where the furnishings have merely structural function. In some of these rooms, the most solemn, the frescoes on the walls and the daedalian ceiling reign alone. Along the dado the few monumental pieces of furniture seem fixed in place, unmovable from their precise, definitive position. In the bedroom, the state bed is like a monumental altar surmounted by its canopy.[31] Since the humanists lacked Classical models for many articles of furniture, they sought inspiration in architecture, they translated into wood forms that had been conceived for stone, and cornices, pilasters, modillions, became elements of the cabinet-maker as they were of the architect. In the late Renaissance the architectural forms were complemented by anthropomorphic and theriomorphic elements derived from antiquity: sphinxes, dolphins, chimeras.

Even the solemn forms of the Renaissance can have an intimacy of their own, their own rarified and cerebral exquisiteness, if they are warmed by a mind like that of Poliphilus, the protagonist of the *Hypnerotomachia Poliphili* of Francesco Colonna (1499). The writer's sensual spirit informs all the detailed descriptions of clothes, monuments, ruins and objects, adapting itself lovingly, scrupulously to the shapes of things, and cherishing them with that linear, curling style, which is the exact counterpart of the woodcuts that accompany the text (*Figs.* 47, 48). In such descriptions Poliphilus' world is presented to us with a supreme, crystalline clarity, at times having the gem-like and precious aspect of a room painted by Mantegna.

Here, rendered in the English translation of the *Hypnerotomachia,* of 1592, is a description of the interior of a palace with a "bewtifull and precious Paument:" . . . within a checkered compasse going

about the same, there was a space of sixtie foure Squadrates of three foote, the dyameter of euerye one: Of the which one was of Iaspar, of the colour of Corall, and the other greene, powdered with drops of blood not to bee woorne away: and set togither in manner of a Chesse-boord. . . About this, lastlye was an other marueylous kynde of Pauing of three paces broad, in knottes of Iasper, Praxin, Calcedonie, Agat, and other sortes of stones of price. And about the sides of the walles, compassing the sayde Court paued as you haue heard, there were placed Settles, of the wood of Palme Trees, of colour betwixt a yealow and tawny, passing well turned and fashioned, couered ouer with green Veluet and bowlstered with some soft stuffe or feathers easie to sit upon, the Veluet brought downe to the frame of the Settles or Benches, and fastened to the same with tatch Nayles of Golde, with bossed heades upon a plaine Siluer Nextrule or Cordicell."

And when Poliphilus lingers to describe the silk garden: "The boxes and Cyprus trees were all silke, sauing the bodies and greater branches . . . the rest, as the leaues, flowers, and outermost rynde, was of fine silke, wanting no store of Pearles to beautifie the same . . . and in the bushes were Ringe-doues of silke, as if they had beene feeding of the berries, all along the sides of the square plotted garden walles: ouer the which, in master-like and requisite order, stretched out the beame and Zophor of golde."

How can one not think of certain Elizabethan rooms, where the oak furniture inspired by the French Renaissance, carved over every inch of its surface, stood side by side with a profusion of heavy embroidery, with clumsy, curiously-padded figures, often adorned with little pearls: a mixture of refinement, sophistication, and barbarism which recalls the euphuism and the tortuous casuistry of Sir Philip Sidney's *Arcadia?*

Decorations of this kind, however, take us very far afield from the architectonic delirium of Poliphilus and from his haunted, mineral atmosphere. They carry us back to one of those Northern interiors where the collection of objects does not produce merely an esthetic effect since the nature and the arrangement of the objects always suggest human contact, daily, loving use; back to that sense of furnishing which was born in the houses of the rich and refined bourgeois of the North. Only a bourgeois imagination could conceive and produce those monumental Germanic cupboards of the 16th and 17th centuries, true encyclopedias of ornamentation and architecture, where no distinction is made between the fundamental and the accessory, where the scholar, the architect, the cabinet-maker, and the goldsmith vie in ability, and where within the numerous compartments, decorated on the outside with gems and coins, you find toilet articles, writing materials, playing cards, astrolabes, hourglasses, cupping glasses and clysters. A cupboard of this kind finds its architectural counterpart in the mad designs of Wendel Dietterlin, and its literary twin in John Donne's sermons and his more ambitious poems *(The Anatomie of the World)*.

These complex cupboards, a characteristically bourgeois invention, were above all court pieces. Under Louis XIV came that sharp distinction between court furniture and bourgeois furniture which lasted up until the Neoclassic period: the bourgeois credenza, used to display handsome pottery, corresponded to the patrician cabinet, used for keeping precious objects. The distinction went beyond such comprehensible specializations: for the court, furniture that was merely for show was created so removed from any practical use that such pieces, suggesting no human contact, gave no intimacy to a room. This was furniture that had no function beyond that of supporting the coat-of-arms, or as I said earlier, speaking of certain grim Roman palaces, of standing like stiff, liveried servants. The proportion of these pieces expressed that same taste that involved an abuse of capital letters in handwriting and enlarged the human figure through great wigs and shoes with high, red heels.

But when, in 18th century France the great palaces were neglected in favor of *hôtels,* or the little country houses, *maisons de plaisance,* when in court circles one sought variety, comfort, and gaiety, then the golden age of furnishing was born. Born from the confluence of bourgeois and patrician taste, just as these two kinds of taste were joined in England in the prose of *The Spectator,* giving it that tone of both distinction and affability, of humanity and classic restraint.

And it is precisely in England and in the Anglomane France of Louis XVI that furnishing became the faithful expression of the new spirit. A didactic poet who wished to translate into images this phase of the history of furniture might now sing a cunningly contrived myth of the invention of the commode, which took place at the beginning of the 18th century and contributed greatly to giving rooms a more intimate character. And this poet could also hymn the theogony of other new pieces of furniture: the bookcase, and the numberless progeny of little tables, those that

Figure 21: F. W. Klose.
Writing Room in the Palace of
Friedrich Wilhelm III in Berlin,
watercolor, c. 1830.
COLLECTION CHARLOTTENBURG PALACE,
BERLIN.

went against the wall or stood in the center of a room, game-tables, work-tables, occasional tables, nests of tables, each with their characteristic form and attributes. And he could sing of the long list of furniture with imaginative and charming feminine names, the *bergère*, the *marquise*, the *duchesse*, the *turquoise*, the *veilleuse*, the *voyeuse*, the *athénienne*, the *psyché*, a theme worthy of a new *Metamorphoses*.

In 17th century Holland furnishing was aimed above all at achieving an effect of prosperity and intimacy. The bourgeois neatness, the distinction and solidity in the rooms of Vermeer, of Pieter de Hooch, of Terborch, and Metsu! As if the world were becalmed forever in a season of grace and sweet reason, absorbed in memories, content with small pleasures: a harpsichord being played, choice wine drunk from clear crystal, the visit of a beloved person. The contrast to magniloquent pomp that the author of the *Argenis*, as transcribed by Crashaw, saw in a religious house could be applied to these peaceful Dutch interiors:

Figure 22: E. Biermann.
Drawing Room of the Princess Elizabeth
in the Palace at Berlin,
watercolor, 1829.
COLLECTION SANSSOUCI,
POTSDAM.

"No roofes of gold o're riotous tables shining
Whole dayes & suns deuour'd with endless dining;
No sailes of tyrian sylk proud pauements sweeping;
Nor iuory couches costlyer slumbers keeping;
False lights of flairing gemmes; tumultuous joyes;
Halls full of flattering men & frisking boyes;
Whate're false showes of short & slippery good
Mix the mad sons of men in mutuall blood . . .
. . . peace, & pure ioyes;
Kind loues keep house, ly close, and make no noise . . ."

In the familiar rotation of daily tasks, in the rhythm
of the tranquil hours, "The self-remembring *Soul*
sweetly recovers, Her kindred with the starrs . . ." All
this was expressed in the Dutch house.

Then in the course of the 18th century, for that other
great bourgeoisie of the North, the English, another
style of furnishing was born, also filled with *Stimmung*. Before Robert Adam, the classic, Palladian
buildings which had been so fashionable in England
were modeled on the temples of the ancients, not their
houses. Therefore interiors had always seemed monumental, unsuited to the needs of a society like that of
the 18th century, with its sense of intimacy, of quiet
well-being beside the hearth. From the remarkable
ruins of Diocletian's palace at Spalato, from the
stucco work in the tombs along Rome's Via Latina,
from Raphael's loggias in the Vatican and those of
Villa Madama, and from the ceilings of white stucco
on a blue ground made by Algardi at the Villa Doria-
Pamphili, Robert Adam conceived his idea of an
interior decoration: all grace and delicacy, with stucco
arabesques enlivened here and there by little colored
medallions of mythological scenes.

Rome, Adam observed, "was tasteful, not profuse."
The private apartments of the Romans were not a
series of monotonous, solemn halls, as their imitators
had claimed; on the contrary, the Romans were careful to adjust the form and dimensions, with the happy
effect of introducing into their buildings a variety
which, if it did not constitute beauty in itself, at least
considerably enhanced the beauty of the apartment.

Adam's ideal was to substitute the massive grandeur
of the interior architecture of the Georgian palaces
with a system of decoration in relief, having no tectonic significance, or at least to retain in the tectonic
parts (stucco columns, flattened barrel vaults) a light
and elegant character. "Elegant" is a word that recurs
often in Adam's writing, just as it is to recur in the
pages of Jane Austen. Reason, the sense of proportion,
elegance were associated concepts for all these 18th
century people, concepts which were also connected to
the Roman tradition renewed by Boileau in French
literature and by Pope in the English: a Rome not
solemn or grandiose, but charming, Alexandrine,
Horatian; a Rome no longer regarded as the triumph
of the Mighty of the earth, but adapted to the urbanity
and the intimacy of the bourgeoisie. To make lighter
the exterior design of the buildings, to lighten the
interior and make it more natural and picturesque
with the play of light and shadow which lent animation
and grace—this was the idea. Rousseau had not
preached and Gray had not sung in vain. Decorating
their interiors (and Adam was thinking of Spalato, of
Pompeii), the ancients never lost sight of the proportions of the occupants, both the people and the furni-

ture; the first modern Italian artists had erroneously conceived everything according to a canon of magnificence, and for three centuries all of Europe had simply groaned slavishly under the weight of this error.

So a domestic, accessible Neoclassicism began, whose full spring came in the France of Louis XVI, whose summer was the Empire of Napoleon, and whose languid autumn the delicious awkwardness of Biedermeier. If the Dutch interior was the first to give *Stimmung* its proper importance in furnishing, the Adam's Neoclassic interior, Etruscan as it was called, or Pompeiian, established a new kind of *Stimmung* which reconciled bourgeois intimacy with the dignity and sobriety of classical furniture. Unlike the continent's Roçoco, where functional significance was obliterated in a succession of curves which fused furniture with the decoration of the whole wall, Chippendale chairs imparted a lesson of sanity and balance. There was no attempt to conceal the practical purpose of the piece, asserted by its simple solid, straight legs. But on the back of the chair, delicately varied in Rococo or Gothic or exotic motifs and crowned with Cupid's bow, the decorative imagination was expressed. This chair was a perfect mirror of the bourgeois soul, positive and practical, yes, but not averse to fantasy, to dreaming, reconciling these two aspects with a refined sense of proportion and of measure which was pure enchantment. The *Stimmung* of those bright, fresh rooms, soberly adorned with stuccos and medallions, backgrounds to the well-defined, independent outlines of the furniture of polished mahogany, the silver objects, the crystal, marks a phase in human civilization which has perhaps never been surpassed; a time when reserve was not separated from affability, use from elegance, the positive spirit from the dream. Like the essays of *The Spectator*, these rooms in their very gracefulness express an ethical significance.

This spirit continues in Empire furnishing. That character of Thomas Mann's (Spinelli in *Tristan*) was not wrong when he argued: "There are times when I cannot do without Empire, when I simply must have it in order to attain any sense of well-being. Obviously, people feel one way among furniture that is soft and comfortable and voluptuous, and quite another among the straight lines of these tables, chairs, and draperies. This brightness and hardness, this cold, austere simplicity and reserved strength . . . has upon me the ultimate effect of an inward purification and rebirth. Beyond a doubt, it is morally elevating."

In Empire furnishing nevertheless a curious pedantic spirit was insinuated, fostered by the same logic that allowed Milizia, in his *Dictionary of Fine Arts,* to deny the appellation of beautiful to anything that contradicted a geometric *raison* (whereby the façades of churches with more orders of columns than there were divisions in the interior could not be beautiful), and that caused Ledoux to feel ideas of oppression and burial in the architecture of the prison of Aix, and Délépine to give the form of a globe to his monument to Newton, and Vaudoyer the same form to the House of a Cosmopolite. Empire furnishing aimed at being apposite to the spirit of the owner, so that, for example, hunting attributes must dominate in the house of an enthusiast of the hunt; helmets, swords, and winged Victories should distinguish the house of a soldier, and so on, according to a rational principle already expressed in the sixth book of Lomazzo's *Treatise on the*

Figure 23: Eugène Lami.
The Great Hall in the Château
of Baron James de Rothschild
at Ferrières, watercolor, 1863.

Art of Painting (1585). Lomazzo prescribed the place suited to every kind of painting, whereby for example portraits of princes and sovereigns should be seen only in royal palaces, battles only in *salles d'armes*, paintings with fruit and vegetables in kitchens. The congruence of the furnishing with the sentiments of the owner dated back to a tradition older than 18th century rationalism. And so the etiquette which demanded only black walls in the apartments of the widow of the Duc de Berry at the Pavillon de Marsan (with black veils on the mirrors and the gilt; candles of yellow wax which gave the rooms a sepulchral tone) recalled the expedient of the Greek sophist who, having lost his wife, in order to see nothing white around him, had himself waited on by black servants; or the funereal ingenuity of the Spanish knight who, not content with decking his house in

*Figure 24: Living Room in
the Villa Wolkonsky in Rome,
watercolor.*
COLLECTION LEMMERMANN,
ROME.

black, burned black candles and installed other funereal inventions of which Father Le Moine speaks in his *Art des devises*.[32] It recalls also Montezuma's House of Grief, which had black walls, roofs, ornaments, and an extremely dim light, admitted through very narrow slits. Translated into white, such uniformity could be no less funereal, as Madame d'Agoult found in the bedroom of the Principessa Belgiojoso: "A bedroom decked in white, with a great bed trimmed in opaque silver, like the catafalque of a virgin. A turbaned Negro, who slept in the antechamber, had a melodramatic effect, in the midst of all that candor."

Different from that of a Neoclassical room is the *Stimmung* of a Biedermeier or Victorian apartment, with its conversation of divan and easy chairs around the tea table, the glass cabinet of porcelains, the *petit-point*, and the contamination of Classical, Gothic, and exotic motifs. The bourgeoisie becomes heavier, loses its purity and grace, thickens with curious superfluities. The Apollo Belvedere puts on a dressing gown and slippers and grasps a pipe. The *athénienne*, the tripod for the sacrificial incense, is turned into a washstand, complemented with flowered porcelains, and then becomes a stand to support the basin of enamelled iron. "Muse, let us fill with tears the basin / which once laughed with counterfeit roses," our didactic poet might sing. Musset in his *Confession d'un enfant du siècle* deplores the apartments just after 1830, "where one found, assembled and confused, the furniture of every age and every country. Our age has no form. We haven't given the imprint of our age to our houses or to our gardens or to anything ... The apartments of the rich are cabinets of curios: the ancient, the Gothic,

the taste of the Renaissance, of Louis XIII, all jumbled together. In short, we have something from every century except our own: a condition unknown in any other age. Eclecticism is our taste; we take what we find, this for its beauty, that for its convenience, and that for its antiquity, and another thing even for its ugliness; thus we live amid flotsam, as if the end of the world were near."

Shapeless, rhetorical, cumbersome, the rooms of the mature 19th century still have a *Stimmung* all their own, derived from the picturesque, from their colorfulness. At times the predilection for a dominant note of bright red, of crimson, betrays Romantic emotionalism, and the surprise of finding, behind a severe Neo-Gothic façade with ecclesiastic reminiscences, a crimson drawing room, is like the surprise that comes from the red flannel underwear that many very worthy Victorian ladies wore around 1860, almost as if to symbolize their startled modesty at the enquiry of male eyes when skirts were lifted revealing the ankle. Poe, in the ideal room described in his *The Philosophy of Furniture*, imagines "crimson-tinted glass" at the windows, and curtains of crimson silk, "an exceedingly rich crimson silk." "The colours of the curtains and their fringe—the tints of crimson and gold—appear everywhere in profusion, and determine the *character* of the room." Even the carpet has a crimson ground on which gilded arabesques stand out, the walls are papered with a shiny silver paper with a paler crimson arabesque design, and crimson is the silk that covers the sofa. "*Repose* speaks in all," Poe says. Repose, we imagine, like that of embers that burn without flames. In all that red, at the slightly curved corners, four large, sumptuous

Sèvres vases are prominent, brimming with an abundance of sweet and vivid flowers.[33]

We seem to perceive a similar effect in a room described by Charlotte Bronte in *Jane Eyre:* "... a very pretty drawing-room, and within it a boudoir, both spread with white carpets, on which seemed laid brilliant garlands of flowers; both ceiled with snowy mouldings of white grapes and vine-leaves, beneath which glowed in rich contrast crimson couches and ottomans; while the ornaments on the pale Parian mantelpiece were of sparkling Bohemian glass, ruby red; and between the windows large mirrors repeated the general blending of snow and fire." A similar room is glimpsed in *Wuthering Heights,* by the prodigious Emily, from the shadowy garden: "and we saw—ah! it was beautiful—a splendid place carpeted with crimson, and crimson-covered chairs and tables, and a pure white ceiling bordered by gold, a shower of glass-drops hanging in silver chains from the centre, and shimmering with little soft tapers."[34] Isn't all this vivid red a symbolic transposition of repressed and sublimated passion?

That taste for the picturesque which, in the first part of the century, was still restrained within the patterns of a die-hard classicism, gradually got the upper hand in the Neo-Rococo period and triumphed in the chaotic anarchy of styles at the end of the century. The house described in Tennyson's *The Princess,* 1847 (this was Park House, near Maidstone, inhabited by the family of the poet's brother-in-law Edmund Lushington) already presents, with the Neoclassic framework, a jumbling of objects that recalls the *Wunderkammern* of the 16th and 17th centuries.

"And me that morning Walter show'd the house,
Greek, set with busts: from vases in the hall
Flowers of all heavens, and lovelier than their names,
Grew side by side; and on the pavement lay
Carved stones of the Abbey-ruin in the park,
Huge Ammonites, and the first bones of Time:
And on the tables every clime and age
Jumbled together; celts and calumets,
Claymore and snowshoe, toys in lava, fans
Of sandal, amber, ancient rosaries,
Laborious orient ivory sphere in sphere,
The cursed Malayan crease, and battle-clubs
From the isles of palm: and higher on the walls,
Betwixt the monstrous horns of elk and deer,
His own forefathers' arms and armor hung."

And here is an English drawing room of 1855 in the description of Mrs. Gaskell (in *North and South*): "There was no one in the drawing-room. It seemed as though no one had ever been in it since the day when the furniture was bagged up with as much care as if the house was to be overwhelmed with lava, and discovered a thousand years hence. The walls were pink and gold; the pattern on the carpet represented bunches of flowers on a lit ground, but it was carefully covered up in the centre by a linen drugget, glazed and colourless. The window-curtains were lace; each chair and sofa had its own particular veil of netting or knitting. Great alabaster groups occupied every flat surface, safe from dust under their glass shades. In the middle of the room, right under the bagged-up chandelier, was a large circular table, with smartly bound books arranged at regular intervals round the circumference of its polished surface, like gaily coloured spokes of a wheel. Everything reflected light, nothing absorbed it. The whole room had a painfully spotted, spangled, speckled look about it, which impressed Margaret so unpleasantly that she was hardly conscious of the peculiar cleanliness required to keep everything so white and pure in such an atmosphere, or of the trouble that must be willingly expended to secure the effect of icy, snowy discomfort. Wherever she looked there was evidence of care and labour, but not care and labour to procure ease, to help on habits of tranquil home enjoyment; solely to ornament and then to preserve ornament from dirt or destruction."

In one of his American lectures on house decoration Oscar Wilde lashed out at Victorian furnishings: "Strange ornaments to be seen in the houses of very charming people . . . wax flowers, horrible things perpetrated in berlin wool, endless antimacassars . . . which seem to reduce life to the level of an eternal washing day. . ." He also said: "The wax peach no longer ripens in the glass shade."

The accessories, the *petit riens,* the knick-knacks, the whimsical draperies (everything was draped: walls, fireplaces, mirrors, pianos, paintings on easels, flowerpots)[35] finally became the protagonists of a décor.[36] Thus the end of the 19th century, better than any other period, could be fittingly described in Walter Pater's words in *Gaston de Latour* (VIII): "It might perhaps be that . . . things, as distinct from persons, such things as one had so abundantly around one, [had] come to be so much, that the human being seemed suppressed and practically nowhere amid the objects he had projected from himself."

The drawing room at the end of the century was meant, above all, to look "artistic." A volume published in 1896, Henri de Noussanne's *Le Gout dans l'Ameublement,* instructs us on this score: "Imagination, much imagination" is his slogan; *butinant ici, voletant là:* Middle Ages, Renaissance, China, Japan, the most disparate ingredients are mixed in a hotch potch which then passed for "taste." Fairy fingers, with small outlay of money, can create surprises, marvels; only one thing must be avoided: symmetry; one art to be considered above all others: the Oriental. "The Japanese are all artists." If one understands Japanese art, he will prove to have experienced taste; the ideas will come, originality will put in an appearance, and one will know how to furnish a house.[37] William Rothenstein[38] tells about Whistler's house in Paris: "He had found an enchanting apartment set far back in the rue du Bac, a small, late-eighteenth century pavilion which, as he usually did with his houses, he had completely transformed. The outer door, painted a beautiful green and white, gave promise of what was within—a small and exquisite interior: a sitting room simply furnished with a few pieces of Empire furniture, and a dining room filled with his famous blue and white china and beautiful old silver. There was a Japanese bird-cage in the middle of the table, whereon he and Mrs. Whistler used to make lovely, trailing arrangements of flowers in blue and white bowls and little tongue-shaped dishes."

Gothic, exotic, and the "return to nature" are all combined to create a new style: *Art Nouveau.* There has been much laughing at *Art Nouveau,* but no one can deny that, after the last gasp of Neoclassicism in the chaotic eclecticism of the 19th century, this style offered the first kind of decoration with a well-defined personality, with a new *Stimmung*. Rooms again had a coherent character as in the Rococo period. The furniture, which in the classic style had been independent cubes and parallelapipeds, was now reabsorbed into the walls, camouflaged, melting into the general decoration of which they became fixed parts. The curves now took in furniture and rooms all together. One room was no longer separated from the others; they flowed into one another, organized around an atrium like the chapels of a strange Gothic cathedral which has its buttresses on the inside.

All this complex of curved and serpentine lines, alcoves, niches, rooms with whimsical outlines, remind one of the jungle, lianas, water-lilies, Nature, and the East, Byzantium and Kyoto. In these surroundings one breathes a strange pungency, an air that could be synthesized in a verse of D'Annunzio (which echoes for that matter a passage of that guileless writer on agriculture, Pietro Crecenzio): "The sweet grassy flesh grows sodden": that mixture of perfume and mustiness that flowers give off when the water in the vase hasn't been changed. That *je ne sais quoi* of Wagnerian music. In a word, the breath of decadence. A decadence that assumes the pose of springtime. They thought they understood Donatello and Botticelli, but their spokesmen were named Max Slevogt, Khnopff, Klimt, Bistolfi. An *Art Nouveau* lamp, on its slender stem, resilient or limp as a strange insect, like the spider or the mantis, has in the vocabulary of forms a language of its own, just as has a rampant Gothic leaf, a Renaissance candelabra, a Baroque cartouche, or an Empire *appliqué:* each of these forms is a *speculum minus* of the intellec-

tual and emotional life of an age, whose quintessence they contain *in nuce*. In that stiffening of *Art Nouveau,* which was the Dutch phase known as *De Stijl,* came the first hint of the modern taste for the essential nakedness of lines, pure, strongly expressed geometrical forms.

If now we imagine a kind of retrospective exposition of the furnishing of rooms in Europe in the last centuries, we can perceive a constant flux and reflux, we see the multiplicity of aspects reduced to certain formulas whose rise and fall are as regular and inevitable as those of Conservatives and Liberals in the golden age of the English parliamentary rule.

From the geometric Gothic we pass to the curvilinear Gothic and from this to the Perpendicular, with the consequent altering of the decorative composition from closed in the geometric to flowing or flamboyant in the curvilinear. The rectilinear, classic Renaissance is followed by the curvilinear Baroque, with a change in decoration similar to that just mentioned in Gothic. From perfect symmetry we move by degrees to an excess of picturesque dynamism, and even to dancing movement in the Rococo. There is then a reaction to this with an excess of static rigidity in the Neoclassic and Empire. In turn, the crystallized archaeological uniformity gives way to a new return to the picturesque, which is no less archaeological, but eccentric and changeable, inspired by all the defunct styles, until the resolution of dynamic naturalism in *Art Nouveau*. And then this style too, in years closer to our own, provokes a reaction—a reaction based on nakedness of lines, pure, strongly expressed geometric patterns, and an elimination of the distinction between interior and exterior space.[39]

These are phenomena which, of course, cannot be predicted with mathematical precision in their details (obviously not reducible to Spinozan theorems and corollaries), since they originate in the human imagination. Yet they can be ascribed to a general law which relates the rhythm of taste to that of nature and the universe, so that we can distinguish cycles and seasons. And if this is so, should we look ahead to the style of tomorrow, that tomorrow which decorators will find cleared-out, freer than any artist ever dreamed of finding terrain or walls for new projects, emptier than anyone could have wished, with the old houses swept away, illustrious palaces wiped out, so that perhaps this emptiness itself will make designers dizzy? And, on the brink of the world that wants to rise from its ruins, may they not feel lost and uncertain?

If, as is probable, the designers of tomorrow want to express a new hope, a new faith, if they want to translate into decoration the voice of a free people, won't they writhe with nausea at the thought of all the styles buried under that rubble, styles bent one after the other into symbols of doctrines that were broken and pulverized in the great ordeal just as the towers were, and the walls and houses of old Europe?

Old Europe, beautiful were the richly-decorated salons of your palaces, the calm rooms of your old bourgeois houses, the rustic kitchens of your simple dwellings in the mountains; beautiful also was your furniture with its time-stained patina, your objects lovingly worked by generations of cabinet-makers, potters, and goldsmiths! We, who have known all these things in their splendor, who have—if only for a day—made ours the life of so many cities that are no more, how can we forget? As long as there are four walls that still keep the aroma of that vanished Europe, it is among those walls that we wish to die.

October 1944–November 1963

NOTES TO THE INTRODUCTION

1: The reader who is curious about the enormous range of subjects dealt with by didactic poets may consult the essays "Le forme minori della poesia didascalica" and "Le forme maggiori della poesia didascalica" by E. Bertana in *In Arcadia, Saggi e profili*, Naples (1909).

2: Liberty is the name given in Italy to the imported style which was known in France as *Art Nouveau*, in England as Modern or New Style, and *Jugendstil* in Germany. The name is derived from that of one of the English firms which flooded the Continent with New Style furniture. In Italy the style developed later than in northern Europe, and did not produce any daring work: it came in the wake of the industrial development which was mostly due to foreign intervention. Thus in Naples the 1904 law for the economic development of the town had as a consequence the influx of foreign capital and the establishment of foreign firms (Pattison, Hawthorn-Guppy, Armstrong, Schlaepfer, Wenner, Aselmeyer). These foreign firms provided not only capital, technical management and skilled workers, but also a definite orientation of artistic taste. The prevailing taste in the countries to which those firms belonged was, at the beginning of the century, characterized by *Art Nouveau*. Therefore the new districts in Naples were built in that style. (See Renato De Fusci, *Il Floreale a Napoli*, Naples (1959) and M. Praz, *Bellezza e bizzarria*, Milan (1960) p. 73 ff.)

3: *Umbertino*, from the name of King Umberto I (1878–1900), is the name given to the eclectic style which prevailed in the last decades of the 19th c., characterized by a debased classicism and an exuberant ornamentation which utilized Renaissance and Baroque motifs indiscriminately. It corresponded to that phase of Victorian taste which became widespread with the 1851 Exhibition. The Italian Royal palaces, particularly those of Turin, Rome and Naples, were partly redecorated in this style, but the most perfect example of an Umbertine interior is found in the Palazzo Manganelli at Catania. See for illustrations Valentino Brosio, *Ambienti italiani dell'Ottocento*, Milan (1963).

4: Vincent de Paul Brunetière, *Histoire de la littérature française*, Paris (1917) p. 372, on the subject of Balzac: "On dit qu'un paysage est un état d'âme: en tout cas un mobilier ou un costume sont caractéristiques d'un personnage, come la coquille l'est de l'animal: ils révèlent, ils trahissent; quand ils ne sont pas un moyen d'atteindre

un fond de son âme, ils l'expriment encore en fonction de la société de son temps."

5: Joris Karl Huysmans, *A Rebours*.

6: A miniature form of such a retrospective exhibition exists at the Chicago Art Institute, thanks to the patience and the ingenuity of Mrs. Ward Thorne. I discuss it on p. 221 of my book, *La casa della vita*, Milan (1958). The only fault of Mrs. Thorne's delightful creations is their anthological character. The rooms represent a median of the taste of the various periods; they lack therefore the immediate authenticity of contemporary paintings, drawings, or watercolors. The Chicago Art Institute has published two handbooks with reproductions of Mrs. Thorne's little masterpieces (*European Rooms in Miniature* and *American Rooms in Miniature*).

7: Walter Benjamin, *Schriften*, Frankfurt (1955) Vol. I, p. 414, "Louis-Philippe oder der Interieur."

8: The episode is narrated by Matilda Lucas, *Two Englishwomen in Rome, 1871–1900*, London (1939) p. 144.

9: *Op. cit.*, pp. 415–416.

10: Ovid, *Metamorphoses*, III, 424 and 487–90.

11: Henry James, *The Spoils of Poynton*.

12: *Paradoxa*, V.

13: La Bruyère, *De la Mode*.

14: Cf. E. de Goncourt: *La Maison d'un artiste:* "Cette passion . . . ce plaisir solitaire . . . doit son développement au vide, à l'ennui du coeur . . ."

15: Hale White, *The Autobiography of Mark Rutherford*, 1881.

16: The detailed description by Kotzebue is found in the second volume of *Das merkwürdigste Jahr meines Lebens*, 1801.

17: This alarming case of ill-advised patronage is documented in Luise von Kobell's volume, *König Ludwig II von Bayern und die Kunst*, Munich (1898), copiously illustrated. Interior views of Ludwig's castles can be found in the catalogue of an exhibition at the Victoria and Albert Museum, *Designs for the Dream King, The Castles and Palaces of Ludwig II of Bavaria*, London (1978).

18: In an article on D'Annunzio published in the *Frankfurter Zeitung* of August 9, 1893, and reprinted in Loris, *Die Prose des jungen H. von Hofmannsthal*, p. 85 ff.

19: E. and J. de Goncourt, *Histoire de la société française pendant le Directoire*, Paris (1880) pp. 110–11. See the whole chapter, which is nothing but a long lament at the destruction of the houses of the aristocracy, "those châteaux, those thousand little Versailles, those *Folies* of Bouret and Samuel Bernard and others, those *Moulin-Joli* of the great tax-contractors, those princely caprices, those rustic pavilions of marble and gold, which populated all the avenues of the metropolis and made them a girdle of museums, a line of palaces half-hidden in foliage. What have fire and vandalism and man done to these?" A lament which could be repeated today, and on how measureless a scale!

20: J. Reed, *Ten Days That Shook the World*, New York (1919).

21: Giuseppe Tomasi di Lampedusa, *Two Stories and a Memory*, New York (1962), translation by Archibald Colquhoun, pp. 58-59. See also the description of the house at Santa Margherita in Chapter IV of "Places of My Infancy" (same volume), and the pink dining room in Chapter VIII, whose walls were hung with great paintings of the prince and his family at meals, with life-size figures: a series of 18th century conversation pieces rather than paintings of interiors. These canvases, very crudely painted, were later acquired and resold by the antiquarian Luigi Galli of Carate Brianza; at this writing (September, 1963) he has only one left.

22: I speak of this in *La casa della vita*, pp. 302-304.

23: From the little oil painting (*Fig.* 16) apparently was derived the miniature by F. MacDonald (*Fig.* 165) (morganatic husband of Caroline Murat), showing the same scene with some variants.

24: I abandon here the conjecture made in *La casa della vita*, p. 326, concerning the identification of the lady in Spanish costume. Lacoma's little picture dates in fact from before 1830 and the young lady may very well be the future Queen of the Two Sicilies, the same lady who, at a more advanced age, is depicted in the interior painting reproduced in this volume (*Fig.* 189).

25: Duchesse d'Abrantès, *Mémoires*, Paris, Edition Garnier, Vol. VI, p. 349. The Duchesse speaks simply of "Garnerey", and since Auguste was the painter of Queen Hortense and of the Duchesse de Berry and numbered among his patrons also the Empresses Josephine and Marie-Louise, it must certainly be he. Still a problem arises: the watercolor mentioned here in which the three personages are present (the Duchesse de Berry, Francesco I, and Isabella) is dated 1829, the period of the Paris visit of the Neapolitan sovereigns. But Auguste Garnerey died in 1824. Can the picture in question be the work of Garnerey's sister, who completed —as we shall see—a watercolor of his of Malmaison, or the work of his father Jean-François, who lived until 1837 and also painted interiors (though mostly of churches)? Olivier Lefuel, whom I consulted on this matter, writes me: "L'hypothèse la plus vraisemblable qui vient à l'ésprit est que les tableaux de Brunnsee seraient de la main de Jean-François, le père d'Auguste. Comme les caractéristiques de style et les 'mains' sont extrêmement voisines—si ce n'est identiques— il est bien ardu de pouvoir distinguer l'oeuvre du père et celle du fils. Au fond, il vaudrait mieux dire prudemment 'aquarelle de Garnerey', le terme étant général."

26: On p. 38 ff. in the edition J.J. Pauvert, Paris (1954). The attribution to Sade, however, is uncertain.

26a: The painting at the extreme left has been so foreshortened as to be difficult to read. It is similar to a *Madonna* with hands joined in prayer attributed to Niccolò di Pietro Gerini (Christ Church, Oxford; see Shaw's catalogue, p. 34, no. 10). However, the measurements of the latter are only 64.2 × 48.3 cm.

27: It was, in fact, an English gentleman, Sir Archibald Geikie, who first wrote extensively on this subject in *The Love of Nature among the Romans*, London (1912), with chapters on flowers and animals in the Romans' life. And another Englishman, Stanley Casson, wrote a charming essay on the Greeks' love of nature, "L'Exaltation de la fleur", in *Hellenic Studies*, London (1920).

28: Attempts by modern painters to reconstruct the intimacy of rooms of the ancient world betray a mixture of labored archaeology and much 19th century fantasy. See, for example, certain paintings of Alma Tadema, such as *In Confidence* (with that little table laden with vases of flowers, and that niche over the sofa, so *fin de siècle!*) or *Joseph, Overseer of Pharoah's Granaries* (with a vase on a stool which seems wrenched from a Liberty veranda), or *The Picture Gallery* (a 19th century room transparent beneath its Roman mask), or *He Loves Me, He Loves Me Not* (where it is no longer clear whether the scene is taking place in ancient Rome or a modern, "artistic" villa).

29: Clement of Hungary in 1328 had eight tapestries "à ymages et à arbres, à la devise d'une chasse"; the wardrobe of the Palace of the Popes in Avignon has murals of hunting, falconry and fishing, dating from the middle of the 14th century; and 15th century Flemish tapestries with hunting themes are found at Hardwick Hall (Derbyshire) and were listed in the inventories of Cardinal Wolsey.

30: This is a conclusion based on figurative documents which have been left to us, but at the time there was far more variety, more picturesqueness thanks to the decoration of the walls, with tree motifs and painted draperies covering the upper part, while the lower was covered with a wooden dado, or painting in a different manner. The richer citizens employed well-known artists to fresco their walls with isolated figures or stories or allegories. A functional criterion was already operating: battle scenes were painted in the room of a statesman or military man, portraits of famous men and the seven Liberal Arts in a study, in a court room the allegorical figures of the Virtues, in a nuptial chamber episodes from courtly romances, etc. In the apartments of princes was found carved furniture, inlaid and painted, as well as tapestries, paintings, sculptures, ivories, etc. Some pieces were covered with stuffs, which together with the wall-hangings and the rugs must have helped relieve the linearity and rigidity which appear in paintings of the rooms. See Attilio Schiaparelli, *La casa fiorentina e i suoi arredi nei secoli XIV e XV*, Florence (1908).

31: Gregorovius, in the third chapter of the first book of his *Lucrezia Borgia*, tries to reconstruct the furnishing of the house of Vannozza. He notes the "heavy pieces of furniture: large, broad beds, with canopies; tall chairs of dark wood, massive little tables, immense coffers," and the great credenza with showy objects on it. In short, a house with "something grave and sad about it" which—as Gregorovius remarks—still characterized the houses in Rome in his time.

Reduced to smaller dimensions, 16th century decoration has a charm of its own, like a jewel-box. This is exemplified in the windowless little study of Francesco I dei Medici, in the Palazzo Vecchio at Florence, of which the walls are completely encrusted with exquisite oval and rectangular panels, including *The Pearl Fishers* by Alessandro Allori, *The Diamond Mine* by Maso da San Friano, etc.

Not much is to be drawn from the description of interiors by Bandello, who —like Balzac and Baudelaire, later, as in the passages quoted in this volume—was concerned only with giving the idea of a room that inspired voluptuousness and luxury. Such is the description of the room where Pompeo takes Eleonora (*Novelle*, I, 3) or the room of the bold widow (IV, 25) or of the courtesan Imperia (III, 42). In the first we note a rich bed surrounded by "crimson curtains of silk worked in gold with precious, striped bands," a table covered with Alexandrian silk in the centre, and around the walls eight coffers "handsomely carved"; there were also four chairs of crimson velvet, and "several paintings by the hand of Master Lionardo Vinci wondrously adorned the place." The unreality of the description is clear from this last detail, since pictures painted by Leonardo were few in number and that "several" could be found in one house is a manifest impossibility. To make the atmosphere more voluptuous Bandello perfumes it with "aloe wood, with Cyprian birds" (that is to say, pieces of perfumed paste in the form of birds, which were burned in little jars like cages; see M. Wis, "Uccelletti cipriani" in *Neuphilol. Mitteilungen*, LVIII, 1957, and in *Lingua nostra*, XVIII, n. 2, p. 62, and XIX, n. 4, p. 136) "with tempered musks and with other odors". Citing the fashionable scents of their own time, Balzac and Baudelaire do the same thing in the rooms they describe. Also in the room of the widow we find a rich bed "with which any great king would have considered himself honorably satisfied", a table with a drapery "masterfully of gold and silk embroidered in Alexandrian style, upon which in handsome order were ivory and ebony combs to comb hair and beard, with very beautiful caps and cloths to place on the shoulders while being combed or to wipe the hands;" on the little table also a silver candelabra, and also a silver bed-warmer; the chamber was richly draped and most delicately perfumed. In the house of Imperia there were "among other things, a hall and a bedchamber and a little room adorned with such pomp that there was nothing but velvets and brocades and the finest of rugs on the ground. In the little room where she retired, when she was visited by some exalted personage, the coverings of the walls were all of golden cloth, fold upon fold, with many charming and beautiful decorations. There was also a frame, all of gold and ultramarine, masterfully made, over which were beautiful vases of various precious materials, with alabaster, porphyry, serpentine, and a thousand other species. To be seen on every side were many coffers and richly carved strongboxes, all of great price. In the centre was seen a table, the most beautiful in the world, covered with green velvet. Here there was always a lute or a lyre, with books of music and other musical instruments. There were also several books in the vulgar tongue and in Latin, richly adorned."

32: The passage from Father Le Moine is quoted on p. 226 of my *Studi sul concettismo*, Florence (1946). For the Duchesse de Berry, see Vicomte de Reiset, *Marie-Caroline Duchesse de Berry*, Paris (1906), p. 103.

33: The title of Poe's essay follows a fashion of the period. Martin Chuzzlewit, in the Dickens novel (1843–44), wonders when he is in America what the ladies do and learns from Mrs. Brick that they listen to lectures: on Monday, The Philosophy of Crime, on Tuesday, The Philosophy of Government, on Wednesday, The Philosophy of the Soul, and so on for the rest of the week.

Poe deplored the "abomination of flowers, or representations of well-known objects of any kind" on rugs, and he wanted in them "distinct grounds, and vivid circular or cycloid figures, *of no meaning*," a declaration in which it is permissible to see an abstract tendency, but Poe's abstraction was limited to arabesques. That is to say, it was ultimately identified with a kind of exotic, Levantine inspired decoration then in fashion, in the wake of the French conquest of Algeria. Still, his tendency was unquestionably toward a simplification and a harmony obtained rather by the domination of lines and colors than by the juxtaposition of objects and pictures, as was the vogue at that period.

It should be remarked that in the ideal room as described by Poe many pictures break the expanse of the glossy silver paper that covers the walls. They are mostly landscapes of an imaginative cast. There are, nevertheless, three or four female portrait heads in the style of Sully, of an ethereal beauty. The tonality of everything is warm, but dark. There are no "brilliant effects". Everything breathes *repose*. Nothing is of small proportions. Little pictures, Poe feels, give

a room that "spotted" effect, which is the flaw of many fine works of art that have been too-much retouched. In this room of Poe's, the secret inner room of the poet's dream, there is already, *in nuce*, the apartment of des Esseintes, that bloodless French Usher, which Huysmans later describes to us in *A Rebours*. "Là tout n'est que ordre et beauté, Luxe, calme et volupté," according to Baudelaire, another who would have felt perfectly at home in the fantastic and frightfully sanguinary artificial paradise of Poe.

On the subject of rugs, what would Poe have thought of the one in the house of Teresa Guiccoli, after she had become Marquise de Boissy? "A uniform carpet covered the floors of all the rooms, a red ground sown with arms (the Boissy escutcheon) and with legs (the Gamba escutcheon)" (A. Guiccoli, *I Guiccoli, Memorie d'una famiglia*, edited by A. Alberti, Bologna (1935), Vol. II, p. 90).

34: For color combinations in Victorian decoration see *The Art of Decoration* by Mrs. H. R. Haweis, 1881, excerpts of which are quoted in the chapter "The Interior of the Home" in the volume *Home: a Victorian Vignette*, by R. Harling, London (1938).

35: Virginia Woolf in *Orlando* (chapter V) has written some lively pages on this universal mania for covering things: "Thus, stealthily and imperceptibly, none marking the exact day or hour of the change, the constitution of England was altered and nobody knew it. Everywhere the effects were felt. The hardy country gentleman, who had sat down gladly to a meal of ale and beef in a room designed, perhaps by the brothers Adam, with classic dignity, now felt chilly. Rugs appeared; beards were grown; trousers were fastened tight under the instep. The chill which he felt in his legs the country gentleman soon transferred to his house; furniture was muffled; walls and tables were covered; nothing was left bare . . . Outside the house . . . ivy grew in unparalleled profusion. Houses that had been of bare stone were smothered in greenery . . ."

36: See the description of the vestibule in *La Maison d'un artiste* by E. de

Goncourt, Vol. I, p. 4: "Sur ce mur dans un désordre cherché, dans un pittoresque d'antichambre et d'atelier, toutes sortes de choses voyantes et claquantes, des brillants cuivres découpés, des poteries dorées, des broderies du Japon et encore des objets bizarres, inattendus, étonnant par leur originalité, leur exotisme. . ." The caricature of a room based on these principles is described by Aldo Palazzeschi in his *Stampe dell'Ottocento* (La sor' Isabella): "The living room was so heaped with things that it made your head spin. Little easy chairs, straight chairs, columns, tables; . . . and on everything there were *crochets, filets*, embroidered covers which included the little figurines from nougat wrappings or from chocolate boxes or matchboxes; portraits, tiny vases, little paintings, oleographs, sachets, baskets, china shoes, miniature amphoras, *frivolités*, needlework, *coquillages*, fans, spinets, dippers and pots painted with views of Vesuvius, Saint Peter's, the dome of the Florence cathedral, the Leaning Tower, the Bridge of Sighs . . . And all hung with ribbons, cord, bows, cockades, and pompons."

37: To be sure, at the end of the last century people had a different notion of the Japanese from today's idea. For Jean Fautrier (see P. Bucarelli, *Jean Fautrier*, Milan (1960) p. 142): "Une chose qui étonne beaucoup, ce sont les intérieurs. Les japonais vit sans meuble. Tu te trouveras toujours dans des pièces strictement vides entourées de cloisons en papier sans portes. Si tu veux manger on t'apportera une table et un coussin. Si tu veux dormir on mettra sur le sol ton lit et on te donnera ton kimono de nuit. Pour sortir, la japonaise se mettra à genoux et fera glisser une partie de cette cloison et elle se mettra une deuxième fois à genoux pour la faire réglisser derrière elle."

38: *Men and Memories*, Vol. I, London (1931) p. 83.

39: See the article "Our Period Style" by Clement Greenberg in *The Partisan Review*, November, 1949, and J. M. Richards and Elizabeth Mock, *Introduction to Modern Architecture*, Penguin Books, (1947) pp. 57–58.

Figure 25: F. W. Klose.
The Blue Room in the Palace
at Potsdam, watercolor, c. 1840.
COLLECTION CHARLOTTENBURG PALACE,
BERLIN.

Illustrations and Commentary

26: The Loves of Mars and Venus, fresco. HOUSE OF MARCUS LUCRETIUS FRONTO, POMPEII.

Although Greek vase paintings often depict domestic scenes and although paintings on the walls of Roman houses, especially in Pompeii, portray people seated or reclining, it is impossible to reconstruct interiors, properly speaking, from any figurative evidence of the Classical world. A few pieces of furniture and a curtain, as in the bas-relief of the *Visit of Dionysus to Icarius,* are not enough to create an interior. Here the house is indicated only by its outside, in that "doll's house" convention which we shall find again in the Middle Ages. The only recurrent pieces of furniture seem to be: the bed, covered with vari-colored stuffs, often Oriental, and with cushions; the throne or the chair, also draped, as in the Pompeiian wall-painting of *The Loves of Mars and Venus;* the ever-present stool; and the little table, usually three-legged.

The Grammarian Pollux, of the 2nd century A. D., has a long list of epithets (Book X, 42) for bed coverings: delicate, well-woven, glistening, beautifully colored, flowered, decorated, purple, dark green,

scarlet, violet, purple-bordered, gold-woven, animal-figured, gleaming with stars. It was a widespread custom to perfume bed covering. The beds themselves had rectangular legs or legs turned on theriomorphic forms.

The little table with lion's legs, seen in the bas-relief, began to appear in Greece in the 4th century B.C. and enjoyed immense popularity. A very rare example, in wood, was found at Thebes in Egypt in 1905 and is now in the Musée du Cinquantenaire in Brussels. It has antelope legs which terminate, at the top, in swans' heads emerging from acanthus leaves. These same swans' heads appear again many centuries later, in the furniture of the first part of the 19th century. Livy (XXXIX) informs us that "foreign luxury was first introduced to Rome by the army returning from Asia: beds with bronze ornaments, precious coverlets, curtains and other stuffs, and furniture that then seemed unusual, one-legged tables, and serving-tables." When chests and coffers were no longer sufficient to contain

27: *The Visit of Dionysus to Icarius*, Hellenistic bas-relief. MUSEO NAZIONALE, NAPLES.

28: *The Scribe Ezra*, miniature from a late 6th century Bible. BIBLIOTECA LAURENZIANA, FLORENCE.

the objects accumulated with increasing comfort, the cupboard was born, its form not very different from today's wardrobe: a rectangular storage place on legs, provided with shelves and hinged doors and a pediment crowning the top, as seen here in the miniature of *The Scribe Ezra* which decorated a late 6th century Northumbrian Bible.

The gaiety of the stuffs was complemented by that of the mosaic floors and the walls painted in bright colors. Many centuries afterwards, Walter Pater, describing the Villa Ad Vigilias Albas, residence of Marius the Epicurean, tried to recreate the atmosphere of a Roman interior: "Scrupulous sweetness and order reigned within. The old Roman architects seem to have well understood the decorative value of the floor the real economy that there was, in the production of a rich interior effect, by a somewhat lavish expenditure upon the surface they trod on. The pavement of the hall had lost something of its evenness; but, though a little rough to the foot, polished and cared for like a piece of silver, looked, as mosaic-work is apt to do, its best in old age."

Suetonius (*Life of Augustus*, LXXIII) speaks of the parsimonious furnishing of Augustus's house on the Palatine: "The simplicity of his furniture and household goods may be seen from couches and tables still in existence, many of which are scarcely fine enough for a private citizen. They say that he always slept on a low and plainly furnished bed." At the time of Augustus there were still traces of Republican austerity and Horace (*Odes*, II, 18) showed contempt for the luxury of the new rich: "In my house neither gold nor ivory shines, nor beams of Hymettus press on columns cut in the most remote parts of Africa . . ."

29: Pietro Lorenzetti. *Nativity of the Virgin*, 1342.
MUSEO DELL'OPERA DEL DUOMO, SIENA.

A common type of house in the Middle Ages was the two-part or bicellular house. Normally this type of house had two or three stories, and on each of them was a hall, the entrance to which was in the long side of the hall, and beyond the hall was an inner room. The most characteristic feature of houses of the two-part style was the distribution of the floors. The middle floor was reserved for the dwelling, properly speaking, formed of a common hall (*mansio*) and a bedroom. The ground floor was for domestic uses. The upper floor contained the great hall or halls.

For reasons of defense the tower-house or keep was also widespread in medieval times. These towers were

at first rectangular in plan, with hall-like rooms; the accessory rooms were created in the thickness of the walls. Again there were three stories: the provisions floor, in the lower part of the tower, accessible only from above by a trapdoor in its ceiling; the main floor; and the upper floor which, divided by thin partitions, contained the sleeping quarters for children and for the garrison. In another type of tower, on each floor there were two rooms of equal dimensions; the most handsome apartment that of the top floor. To the simple rectangular keep there was later added a lateral annex in the form of a tower, containing living rooms of a more intimate nature. At times these supplemen-

tary towers were multiple and all attached to the main body of the building, forming a powerful fort.

Flanking the tower-house and the bicellular house it was not unusual to find a building containing a great hall used for festivities, for important receptions, for legal trials, and in certain cases for daily gatherings or the meals of the inhabitants. Often a construction of this kind was also arranged in a bicellular form.[1] In the description of the rooms that a medieval castle should contain, the English schoolman, Alexander Neckham lists only the great hall, the bedroom and the rooms for domestic use. The function of the great hall in the Middle Ages was both for gatherings and for daily living. The lord of the castle met his vassals and his retinue there to converse, feast, and keep wassail. The table of honor was set at the end of the room on a platform, as in the miniature of Loyset Liedet (*Fig.* 39). Above the seats of the lords of the castle hung a tapestry surmounted by a canopy. Benches or chests were lined up against the long walls, and at mealtimes movable tables were set up.

The nomadic habits of the fuedal lords, who used to stay first in one, then in another of their castles, meant that a part of their furniture had to be easily transportable. Only the bed stayed in its place. The chests served to contain clothing and crockery during moves, but were also used as seats and storage cupboards. Draperies and folding tables were also carried from one place to another. The draperies were a protection against draughts and, with their brilliant colors, made the rooms more cheerful. One kind of fixed decoration, however, was the wall frescoes of coats-of-arms, hunting scenes, scenes from history and from legend.[2]

Life inside the castle centered around the hall, to which the ladies were also admitted. The bedroom of the lord of the castle was next to the hall. In many cases the lord's immediate subordinates had their beds in this same room. In princely dwellings a great hall for festivities was required, supplemented by a less important hall for ordinary gatherings. The great hall generally connected with the state bedroom, containing the state bed. To the second hall was connected the private bedroom. The common room of the knights had a counterpart in the ladies' common room, which was normally on the upper floor of the tower-house. Chivalric romances would lead us to believe that every lady had her own room in the castle, and it is possible that many rooms were created with partitions, but in the Middle Ages it was quite common for a number of people to live in the same room. As we have already said, guards on duty and servingmaids generally spent the night in the room of the lord or his lady, often sleeping at the foot of the bed.

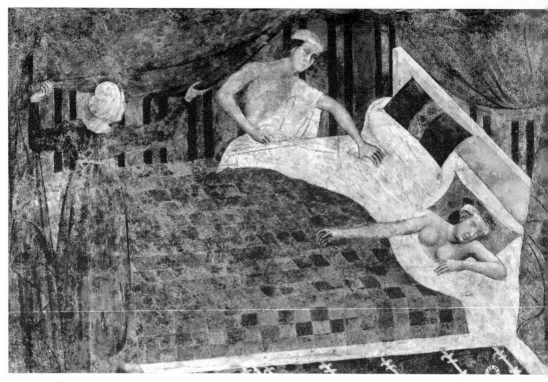

30-31: Anonymous Sienese (Memmo di Filippuccio?).
Conjugal Scenes, frescoes, late 13th century. PALAZZO PUBBLICO, SAN GIMIGNANO.

32: Public Treasurer and his Scribe in their Office, account book cover, 1388. ARCHIVIO STORICO, SIENA.

The search for greater privacy on the part of the rich is borne out by a passage from *Piers Plowman* by William Langland (text B, written in 1377–79):

"Elying is the halle, vche day in the wyke,
There the lord ne the lady liketh noughte to sytte.
Now hath vche riche a reule to eten bi hym-selue
In a pryue parloure, for pore mennes sake,
Or in a chambre with a chymneye, and leue the chief halle
That was made for meles, men to eten inne."

Since there were few kinds of rooms (chiefly the hall and the bedroom) and since furnishings were few, we cannot expect much variety in the depiction of interiors, depictions which are often even more summary than the actual decoration. We see a bedroom furnished with a bed and a chest, and a hanging behind the bed, in the *Nativity of the Virgin* of Lorenzetti (*Fig.* 29). Even more summary are the rooms painted by an anonymous Sienese at the end of the 13th-early 14th century in the tower room of the Palazzo Pubblico of San Gimignano:[3] curtains around the bed, whose occupants, according to the custom of the time, did not wear nightgowns; curtains around the tub in which a man and a woman bathed together. In one of the frescoes a woman raises the bed-curtain and makes a gesture: in the other two people seem to violate the privacy of the bath, slipping in through a door and exchanging impressions. The meaning of these scenes escapes us. Some scholars conjecture that this is a moralistic cycle meant to admonish the podestà or local magistrate, to avoid certain bad companions. On the other hand, it might depict the ceremony of the public bath of a betrothed couple before the wedding, a custom still practised in Albania and elsewhere.[3a] However, there is no mystery in the figure of the *Public Treasurer and his Scribe in their Office.* The counter with writing materials, the two chests behind the counter, the bench in front of the window create an austere and purely functional atmosphere that is timeless.

33: Workshop of Pietro Lorenzetti. *The Last Supper,* fresco, c. 1340–50. LOWER BASILICA OF SAN FRANCESCO, ASSISI.

4: Miniature from the *Book of the Hours of the Maréchal 'e Boucicaut*, 1411–12. MS fr. 165, *Dialogues de Pierre Salmon*, BIBLIOTHÈQUE PUBLIQUE ET UNIVERSITAIRE, GENEVA.

5: Jan van Eyck and Assistants. *Birth of Saint John*, miniature from the *Heures de Milan*, 1416. MUSEO CIVICO, TURIN.

The interiors reproduced in medieval paintings are of the "doll's house" type: a kind of booth whose front part has been removed or perforated to allow a view of the narrow interior, generally a bedroom as we have already seen in the *Nativity of the Virgin* (*Fig. 29*), or, as we shall see, in the study of Saint Jerome or another writer at work. In one of these "doll's houses," a frescoe in the lower basilica at Assisi depicting *The Last Supper*, however, there is a scene which, even in its summary furnishing, represents something new. Here the kitchen, with the blazing hearth, the shelf with a pot and an implement hanging nearby, is the prototype of the domestic interiors of the Flemish painters, while the recess with the crockery could be said to offer the first example of a kind of still life destined later to enjoy great popularity.

The bedroom in the *Book of the Hours of the Maréchal de Boucicaut*, where we see Charles VI conversing with Pierre Salmon, gives an idea of the sumptuousness that could be conferred on even a sparsely furnished room by rich hangings and a rug of simple but effective geometric pattern. The window with the pot of flowers on the sill lends a note of intimacy to a room that is decked out almost like an altar. This kind of interior decoration, which depended more on stuffs than on furniture, continued in princely apartments throughout the 15th century.

The bedroom by Jan van Eyck and assistants, in the miniature *The Birth of Saint John* from the *Heures de Milan* is no longer a summary reproduction of a room. The details are of an extraordinary precision. The invention of the water-saw, which soon spread from Augsburg to other cities, revolutionized the construction of furniture, allowing the making of frames which assured solidity, lightened the mass, and obviated the inconveniences of the wood's warping or shrinking. The table in the center of the room in the *Birth of Saint John* reveals this new kind of construction. Already in the 14th century swallow-tail joints had also been rediscovered, eliminating the necessity of iron bands. In countries where fine woods were rare, such as southern Germany, the use of veneering ordinary (conifer) wood began to spread. Such veneers could be applied even over considerable surfaces.

In the van Eyck miniature not only are the furnishings precisely distinguished (in addition to the table we find the chest and the two triangular stools formed of cylindrical elements, a type of construction dating back to the Romanesque period), but also the objects contained in the chest are minutely depicted, as are those set on the table and on the shelf over the door. A little later Jan van Eyck, in the well-known Arnolfini portrait, freed interior painting from its religious pretext. The relationship between the interior and its occupants thus became the real relationship of daily life, and the *Stimmung* of bourgeois intimacy was explicitly stated.

36: Miniature from the *Livres des fays d'armes* of Christine de Pisan, 1434. BRITISH MUSEUM, LONDON.

The Arnolfini portrait dates from 1434. Also from that year is the codex of the *Livres des fays d'armes* of Christine de Pisan which, in one miniature, represents Christine de Pisan in her writing room. Comparing the Gothic surroundings, summary and conventional, of this miniature with the work of van Eyck, one realizes the remarkable maturity of the latter artist, with his spirit of observation, precise yet poetic.

An even more striking comparison is offered by the miniature by Loyset Liedet (d. 1478) in a codex of the *Histoire de Sainte Hélène* of Jean Wauquelin illuminated for Philip the Good. The scene is the same as that of the van Eyck miniature, and here too, there is a certain desire to portray the furnishings in their individuality: the cradle, for example, is made like the van Eyck stools, with cylindrical elements, which here however are rendered calligraphically without their real volume. And the vessels, the long-handled pan which in such scenes is usually found near the hearth are more listed than represented. They indicate like a stage direction the kind of object which was to be found in such a scene, but do not individualize the object itself. Not merely was van Eyck an incomparably greater painter than Liedet, their whole attitudes were different. Liedet cited; van Eyck observed.

Liedet is also the artist of the solemn *Banquet for the Marriage of Renaut de Montauban*. Though the details of the furnishing are rendered with some care (the late Gothic sideboard, the damask tablecloth, the sumptuous floor), the scene, with the valets who move like figures in a ballet under the eye of the majordomo, the faces all made from the same mould, that heraldic dog, looks more like the illustration of a text on table manners than the reproduction of a real event. More realistic is the *Banquet Scene* in the *Histoire du Grand Alexandre* where, though the faces are somewhat conventionally rendered, the convention is not based on a criterion of abstract beauty, but rather on an attempt at robust characterization. One should note the care in the detail of the furnishings, even the legs of the table, half hidden by the cloth. A peacock on a column is posed in the way in which the fowl was presented when it was served at banquets in those times. The rich hanging behind the guests and the tourney taking place in the square all help to create the impression of a scene from real life.

37: Loyset Liedet. *Birth of Saint John*, miniature from the *Histoire de Sainte Hélène*
BIBLIOTHÈQUE ROYALE, BRUSSELS.

38: Loyset Liedet. *Banquet Scene*, miniature from the *Histoire du Grand Alexandre*. PETIT PALAIS, PARIS.

39: Loyset Liedet. *Banquet for the Marriage of Renaut de Montauban*, miniature.

40: The Translator Jean Miélot Presenting his Manuscript to Philip the Good, miniature from *Avis pour faire le Passage D'Outre-Mer* of Guillaume Adam, 1455. BIBLIOTHÈQUE NATIONALE, PARIS.

Equally alive is the scene from the manuscript of the *Passage D'Outre-Mer* in which Philip the Good receives the work from the hands of the translator. The low chest-bench with its colonettes covered with cushions, the sideboard and shelf filled with vessels, and the rich floor of ornamental tiles furnish precise elements for the reconstruction of a corner of a late Gothic room. It is only in this period of the late Middle Ages as a matter of fact that we begin to have precise indications of furnishings of the epoch. As Julius von Schlosser has observed *(Die Kunst des Mittelalters,* 1923): "The

palace and the private house, though they continued to exist in the Middle Ages, have almost no importance in the history of style. Furthermore, their highly precarious state of preservation makes them much less clear and legible than religious constructions in which the great ecclesiastical communities and religious orders have had an active role and a great historical significance . . . Only in the late Middle Ages when, with the incipient process of secularization especially active in Italy as the lay and bourgeois element began to waken, did the Palazzo del Comune, the City Hall,

41: Monogrammist M. Z. *Gathering at the Court of Duke Albert IV of Bavaria*, engraving.

make its appearance." And what is here said about
buildings might be repeated about furnishings.

In the *Lais* of Marie de France of the second half
of the 12th century, we may well read of the feet and
the sides of a bed *"taillé a or, tot a trifoire—De cipres
et de blanc ivoire."* Yet we still cannot clearly visualize
this chryselephantine bed. But for late Gothic furniture there is an abundance of documentation. Typical
of this furniture is the table which appears in the
engraving depicting a *Gathering at the Court of Duke
Albert IV of Bavaria* (1467-1508). The table is set in an

Erker, or bow-window. On the table there is a German
state cup, typical of the period. The two figures
seated in this window are playing cards, while some
couples are dancing to the sound of the musicians who
have taken their places on the side balconies; and
this movement does not in the least disturb the two
dogs, one crouching and one sitting, in the center of
the room. Still other couples are resting. A gentleman-
in-waiting is near the Duke. From the kitchen a
servant enters carrying a vessel covered with a cloth.
This late Gothic interior is a faithful image of reality.

42: Robert Campin. *Saint Barbara*. PRADO, MA

43: Roger van der Weyden. *Annunciation.* LOUVRE, PARIS.

Late Gothic furnishing does not concern itself with symmetry in the placing of the pieces and is subject to no architectonic scheme. In Northern countries only the fireplace constituted a fixed point of reference; on either side of the fireplace there were generally shelves on which lamps, bottles, etc. were set, as we can see in the *Saint Barbara* of Robert Campin (1375-1444), and in the *Annunciation* of Roger van der Weyden (1399?-1464) (*Figs.* 42, 43). The floor was paved either with ornamental tiles or with wooden planks, as in the *Bathsheba Emerging from the Bath* of Hans Memling (1430/35-1494). *Parquet*, or wood-mosaic floors, were also in use, as can be seen in the Arnolfini portrait by Jan van Eyck already mentioned. The furniture, as we have observed, had no precise location: sometimes the pieces seem to have been set down at random; at other times they are lined up along the wall, but without being an integral part of the architectonic design of the walls themselves. Nevertheless some arrangements recur regularly: the chest-bench with its back to the fireplace, the ewer on the columned cabinet.

The tiny panel of an *Amorous Incantation* by a master of the Lower Rhine was perhaps originally the internal part of a chest like the one seen in the painting itself which is set on a three-legged stool. This chest was meant to contain the instruments of the magic which the young girl in the painting is practicing. (The inside of the cover and the bottom of little German chests which bore the Holy Sacrament were generally decorated with paintings, and it is not surprising that a secular magic chest should imitate the liturgical ones.) Our attention is distracted from the room itself by the curiosity of the scene. The maiden, naked like a Venus, pronounces ritual formulas which were once probably legible in the elegant scrolls. She holds in her right hand a sponge and a flint, and in her left the steel of a tinder-box, while the floor is scattered with roses and narcissus, which flower in May.[4] The room contains a cupboard at the back, surmounted by a shelf with various vessels and vases. From the door a young man, probably the object of the maiden's incantation, peers in. At the right beneath the window is a cupboard with toilet articles. A little bird and a dog, each equipped with his own scroll, witness this strange scene unmoved.

An interesting detail is offered by the bath in the painting by Memling. The tub was usually of wood. As we have seen in the San Gimignano frescoes (*Fig.* 31) it was sometimes round in shape. At other times it was elongated like the modern tub, not, however, to allow the bather to lie down, but to make the tub large enough for more than one person. This obviated the problem of procuring enough water, since the transportation of hot water was not an easy task. While the water was hot, as many members of the family (and guests) as possible immersed themselves in it. We have already seen a couple in the tub in the San Gimignano fresco. At times similar

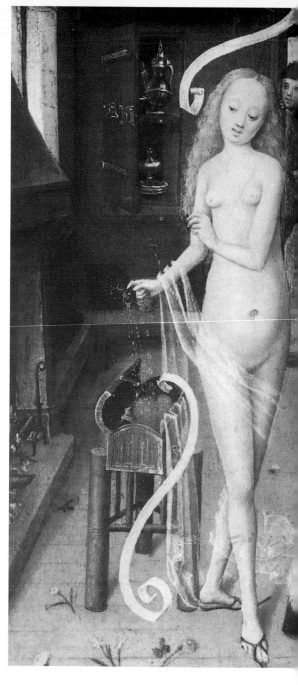

pictures show a plank or a tray between the two bathers, covered with food: doctors warned against excessive drinking during the bath. In medieval love stories lovers often begin the evening by bathing together. The tub often had a decorative or protective canopy, as in the Memling painting, and it could also be lined with cloth.[5] The water was generally emptied with a pail; in exceptional cases there was a drain. In princely houses there were actual built-in baths, and even hot and cold running water.[6]

44: Master of the Lower Rhine.
Amorous Incantation. MUSEUM
DER BILDENDEN KÜNSTE, LEIPZIG.

45: Hans Memling. *Bathsheba
Emerging from the Bath*.
STAATSGALERIE, STUTTGART.

46: Interior with Women Spinning and Playing Checkers, and a Juggler, fresco, c. 1450. CASTELLO, BRACCIANO.

In Flanders in the 15th century the depiction of interiors had already assumed a detailed, realistic character which not only gave each object its distinct individuality but also rendered the atmosphere, the *Stimmung* of the room. In Italy the summary "doll's house" description continued, with bare indications of the indispensable pieces of furniture. These were hints, not proper images from reality, as can be seen here in the tables and stools in the fresco of an *Interior with Women Spinning and Playing Checkers, and a Juggler* (c. 1450) in the Castello at Bracciano, and also from the sparse furnishing of the bedroom in one of the frescoes by Antoniazzo Romano (c. 1430 1509?) in the Pia Casa di Tor Specchi in Rome.

Also schematic are the 15th century furnishings seen in the woodcuts from the famous original edition of the *Hypnerotomachia Poliphili* of Francesco Colonna, published in Venice by Aldo Manuzio in 1499. If there was ever an author who felt objects as living things it was Francesco Colonna. His text speaks with passion of precious materials,[7] and yet the illustrations show bare conventional rooms: one with a table, the other with a bed with slender columns on which there are summary indications of ornaments of classic taste, and steps at the sides of the bed. Along the walls are the inevitable chests. (It took a genius to place these chests one on top of the other and thus create the chest of drawers.)

49: Antoniazzo Romano.
Bedroom Interior, fresco.
PIA CASA DI TOR DI
SPECCHI, ROME.

50: Vittore Carpaccio. *The Dream of Saint Ursula.* GALLERIA DELL' ACCADEMIA, VENICE.

The bed just seen in the woodcut from the *Hypnerotomachia* is of the same type as that in the bedroom of Saint Ursula in the famous painting by Vittore Carpaccio (1486–1525), *The Dream of Saint Ursula*. But here everything is precise, detailed, and taken from life, as in a Flemish painting, even down to the opened door which allows a glimpse of the other rooms. The corner to the right in the back, with the shelf of books, the hourglass, and the little volume, its binding warped from wear, (which in the case of a saint must be a book of devotions, but which otherwise could easily be a little Petrarch) constitutes in itself a still

51: Vittore Carpaccio. *The Nativity of the Virgin.* ACCADEMIA CARRARA, BERGAMO.

life similar to the still lifes as independent subjects
which were born in Italy in the 15th century.[8]
The room depicted in *The Dream of Saint Ursula*
has a fascination similar to that of Flemish interiors,
a fascination which Carpaccio was able to grasp.
His *Nativity of the Virgin* in the Accademia Carrara,

Bergamo, with its series of rooms seen through an
open door, the serving women busy at various tasks,
the whole filled with the atmosphere of domesticity,
is a prelude to certain themes of Dutch interiors of the
17th century, such as the one in Emanuel de Witte's
painting, *Girl at the Spinet* (Fig. 90).

52: Domenico Ghirlandaio. *The Nativity of the Virgin*, fresco. SANTA MARIA NOVELLA, FLORENCE.

The case of Carpaccio, however, is virtually unique.
The architectonic interiors of Ghirlandaio (1449–
1494) and of Andrea del Sarto (1486–1531) as seen
here in their respective frescoes of the *Nativity of the
Virgin* have nothing intimate about them. In the
del Sarto, for example, the door that leads to the
other rooms reveals only two women busy watching
the scene; that sense of the room and that bourgeois
domesticity which Carpaccio seized are lacking.
The room in which Ghirlandaio places the birth of
the Virgin has all the measured Alexandrine affectation of one of those Neoclassic "interior decorations"
which Percier and Fontaine were later to popularize
at the beginning of the 19th century. In this stately
solemnity we lose the more intimate aspect of the
embrace of the two saints at the top of the staircase
to the left. The fresco of Ghirlandaio is a procession
of mannequins (and as such it is often reproduced
in works on the history of dress) in an ideal room
imagined by a lover of the antique.

The sumptuousness of Ghirlandaio's setting did
indeed correspond to reality: the supporting pilasters
in Corinthian style decorated with elegant grotesques,
the inlaid paneling, the carved cornices and parapets
of this room find comparable details in an inventory of
a room in the Medici palace in Via Larga in Florence.
A vivid idea of the elaborate paneling, which once
adorned the most sumptuous Florentine residences,
can be had by observing the sacristy of Santa Croce
in Florence, the Sala del Cambio in Perugia, and
the study of Duke Federigo in the Palazzo Ducale
in Urbino, all works of Florentine masters.

53: Andrea del Sarto. *The Nativity of the Virgin*, fresco. SANTISSIMA ANNUNZIATA, FLORENCE.

54: *Petrarch in his Study,* miniature from the
codex of the *Canzoniere.* BIBLIOTECA TRIVULZIANA, MILAN.

55: Albrecht Dürer. *Saint Jerome in his Study,* engraving.

The scholar's cell, with its obvious invitation to
meditation, was naturally one of the first themes to
suggest the pictorial rendering of an intimate room.
In both the *Petrarch in his Study* and in the various
renderings of *Saint Jerome in his Cell,* the most
striking note is the bookshelf, the still life fixity of
objects which have become symbolic of an interior
furnishing. In Saint Jerome's little study, Faust's
monologue is already being prepared: *Habe nun, ach!*
Philosophie!... The volumes lie in disorder on the
shelves, mixed with hourglasses and astrolabes; or in
the panel by Antonello da Messina (c. 1430–1479)
they are arranged in neat order, pages opened, almost
on display. In these scenes all the details are minutely
depicted, as if the painter, centuries ahead of Robbe-

56: Colantonio, Neapolitan, mid-15th
century. *Saint Jerome in his Study.*
MUSEO DI CAPODIMONTE, NAPLES.

57: Antonello da Messina. *Saint Jerome in his Study*. NATIONAL GALLERY, LONDON.

Grillet, were resolving in the description of objects an interior situation: perhaps a lofty dialogue like that of Petrarch with Saint Augustine in the presence of Truth in the *Secretum*, on a crisis so unlikely of solution that it is better to distract the eye with the materiality of surrounding things, just as the hands would busy themselves with the beads of the rosary. The intense reconstruction of place, as Saint Ignatius, was soon to teach in his *Spiritual Exercises*, is a stage towards ecstasy. All those lifeless objects bear a message, which is the message of vanity and melancholy. Contact with the natural world is assured, by the lion in the case of Saint Jerome, by the white cat in the case of Petrarch. As to a sense of the interior, it is found above all in the Dürer engraving of *Saint Jerome in his Study*, which almost breathes the odor of old wood and old books, warmed and made aromatic by the sun which comes through the windows. But Antonello's is hardly an interior: it is more of a stage on which the saint poses, glancing out of the corner of his eye to see if the painter is about to set down his brushes. The peacock, the partridge, and the two elegant pots of flowers add a decorative note which, with the neat order of the books, gives the composition rather too much the quality of an attitude, which strongly attenuates—if it doesn't nullify completely—any feeling of intimacy.

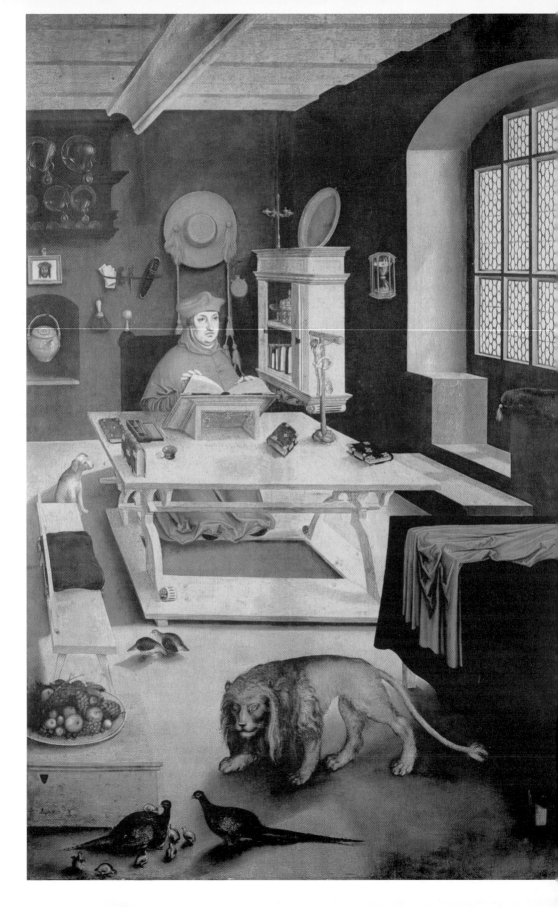

59: Lorenzo Lotto. *A Prelate in his Study*, drawing. BRITISH MUSEUM, LONDON.

60: *Massimiliano Sforza and his Tutor*, miniature, early 16th century. BIBLIOTECA TRIVULZIANA, MILAN.

In Lucas Cranach's *Cardinal Albrecht von Brandenburg as Saint Jerome in his Study*, the animals are more numerous and the picture is a sample-case of still life, of which various types are represented: the shelf of books, the cabinet of pewter pieces, the table with its dish of fruit. If the animals did not provide a certain disorder, everything would be neat, as orderly as the kernels in an ear of corn. Rigid as a wax portrait, Cardinal Albrecht von Brandenburg poses as Saint Jerome. He is no more alive than the copper kettle in the niche or the red cardinal's hat hanging on the wall; in other words, he too is a still life. The masquerade is a success, like those which Reynolds arranged in the 18th century, presenting ladies of the aristocracy in the guise of pagan divinities. Note the care with which the painter has rendered the details of the furnishing: the path for painters of Biedermeier interiors is already defined.

The miniature of Massimiliano Sforza and his tutor is above all a court scene, including the dwarf jester

and some pet animals with which the pages are playing. The castle in the background asserts the family's might. But, as representation of everyday life, seen in *déshabillé*, the drawing by Lorenzo Lotto (c. 1480–1556) of a *Prelate in his Study* introduces us into the rather dusty and casual disorder of a room and its objects very different from the neatness seen in Cardinal Albrecht von Brandenburg's study. The shelf crammed with vases, books, and various vessels, the knick-knacks, the urns, the rubbish, and the bell which clutter the table give us the impression of the bizarre way of life which the effeminate face of the prelate and the little dog on the nearby cushion merely confirm. Here there is none of the enchanted fixity of Cranach's picture, here is no idealization of intimacy; but perhaps this snapshot brings us closer to the everyday life of the 16th century than many more studied compositions. The drawing can be read as a chronicle, a "small-beer chronicle," Thackeray would have said.

58: Lucas Cranach the Elder. *Cardinal Albrecht von Brandenburg as Saint Jerome in his Study*, 1525. HESSISCHES LANDESMUSEUM, DARMSTADT.

61: Hans Eworth. *Henry Stuart, Lord Darnley, and his Younger Brother.*
WINDSOR CASTLE. (Reproduced by the gracious permission of H. M. the Queen)

It takes a great deal of unconcern, or Anglo-Saxon indifference, to consider the background independently of the figures as in the painting of *Henry Stuart, Lord Darnley, with his Younger Brother* by Hans Eworth (born at Antwerp, active in London between 1545 and 1574). The painting is about two feet high, but it looks very much like a large size miniature, miniatures then being much in vogue in England. The background is one of those long galleries which occupied the top of Elizabethan manors, and can be traced back to the kind of *solaria* widespread in the Frankish Empire and in neighboring states in the centuries following the great barbarian invasions. The *solarium* could be a loggia, a gallery, or a promenade, or even a great hall with many windows, as in this picture. The common feature of all *solaria* was their location at the top of the house. We remember one *solarium* especially, that at Chastleton House, near Moreton-in-the-Marsh, a town, as its name states, beside a swamp: an oddly bewitched place where you breathe the air of Poe's House of

Usher. Poe was in England as a boy and was, it is said, deeply impressed by these Elizabethan manors Chastleton is on the border of three counties, Oxfo Gloucester, and Warwick, but the confluence of names can be misleading. It is an absolutely dead corner of the countryside, and the greenery—also because of the relative neglect of the park around t house—reaches even the threshhold of the long gallery on the top floor. This gallery has a barrel-vault decorated with white stucco work and walls paneled with arid, grey wood, which has a greenish patina in the reflection of the light that comes thro the windows. As to the furniture, there is a large chest which recalls the tragic story which really happened, of a girl who one Christmas Eve, playing at hide-and-seek, hid in such a chest whose lock snapped, and she was found only a long time there-after, a corpse in a desperate attitude. Hardly less tragic is the personage represented in this portrait b Hans Eworth. The face of the seventeen year old young man is that of which it was said: "No woma

62: Ludger Tom Ring the Younger. *Marriage Feast of Cana.* Formerly KAISER-FRIEDRICH MUSEUM, BERLIN. (destroyed)

of spirit would make choice of such a man that was liker a woman than a man, for he is lovely, beardless, and lady-faced." And yet, this creature with a "heart of wax" (the words are Mary Stuart's) so turned her head that she married him in 1565. The dramatic events that followed, the murder of the Queen's counsellor and musician, David Rizzio, with the complicity of Darnley, and the murder of Darnley himself in February of 1567, are so well-known that it is unnecessary to recall them here, where they are not pertinent. A single detail of this final tragedy is concerned with furnishing. In the solitary country house at Kirk o'Field, where Darnley was lying ill, there was a costly bed of Mary Stuart's with fur covering, which she ordered removed to Holyrood on the pretext that she wanted to sleep there that night (we must remember the medieval custom, already noted, of the transportation of the nobles' furniture from one house to another). At eleven in the evening the Queen lovingly took leave of her ailing husband. At two in the morning a terrible

explosion was heard, "as if five-and twenty cannon had been fired simultaneously." The solitary house had blown up, and the young man with the feminine face and the waxen heart along with it. For those who wish to know more, there is the beautiful, if prolix trilogy on Mary Stuart by Swinburne or the biography by Stefan Zweig.

The interior scene by Ludger Tom Ring the Younger (1522–1583) suggests associations of quite a different kind. In this *Marriage feast of Cana* everything has become still life. The wedding feast of Cana has been pushed into another room: it is only a background episode, as if the wedding were hanging on the wall like a picture. In the foreground are still lifes of every kind, two subsidiary figures and the mistress with her little girl, posing as if for a portrait, plus many tiny details of furnishing, including the significant one of the two miniatures hanging on the sideboard. This is a veritable multiplication of loaves and fishes, and the room is so crowded that one thinks of the *horror vacui* of 19th century middle class interiors.

LAPIS POLARIS, MAGNES.

Lapis reclusit iste Flauio abditum   *Poli suum hunc amorem, at ipse nauitæ.*

63: Jan van der Straet (Giovanni Stradano). *The Astronomer's Chamber.* Engraving by Philip Galle.

Lorenzo Lotto's drawing of the *Prelate in his Study,* which we have seen, shows an interest rare among Italian artists of the 16th century, who were largely indifferent to details of furnishing and of everyday life. In Italian 16th century dramas, references to everyday life are rare or even non-existent in the toga-ed and boring tragedies of Giraldi Cinthio, Sperone Speroni, etc., and infrequent where they might have been present in the comedies which were not hampered by abstract considerations of *deeorum.* But such references abound in the Elizabethan plays of Shakespeare, Webster, Ben Johnson. One recalls that, even in our own century, an Italian translator was unwilling to render literally the simple expression "Pray you, undo this button" from *King Lear* (Act V, scene iii, 310) but had recourse to the vague "Liberatemi," "Free me." *La fiera* (1619) by Michelangelo Buonarroti il Giovane (1568-1646), whose intent was to give a sampling of words and idioms in Florentine usage, cannot compare, as to depiction of real life and everyday environment, with Ben Johnson's *Bartholomew's Fair* (1614). Still a certain interest in furnishing can be observed in Buonarroti. Here, for example, is a description of a necromancer's laboratory:

Ne te fatidicis Tyrrhenus terreat augur
Graccus ait monitis, Cornelia, non mihi vitae

Tantus amor, tantæ post funera coniugis vnquam
Vt superesse velim, iugulum sed masculus anguis

Prebebit prior, immineant vt summa præ
Fata mihi, vitamq; tuis virtutibus æque

64: Jan van der Straet (Giovanni Stradano). *Women Embroidering.* Engraving by Philip Galle.

". . . *I observed distinctly*
On certain shelves,
Divers bizarre oddities
Of Nature and also of Art
Marine fantasies, minerals,
Whimsical roots, grim rocks,
Freakish stones,
Which display various aspects in their mixtures,
And mummies and fish-scales, tails and horrid skulls
Of beasts and of serpents
And I noticed there strange instruments,
Of eccentric arts and new operations

Which I consider more imaginary than real
For instance huge bells,
And also huge spikes . . .
He has many cauldrons,
Where, amid many curious processes
To give hardness to watery substances,
He has undertaken to petrify
Tears from women . . ."

Buonarroti, *La Fiera*, Seconda Giornata,
Act IV, scene xviii.

97

65: Jan van der Straet (Giovanni Stradano). *Women Cultivating Silk Worms.* Engraving by Philip Galle.

It is not in Italian, but in Northern art that we find depicted rooms like the necromancer's laboratory described by Buonarroti. Observe, for example, *The Astronomer's Chamber* (*Fig.* 63) by Ian van der Straet (Bruges, 1523—Florence, 1605), a Fleming who lived in Italy, where he was called Giovanni Stradano. In this engraving compass, calipers, armillary sphere, globe, hour-glass, books and papers are inventoried, as well as the miniature caravel hanging from the ceiling, and the furniture around the room. As in the case of

Lorenzo Lotto's ecclesiastic, and in other cases, the bed is found in the work- and living-room. This is also true in the engraving by van der Straet of *Women Embroidering* (*Fig.* 64), where the left part of the room functions as a dining room, the right as bedroom, with the ever-present chests. The scene at the extreme right of two men, one of whom is slitting a serpent's throat, is a symbolic illustration of the verses printed below the composition. The women seated in the center of the room illustrate the various methods of embroider-

HYACVM, ET LVES VENEREA.

Grauata morbo ab hocce membra mollia   *Leuabit iſta ſorpta coɛtio arboris.*

66: Jan van der Straet (Giovanni Stradano). *The Treatment of Syphilis.* Engraving by Philip Galle.

ing. Another typically bourgeois piece of furniture is the sideboard to the left, with its display of dishes. The engraving by van der Straet of *Women Cultivating Silk Worms* shows the same combination of bed- and living-room, while in the print which illustrates the *Treatment of Syphilis* (with a decoction of *lignum vitae*) or holy wood, the first remedy invented for the disease which was slaughtering the population at the beginning of the 16th century) the bedroom and the dining room are two different rooms. The picture hanging on the bedroom wall is allusive, as the pictures and other objects which Hogarth was later to introduce into his satirical and moralistic compositions: it illustrates the pleasures of the table and the bed, afterwards dearly paid for with the disease contracted in illadvised lovemaking. In the kitchen-dining room we see the medicine being prepared by extracting it from the resin of the holy wood. The furnishing includes the usual credenza with display of dishes, and the table of a typically 16th century form.

67: Frans Francken II. *Living Room of Peter Paul Rubens' House in Antwerp.* NATIONALMUSEUM, STOCKHOLM.

The 17th century was the age of oak furniture. The most interesting developments are found in the furnishings in the Low Countries. In the *Living Room of Peter Paul Rubens' House in Antwerp,* painted by Frans Francken II (1581–1642), we see at the right the simplification of the type of credenza which we have already seen elsewhere: the monumental high stand for crockery is replaced by two low steps. This piece is in the style of Vredeman de Vries. The space above is occupied by a painting. This painting is not so easily identifiable (it belongs to the same series as the portraits of Charles the Bold and the Emperor Maximilian in the Kunsthistorisches Museum, Vienna) as are the other

two Rubens paintings which hang on the wall at the back of the room: *Lot and his Daughters* (which later went to the Jules Féral collection in Paris) and the *Fall of the Damned* (now in the Munich Pinakothek). Though Leo van Puyvelde[9] insists that the house Rubens had built for himself at Antwerp was not the sumptuous palace which is generally mentioned, the room depicted here by his pupil Frans Francken, a kind of room that will be then found a few years later (c. 1630) enriched and enlarged in the interiors of Bartholomäeus van Bassen, already reveals elements of harmony and luxury.

As for Hans Vredeman de Vries (1527–1604),

68: Frans Francken II. *The Study of a Collector.* M. GOFFI COLLECTION, ROME.

he was active in northern Germany and in Holland, and was the author of a series of architectonic and ornamental projects, as well as a designer of furniture (*Differents pourtraicts de menuiserie*, the first part in 1583, and second published posthumously in 1630) and he adapted current types of furniture to the taste of the 16th century. He found his models in part in the strongly Italianate, Mannerist furniture, of Jacques Androuet Ducerceau (c. 1510–89), which anticipated the proto-Baroque of the Louis XIII style and achieved the first systematic attempt to conceive furniture in perfect accord with contemporary art (use of grotesques, herms, etc. according to the taste of the

School of Fontainebleau).

The other Francken picture depicts the *Study of a Collector,* with a variety of interests (natural history, fish and crustaceans, books and manuscripts, paintings of every kind, sacred subjects, portraits, still life) which we shall see below in other *Wunderkammern.* Against the rear wall, an altar decorated with figures of the virtues bears shells of unusual shapes; other shells, medals, an armillary sphere and a globe are seen on the table at the left, where two people are sitting, one of them that Justus Lipsius, the naturalist, who figures also in the Rubens painting (of 1602) in the Pitti in Florence. The other might be Paulus de Praun.[10]

69: Claes Janszoon Visscher. *Prayers before a Meal*. Engraving of 1609 by Petrus Kaerius.

Dutch engravings of the 17th century, especially those that illustrate the emblem books then in great vogue, afford copious documentation of the Dutch interiors of the period. Particularly noteworthy in this respect are the volumes of Jacob Cats, which are still one of the adornments of the Dutch house. Cats took his inspiration from proverbs and everyday life; these emblems in a realistic vein take a place parallel to genre painting and also illustrate the history of costume. Worth remembering among others are the *Emblemata* *of Zinnewerck* by Johannes de Brune, Amsterdam 1624.[11] Dutch interiors do not have the elegant pretensions often found in Flemish ones, but their sobriety is not without a sense of ease and warm bourgeois intimacy. In the engraving of Claes Janszoon Visscher, *Prayers before a Meal* (1609), we have a smaller-scale version of the same kind of room that we have already seen in Rubens' house in Antwerp. On the rear wall, the mantle is supported by elegant caryatids and surmounted by a triptych; at the right, the wall with

70 (upper): Engraving by P. Serwouter, from *Houwelijck* of Jacob Cats, 1625.
71 (lower): Engraving from *Spiegel etc.* of Jacob Cats, 1632.

windows under which the table is laid; against the opposite wall is the bed. Shelves of books are arranged with the spines against the wall as was then customary, and a shelf with dishes, crockery, and mugs completes the furnishing. Through a door at the back we glimpse the maid busy cooking at another hearth. In the engraving of P. Serwouter from *Houwelijck* of Jacob Cats (*Fig.* 70), the curtained bed, the chest, and the table with turned legs covered with a cloth, are accompanied by an X-shaped chair, a very popular

piece at that period, probably of walnut, its legs faintly decorated with a loricated frieze (in other cases this part of the piece was embellished with more elaborate motifs.) The same kind of chair is found in the following plate (*Fig.* 71), from Jacob Cats' *Spiegel van den Ouden ende Nieuwen Tijdt*, where in addition to the usual elements of furnishing (curtained bed, table with turned legs covered by a cloth, chest) we see the toilette table, this being a lighter table on which a mirror is placed. This room is decorated with hangings, but at

72: Engraving of Emblem XIII, from
Emblemata of Zinne-werck of
Johannes de Brune, Amsterdam, 1624.

73: Engraving of Emblem X, from
Emblemata of Zinne-werck of
Johannes de Brune, Amsterdam, 1624.

other times the walls were covered with wooden panels which also embraced the bed. This is the case in the engraving from the *Emblemata of Zinne-werck* (*Fig.* 72), which also reproduces humble everyday details such as the urinal and the straw toilet seat.[12] Another X-shaped chair and a toilette table are seen in the engraving by P. Serwouter for Jacob van Zevecote's *Emblemata ofte sinnebeelden met dichten verciert,* Ludg. Batav. ex officina Elzeviriana, 1626. Here we also observe the bourgeois tendency to cover with stuffs the flat surfaces of furniture unsuited for such covering (in the present case a tall cupboard), a tendency which becomes even more widespread in the bourgeois 19th century. In *Figure 73* there is the customary display of dishes and mugs on the credenza under the window. A father in a houserobe tries to comfort a crying baby. Here the cradle is of wicker, whereas in *Prayers before a Meal* (*Fig.* 69) it is of carved wood, as befitting the higher station of the family. In *Figure 74* we see a painter's studio, its walls draped with hangings and decorated with pictures, while on a table some sculptures have been set. More curious are the objects which cover the walls of the laboratory in *Figure 76*: jars, basins, shears, musical instruments.

74: Engraving by P. Serwouter, from *Emblemata ofte sinnebeelden met dichten verciert* of Jacob van Zevecote, 1626.

75: Engraving by P. Serwouter from
Houwelijck of Jacob Cats, 1625.

76: Engraving of Emblem I, from *Emblemata of Zinne-werck*
of Johannes de Brune, Amsterdam, 1624.

77: Bartholomäus van Bassen. *Flemish Interior.*
MUSÉE DES ARTS DÉCORATIFS, PARIS.

Flemish furniture, richer than Dutch, has more jagged
profiles, more elaborate carving. Though it adopts
classical elements, its exuberance identifies it as Nordic
just as the teeming imagery of Shakespeare's little
Ovidian poems is Nordic *(Venus and Adonis, The
Rape of Lucrece)*, as indeed is the imagery of other
Elizabethans. The wood generally used was oak, but
in Antwerp they began also to make furniture of
walnut, veneered with exotic woods like ebony and
rosewood. With commercial prosperity even the Dutch
furniture became more elaborate and precious,
assuming showy forms, rich with moulding and with
panels faceted like diamonds. This is especially true in

the characteristic cupboards, whose massive aspect
testifies to the opulent solidity of the prosperous merchant class. The imaginary interiors of Bartholomäus
van Bassen (c. 1590–1625) give us the supreme
expression of the taste of this sumptuous late Northern
Renaissance, inspired by the French interpretation of
Italian Mannerism. In these interiors the artist's
imagination runs riot and creates variations on the
same type of room found in the Rubens house in
Antwerp. In van Bassen's *Interior* belonging to the
Musée des Arts Décoratifs, Paris, the ceiling still has
simple beams, supported by rich corbels, but the
tabernacle which frames the entrance door is

78: Bartholomäus van Bassen. *Flemish Interior.*
STATENS MUSEUM FOR KUNST, COPENHAGEN.

79: Bartholomäus van Bassen. *Flemish Interior.*
STATENS MUSEUM FOR KUNST, COPENHAGEN.

elaborately contrived like the architectonic projects of the German Wendel Dietterlin. (Dietterlin worked in the late 16th century, while van Bassen's interiors can be dated around 1630.) Above the high, carved panels which run all around the room there are paintings and recesses for precious vessels. The credenza with caryatids of French inspiration is covered by a cloth and on the cloth are set earthenware and a slender Mannerist statuette of Venus and Cupid. At the left the room opens onto a court with flowerbeds. This room functions—this may strike a modern observer as strange—as both bedroom and dining room, as in the case of the room in the engraving by Claes Janszoon

Visscher (*Fig.* 69). In the other paintings by van Bassen we see impressive coffered ceilings, like those in Italian palaces. The two focal points of the room are always the fireplace and the credenza: both these and the door frames are richly ornamented. In van Bassen's *Interior* in the Hessisches Landesmuseum, Darmstadt (*Fig.* 80), the bed is in the adjacent room at the back. In these interior scenes by van Bassen we see people banqueting and amusing themselves. Through open doors we glimpse gardens or other vast apartments. Servants are busy carrying food, in one instance a peacock, so highly prized at banquets of the period. Here is the whole panorama of a regal way of life.

80: Bartholomäus van Bassen. *Flemish Interior.* HESSISCHES LANDESMUSEUM, DARMSTADT.

81 (above): Abraham Bosse. *The Visit to the New Mother*, engraving.   *82 (below):* Abraham Bosse. *The Blood-Letting*, engra

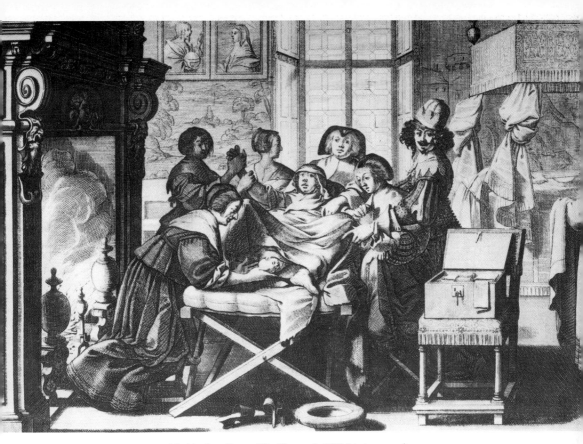

83: Abraham Bosse. *The Woman in Childbirth,* engraving.

Abraham Bosse (1602-1676) was a considerable artist who combined the light effects of Caravaggio with a taste for classical composition, and approached Louis Le Nain's objective naturalism. He is especially famous for engravings which faithfully reflect French 17th century society, particularly the *haute bourgeoisie,* the *noblesse de robe.* Without any romantic, sentimental attitudes, Bosse does not lack a satirical vein when he depicts the aristocracy. A sound draughtsman, without flights of fantasy, Bosse represents the classic phase of French engraving, as Callot — with his light and witty touch, his sinuous movement — represents the Mannerist phase.

The bedroom that appears in *The Visit to the New Mother* presents elements which we already know: the bed with columns and hangings, the cupboard covered with a cloth, the fireplace; the room is decked with elegantly ornamented stuff. Both aristocratic ladies and *bourgeoises* received in their bedrooms. We have already observed in preceding plates (interiors of van Bassen, etc.) the bed's presence in the main room of the house. Though landscapes and scenes with figures often decorated the walls, paintings and mirrors were hung over them, as can be seen in the engravings of *The Blood-Letting, The Woman in Childbirth* and the *Allegory of the Sense of Touch.* Tables disappear under

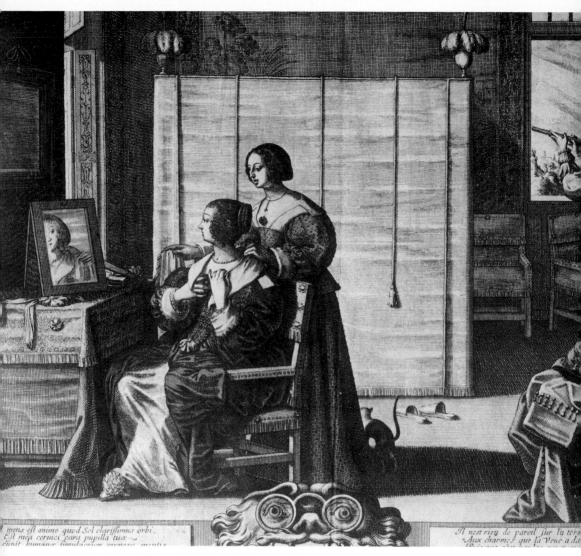

mens est animo quod Sol clarissimus orbi,
Est mea cervici cara pupilla tuæ—
cunit humanæ simulacrum speciem mentis

Il nest rien de pareil sur la terr
Aux charmes que la Veue a da

84: Abraham Bosse. *Allegory of the Sense of Sight*, engraving.

heavy covers. The chairs, lined up in a row along the walls, have very low backs and stiff legs joined by stretchers. These chairs are covered with gold-fringed velvet. Often they have no arms so that the full-skirted women may be more comfortable *(chaises à vertugadins)*. Such was the French furnishing of the 1630's. Later tall chairbacks came into fashion again. They were prevalent in the age of Louis XIV, when French furniture developed independent tendencies, created new kinds of furniture (the *lit de repos*, the *commode*), and displayed a luxury and a polychromy of rich materials (Boulle furniture decorated with

precious panels of metal and tortoiseshell) which took it far from the austerity of Bosse's period, in which the influence of Spanish taste is perceptible. In the *Allegory of the Sense of Hearing* we see clearly the tapestried walls, and in the left background a stiff precursor of the *lit de repos* which began to appear in those years. Under Louis XIV, the shrouded bed we have seen in *The Visit to a New Mother* or in the *Allegory of a Sense of Touch* was replaced by two new forms: *à la duchesse*, with the canopy free of supports in the front; *d'ange*, with the canopy shorter than the bedstead itself, often set in an alcove.

86 *(at right)*: Abraham Bosse. *Allegory of the Sense of Touch*, engra

87: Monogrammist R. W. *Dutch Interior of the Seventeenth Century.* FABRIZIO CLERICI COLLECTION.

Those sober, fairly monotonous interiors with their walls decorated with *verdures* (tapestries with trees, meadows, etc.) or with Cordovan leather, their chairs with stiff lines, and the stuffs that covered the tables and the tops of the cupboards, were for a long time typical of the Jansenist bourgeoisie in France. For that matter Louis XIV style at its height, because of its sumptuous, state character, did not lend itself to the furnishing of bourgeois houses, except through adaptations like those in Holland, for instance, where elements of the Louis XIV style are to be found up till the mid-18th century. Sobriety does not necessarily mean intimacy: it would be hard to imagine a colder room than the one represented in *Dutch Interior of the*

Seventeenth Century, which bears the mark of the monogrammist R. W. The vast room has the atmosphere of a vestibule or a sacristy; bristling with cornices and angles, wooden and marble, it could hardly be considered suitable for conversation and daily life. And yet this is both living- and bedroom, as we can tell from the table, covered by a heavy rug on which musical instruments are set, and from the alcove in the back at right, where part of the bed can be seen, the type of bed enclosed in a projection of the paneling that runs all around the room.

The *Interior with Family Group* by Hieronymus Janssen (1624–1693) is, on the other hand, a room like those we have seen in the engravings

88: Hieronymus Janssen. *Interior with Family Group.* LIECHTENSTEIN COLLECTION, VIENNA.

of Abraham Bosse, though this room is more sumptuous, also recalling the room in Rubens's house. The cupboard against the back wall belongs to a very popular 16th century kind of furniture, with a drop-door and little inner drawers (in France known as *cabinet d'Allemagne*), or decorated with semi-precious stones *(cabinet façon de Gênes,* or *de Florence).* In this type of piece the taste of the artisans indulged itself to such an extent that finally the decorative and architectonic aspect became far more important than the practical one (for example, in the monumental cupboard made in 1555 at Augsburg by Lienhart Strohmeier for the Emperor Charles V). The precious Florentine cupboards in the course of the 17th century won the primacy over the German cupboards which had held first place in the preceding century. A number of Florentine type cupboards are found in the inventory of Cardinal Mazarin's collection, adorned with columns, pilasters, niches, busts, statues, plated with mother-of-pearl, ivory, lapis lazuli, precious metals, miniatures, silver capitals, mosaic flowers. Such cupboards were generally found also in the treasure rooms of sovereigns. The artists of Antwerp specialized in a kind of cabinet veneered with ebony and tortoise-shell and decorated with paintings. This, in fact, is the style of the cabinet that we see in the *Interior with Family Group.*

89: Pieter de Hooch. *The Good Housewife*, c. 1650. RIJKSMUSEUM, AMSTERDAM.

Dutch painting in the 17th century affords valuable documentation of the furnishing of the period. So in *The Good Housewife of* Pieter de Hooch (1629–1688) we see all the colored vivacity (tawny wood, with ebony inlays) of the cupboard, originally a functional piece invented to contain more conveniently the clothing formerly kept in chests, and which was now made less dull by accentuating its architectonic character, decorating the cornice with masks, inserting in the pilasters mirrors of precious woods, as in this illustration. But the Dutch painters wanted to depict not only the house's furnishing, but also its life; not only an interior, but the way this interior was articulated with the other rooms. Hence the side

views, the lengthwise glimpses that these paintings offer of other rooms and adjacent courtyards, and also the way in which these interiors are related to the world around them, through nature glimpsed at the doors and windows, and above all by the use of light. From this point of view the *Girl at the Spinet* of Emanuel de Witte (1617–1692) can be called an exemplary picture. Very appropriately Fritz Laufer[13] has underlined the contrast between this kind of interior painting, in which man is not isolated from the outside world, and the interior painting in vogue in the 19th century, which is nevertheless connected with the Dutch tradition. In Biedermeier painting the aim is to render an interior as a space

90: Emanuel de Witte. *Girl at the Spinet*. PRIVATE COLLECTION, DIEPENVEEN.

sealed off from the world outside, a little universe
carefully prepared for an escape into the past and into
the exotic. Our primitive need for security against
a hostile external world is satisfied by a closed place.
Read here what Gordon Logie says,[14] speaking
about one of the reasons for the charm of Rome's
Piazza Navona: "This need has now sunk into our
subconscious but it is important enough to affect
our reactions so that for this reason alone it is better
to restrict the entries into a place to a minimum
and to make them as small as possible so that the
place shall seem to be completely enclosed."

On the other hand, when the Dutch wanted to depict
not the life of the house, but the very materiality of
the furnishing, they had the series of the rooms
of an apartment reproduced in miniature in those
capacious cupboards which have improperly been
called dolls' houses. Such faithful reproductions,
often the work of the same artists who had made the
objects of normal proportions for the house, were
destined to hand down to posterity the memory of the
handsome furnishings which those refined bourgeois
evidently imagined would not survive the revolutions
of taste. Peter the Great also ordered for himself
such a miniature house, but when, after five years,
it was delivered to his agent in Holland, the sovereign
refused it because of its high price (twenty thousand
florins).

91: Pieter de Hooch. *A Young Woman at the Cellar Door with a Child.* RIJKSMUSEUM, AMSTERDAM.

92: Hendrick Gerritsz Pot. *Struggle for the Inheritance.* Formerly KAISER-FRIEDRICH MUSEUM, BERLIN.

In Pieter de Hooch there is the barest hint of a relationship among the human figures that appear in his interiors: In the *Young Woman at the Cellar Door with a Child* the maidservant smiles, handing a small pitcher to the little daughter of the house. The true protagonist of these pictures, as Edouard Huttinger has observed, is the space which "prend doucement en sa garde les hommes, à tel point qu'ils se fondent indissolublement en lui."[15] But often, with the majority of Northern genre painters, the room serves only to frame the anecdote and presents a richness of objects meant to illustrate some moral. Thus in the *Struggle for the Inheritance* of Hendrick Gerritsz Pot (c. 1585–1657) things of every kind, crockery, jewels, coins, books, even large cheese cakes are piled on a shelf in the background while, next to the corpse watched over by the faithful dog and stared at, wide-eyed, by the cat, the heirs—insensitive to any stimulus save their own greed—assault the riches left by the deceased.

93 *(above):* Jan Mienze Molenaer. *Allegory of Vanity.* JULIUS S. HELD COLLECTION, NEW YORK.

94 *(at right):* Wolfgang Heimbach. *Reading by Lamplight,* c. 1645. GALLERIA BORGHESE, R(

The necklaces and coffers that clutter the table, and the scattering of musical instruments in the *Allegory of Vanity* by Jan Mienze Molenaer (1610–1668) are meant only to illustrate the allegorical subject which is also alluded to by the little monkey on a chain near its mistress. Probably, on the other hand, there is no hidden meaning at all in the presence of the painting of Cain and Abel on the wall of the room where two men (who might also be brothers) are examining some papers and discussing business in the

Reading by Lamplight by the German painter Wolfgang Heimbach (c. 1615–d. after 1678). Here the painter is chiefly concerned with the effects of light on the face of the man who is reading and the other who is listening, or on that of the woman in the next room who is offering drink to another figure who seems to refuse. The furnishings are those usual in the first part of the 17th century: stiff chairs, table with bottle legs, and a display of dishes and utensils which we glimpse in the far room.

95: Jan Vermeer. *Girl Drinking with a Gentleman.* KAISER-FRIEDRICH MUSEUM, BERLIN.

One does not want to degrade the incomparable painting of Jan Vermeer van Delft (1632–1675) to mere documentation of customs and furnishings; it is far more than that, just as the novels of Jane Austen are more than the curious documentation of the manners and civil conversation of England at the end of the 18th and beginning of the 19th century. To begin with, in the paintings of Vermeer the human figure predominates; it is not, as in the work of Pieter de Hooch, only a point of reference in a play of spaces and light. But what does the human figure in Vermeer say? A gentleman observes a lady as she sips from a goblet a drink he has poured for her

from a jug (*Girl Drinking with a Gentleman,* Kaiser-Friedrich Museum, Berlin); a painter paints a model dressed as Fame, with the proper attribute, the trumpet (*Artist in His Studio,* Kunsthistorisches Museum, Vienna); in other famous pictures by Vermeer, a maidservant pours milk from a pitcher; a girl reads a letter; another is intent on her embroidery; yet another is putting on a necklace in front of a mirror; a lady plays a spinet in the presence of a cavalier ... To classify these scenes as genre painting would be like putting Dante's masterpiece in the same category with the vast literature of visions of the next world. Moreover, rather than scenes, these

96: Jan Vermeer. *The Artist in his Studio.* KUNSTHISTORISCHES MUSEUM, VIENNA.

are moments: moments caught in their fleeting
essence, which here remains eternal. The realism is
spiritualized in the intensity of the artist's vision;
he has held up a mirror to the world, but the mirror
is enchanted. Everyday things assume a silent
magnificence, immersed in an atmosphere purer than
the earth's. Without invoking any divine presence
in his paintings, Vermeer creates a peace that is more
divine than in the Paradises depicted in the canvases
of other painters: the pearly light translates the
feeling of peace into purely visual terms. The sense
of pleasure in the surroundings, the rare stuffs,
the gleaming crystal, the carefully arranged objects,

becomes ecstatic; the contemplater's soul is taken
outside itself, is plunged into the object, and in fusing
with it, creates a divinity. Painted by Vermeer, a map
hanging on the wall, a majolica vase, a pearl adorning
a woman's ear have an almost Platonic, archetypal
value: they are, *par excellence*, the object they
represent. The transfiguration of everyday things
could not go further. So Vermeer, from the very
beginning of this bourgeois art, is the precursor in
painting of what, at a distance of centuries, was to be
the supreme result of that art in literature; generations
of realist novelists had to come and go before literature achieved such a transfiguration of the everyday.

97: Jacob Ochtervelt. *Lady with Maidservant and Little Dog.* CARNEGIE INSTITUTE, PITTSBURGH.

98: Emanuel de Witte. *Family Group,* 1673. LEWIS S. FRY COLLECTION.

Such heights are not reached by other Dutch painters, who generally indulge in the anecdote. In the *Lady with Maidservant and Little Dog* of Jacob Ochtervelt (1634/5–1708/10) the splendidly dressed blonde lady offers a sweetmeat to a little dog, the maid smiles encouragingly at the pet, a gentleman beyond the door seems to take part in the scene; the moment has none of the ecstatic quality which belongs only to Vermeer. Our gaze wanders over the furnishings, the dark cube of the bed with its curtains drawn, the table hidden by the rug, the rigid chair with the twisted legs according to the fashion prevalent in the mid-17th century. Here, too, as in certain pictures of Vermeer, a map is considered a pleasant wall decoration. A little dog also enlivens the *Family*

Group painted by Emanuel de Witte in 1673. Here we see Chinese vases on the fireplace, according to the fashion which caught on under Louis XIV, Cordovan leather covering the lower part of the walls, and a mirror with a gilded intricate frame, like the other mirror which appears in the *Girl at the Spinet* of the same painter (*Fig.* 90). Around 1650 Ian Lutma (1609–1689) launched the fashion of the so-called ear-shaped style frames for mirrors, a style characterized by the richness of ornamental motifs such as shells, *putti,* musical instruments and cartouches, which indeed gave to these frames the appearance of the auricle. The curve of the leg of the table has the late Baroque character which came into fashion in the very years in which this picture was painted.

99: Michiel van Musscher. *Thomas Hees with his Nephews and a Negro Servant*, 1687. RIJKSMUSEUM, AMSTERDAM.

In the portrait of *Thomas Hees with his Nephews and a Negro Servant* painted in 1687 by Michiel van Musscher (1645–1705) the whole room has an exotic air, from the coral hung around the Dutch coat-of-arms, which attests the colonial power of the Low Countries, to the scimitars and Arab carbines hanging on the wall, the Atlas open to the page of the Barbary Coast, the book with an Arabic title (the Koran) set beside the Bible, and even the dress of the central figure. The mirror reflects two Algerians looking in from the courtyard. Thomas Hees (born in 1635) was sent by the States General to Algiers in 1675 to make a treaty of peace and commerce with that government. Presumably he left Algiers in 1680, the year following the ratification of the treaty, and brought back gifts from the Algerian government including three cummerbunds, three guns, and three scimitars, some of which are hanging on the wall. In 1684 he was sent, as Commissioner General, to Tunis and to Tripoli, whence he returned in 1685. In the

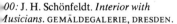
100: J. H. Schönfeldt. *Interior with Musicians*. GEMÄLDEGALERIE, DRESDEN.

101: J. H. Schönfeldt. *Interior with Musicians*. GEMÄLDEGALERIE, DRESDEN.

painting, one of his nephews, Andrew, is handing him a letter in which we can distinctly read the name and office of the man, while the younger nephew, Jan, holds his tobacco pot. The name of Hees, with the date of 1676, is worked into the golden embroidery of the red bag for his official papers on the table.[16] As to the furnishing, the foot of the table, a dolphin's head, which protrudes from beneath the rug, is of interest because feet in the form of dolphins' heads are often mentioned as an innovation introduced only in the following century, in Chippendale furniture.[17]

The two paintings of an *Interior with Musicians* by J. H. Schönfeldt (1609–1675) apparently show the same room seen from opposite ends. The kind of chair depicted in the hall with the harpsichord is earlier than the chair shown in the other painting, but the date of both paintings is somewhere around the middle of the century. This type of gallery room, its walls covered with paintings up to the ceiling, can still be seen in certain patrician homes in Italy and elsewhere.

102: Johann Georg Platzer. *Allegory of Winter.* INSTITUTE OF ARTS, MINNEAPOLIS.

This interior from the series of the seasons by the Austrian Johann Georg Platzer (1702-1760) shows the influence of Rubens and the Dutch painters: the forms of the furniture may seem luxuriant, but they correspond to types that date back to the end of the 17th century.[18] In this painting there predominates an atmosphere of warm, voluptuous abandonment to pleasure in a room protected against the rigors of the season, which can be glimpsed through the arches of the portico: a cloudy sky, icy mountains, bare branches, a peasant struggling with his horse. In this room, decorated with gay and lascivious paintings (a village dance to the sound of bagpipes, a seduction scene where the man has the expression of a satyr),

there are two young men with masks courting: one accosts a young woman at the door who seems attracted, though at the same time she draws back; the other approaches a married woman who pretends to caress her frowning husband, who is warming himself at the fire and will soon seek consolation in wine. At the table the old lady ponders the cards to play in a game with another swain, for whom an accomplice with a mirror reveals the lady's hand, treacherously pretending to give her advice at the same time. At the right of the picture, an ewer, a goblet and a little crystal bottle on a table covered with a rich rug offer a Dutch-style still life in the taste of Willem Kalf and Barend van der Meer.

The first collections of modern times brought together every kind of curiosity: elephants' tusks and sharks' teeth, ostrich eggs, coconuts and bezoar-stones were given an enormous value, even higher than the value set on works of human ingenuity and art. Some of these objects were believed to possess special qualities. A rhinoceros horn, for example, could detect the presence of a poison. Every precious stone had its occult power. This explains the composite aspect of those collections—church treasuries, the *Schatz-* and *Wunderkammern* of princes—which has been preserved for us in the paintings of the period. One of the first collectors in the modern sense was the Duc de Berry (1340-1416), who did not so much consider the curosity of objects as their artistic qualities. Archduke Ferdinand of the Tyrol (1520-1595) in his castle at Ambras collected treasures which were later scattered at the time of the French Revolution. In a description of the varied contents of his *grosse Kunstkammer* at Ambras,[19] not only is the Cellini salt-cellar listed there, but also a coconut mounted in silver, as well as lamps and inkwells made of shells, objects which we would not hesitate to call in bad taste. Musical and mathematical instruments, automata, mosaics of hummingbirds' wings, Mexican curios, feathers, objects of ivory and coral, curiosities like those boasted of by Frate Cipolla in Boccaccio's tale, such as "a length of the rope with which Judas hanged himself, carried off from the basilica of Saint Peter's by Sebastian Schertlin during the Sack of Rome" and a peg made from one of the cedars of Lebanon which were used in the construction of Solomon's temple, a male and a female mandrake elegantly set on a bed of blue taffeta, carved cherry-pits, collections of portraits of famous jurists and beautiful women, the latter painted on an assembly-line by the court painter Francesco Terzio. These and similar marvels were found in the treasure rooms of Ambras on whose walls and from whose ceilings were hung stuffed serpents, crocodiles, birds, elk horns, bones of prehistoric animals, and other oddities. Another famous collector was the Emperor Rudolph II, whose museum in Prague was a perfect mirror of the 16th century taste for the rare and the odd. Suffice it to say that he commissioned from Guiseppe Arcimboldo many of those composite paintings which have delighted the Surrealists of our own time. Among the objects he collected there was "a fine veil, which had fallen miraculously from the sky into the camp of His Majesty in Hungary." The collection of Rudolph II was broken up during the Thirty Years' War; a great part of it was the booty of the Swedes at Königsmark, and the barges went slowly down the Elbe bearing shipments of paintings to Queen Christina. After many peregrinations some of these objects returned to Austria, including a marvelous cupboard adorned with sculptures, medals, and marine plants, in whose drawers nothing was found, except—in a secret compartment—a blonde lock of woman's hair.

HÆC ARTIS ET NATVRÆ   MACHINAMENTA AD EXCITANDAM

103: The Collection of Ferdinando Cospi. Frontispiece of the *Museo Cospiano*, Bologna, 1677.

104: *The Collection of Coins and Gems of the Elector of Brandenburg.*
Frontispiece of the *Thesaurus Brandenburgius selectus*, 1696.

In Italy the universal curiosity of the German princes was lacking: there were few *Schatz-* and *Wunderkammern* in Italy. One may think of Rome's Museo Kircheriano, but Kircher was a German Jesuit. There was the collection of the Bolognese nobleman Ferdinando Cospi, which later became the Museo Comunale of Bologna, along with the collection of the Bolognese naturalist Ulisse Aldrovandi (that same Aldrovandi who considered the objects of Mexican feather work, collected in his famous museum, more beautiful than the works of Apelles). The Museo Cospiano, whose catalogue was printed in 1677, had rather an ethnographic character, and kept natural objects distinct from products of art, but the latter were considered from the point of view of technical curiosity, as transformations of natural

materials, or from the ethnographic antiquarian point of view. For example, Egyptian and Mexican idols illustrate mythology, Etruscan cists and Roman lamps document the furnishing of tombs. Nearer to the kind of museum created by the German princes was Manfredo Settala's in Milan, concerning which there also exists the publication *Museum Septalianum*, dated 1664. From Neickel's description of what constituted a museum at the end of the 17th century in his *Museographia* (1727), one realizes the small importance given here to pictures: paintings of famous masters were used only to fill the empty space over the doors and windows. But most certainly many important collections were formed at this time of which great paintings constituted a major part and the curious aspect of collecting we are discussing

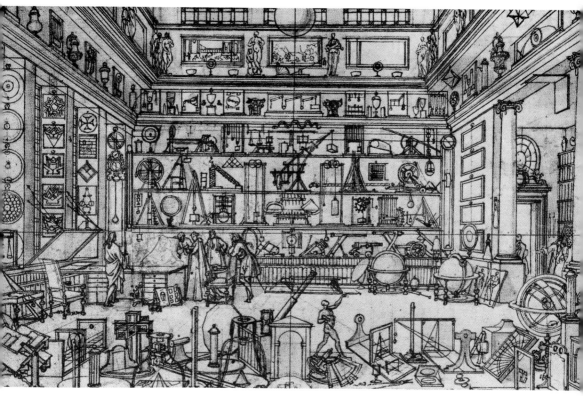

105: Sebastien Le Clerc. *Cabinet of Physics,* drawing.
BIBLIOTHÈQUE DE L'ÉCOLE DES BEAUX-ARTS, PARIS.

here was only incidental.[20]

The Collection of Coins and Gems of the Elector of Brandenburg is the subject of the frontispiece of the *Thesaurus Brandenburgius selectus* of 1696, a publication commented and illustrated by L. Beyer. The ample hall, furnished with cabinets and tables with many drawers containing the collections, has nothing of the fantastic aspect of the *Wunderkammern.* Still the statuary groups on the cabinets, the busts, the bas-reliefs, and the innumerable statuettes on the tables look, at a distance, like so many hens surrounded by chicks, and the table against the wall at the back, supported by sirens astride dolphins, is a *Prunktisch* similar to those of late Italian baroque tables such as those made by Andrea Brustolon (1662–1732) in Venice.

The following plate illustrates the *Cabinet of Physics* of Sebastien Le Clerc (1637–1714). A professor of drawing, Le Clerc left among his most significant works a *Traité de Géométrie,* a *Système sur la Vision,* and an album of medals and coins of France. This drawing shows him in his vast laboratory where there are accumulated, in a jumble typical of the museum of the period, models of machines, optical instruments, a flayed figure by the sculpture Antoine Coysevox and some antiquities. Crowded compositions were popular in the 17th and 18th centuries. Before Piranesi turned them into nightmares in his *Prisons,* many artists took pleasure in reproducing places unthinkably crammed with things: Jan Bruegel, for example, and later John Zoffany, as in his *Portrait of Charles Towneley* among his statues.[21]

106: Jan Bruegel the Elder. *Allegory of the Sense of Sight.* PRADO, MADRID.

Jan Bruegel's *Allegory of the Sense of Sight,* painted about 1618, gives a good idea of a museum as it was then conceived. Fabrizio Clerici[22] having recognized many paintings of Rubens among those depicted in this painting, believes that the composition was inspired by one of the rooms in Ruben's house in Antwerp of which we have already spoken. But

even if this were so, the painter has added a great deal f his own imagination, creating an apotheosis of still life we find in the Garden of Pleasure in Giovanni Battista Marino's *Adone* (Cantos VI-VIII),[23] and also adding that female figure whose meditative pose recalls Dürer's *Melancholia.* The cupid sets before her eyes an edifying

re, an episode from the Gospels, and the woman seems
 considering, with an afflicted expression, the chains,
ng, the medallions set on the table as if they were so
 vanities. Almost overwhelmed by the multitude of so
 sensual presences, the female figure seems to express
residue of melancholy that is found in the spirit of

all collectors. In fact, Bruegel's paintings were meant as a
diversion for melancholy princes, the most melancholy that
ever existed, those of Spain, to distract them with the display
of everything that was beautiful, appetizing, or elegant. The
vibrant opulence of Bruegel's encyclopedic rendering of the
world's riches served to stimulate their own languid appetites.

107: K. Werner. *A Room in the Palazzo Rospigliosi-Pallavicini*, painted in 1882. PRIVATE COLLECTION, ROME.

Of the great painting collections of the patrician Italian families, only a few have been preserved. Among them is the Pallavicini collection in Rome, whose vicissitudes and whose catalogue are the subject of a learned volume by Federico Zeri.[24] The Rospigliosi-Pallavicini families were divided at the mar-

riage of Giulio Cesare Rospigliosi-Pallavicini to Marg[...] Colonna: two lines stem from this couple's first-born Clemente Rospigliosi, and the second son, Francesco Pallavicini. Separated, the two branches met quite dif[...] fates: When the Rospigliosi branch, around 1920-193[...]

et by grave financial reverses, they were forced to sell
ir part of the palazzo on the Quirinal which had been
irs since 1704. The Galleria Rospigliosi, despite the efforts
he Pallavicini branch, who did everything to save it for
palazzo, was then broken up.

The watercolor painted by K. Werner in 1882 shows a room
of the Rospigliosi apartments in the Palazzo Rospigliosi-
Pallavicini. The room as seen here still retains its 18th century
aspect, the pictures hung with no concern for their visibility.
The harpsichord is 17th century.

108: William Hogarth. *The Breakfast,* from the series of the *Marriage à la Mode,* 1743. NATIONAL GALLERY, LONDON.

109: Charles Philips. *Algernon, Seventh Duke of Somerset, with his Family,* 1743.
DUKE OF NORTHUMBERLAND COLLECTION. (Copyright Country Life)

110: Elias Martin. *Eighteenth Century Swedish Interior.* NATIONAL MUSEUM, STOCKHOLM.

The moralizing tendency already perceptible in a Dutch painter like Jan Steen was carried to its extreme in England by William Hogarth (1697–1764) in the edifying cycles of paintings known all over the world from the engravings which were made after them. It is indeed from one of the "dissolute families" of Steen that Hogarth derived the *Breakfast* scene in the *Marriage à la mode* cycle, finished in 1743 (the engravings date from 1745).[25] Even the Hogarthian way of underlining the moral of the painting with an object or a symbolical animal has its antecedents in Steen. The fantastic clock in the living room in the breakfast scene is a hybrid jumble: a porcelain cat on an *ormolu* clock, surrounded by foliage among which fish are swimming, and below, a figure like a Buddha, from whose navel snakelike arms emerge, holding candles. This clock, almost a surrealistic symbol of the ill-matched marriage, must not be considered an object that really existed, as did the chinoiserie on the mantelpiece and the typical early 18th century English chairs, the form of which bears the name of

Queen Anne and of Hogarth himself. This room has the richness of an aristocratic manor.

About ten years earlier, the family group by Charles Philips (*Algernon, Seventh Duke of Somerset, with his Family,* 1743) shows a solemn, classic English interior, with architectonic panels which recall the wood decorations of Grinling Gibbons (1648–1720) with their rich festoons. The gilt console at the right is in the late Baroque style of continental derivation in which the architect William Kent designed the state furniture of the palaces of the nobility.

The *Eighteenth Century Swedish Interior* painted by Elias Martin (1739–1818) shows the influence of the Hogarthian satirical vein, and this even in the decoration: the horned bust in the niche. It is a spacious hall, where an agitated *lever* is taking place. It is similar to scenes in the Hogarth cycles, for example, *The Rake's Progress.* In the center of the picture, the hairdresser surrounded by the cloud of powder which he is pouring onto the wig, seems as evanescent as a ghost.

The portrait of *Count Vries and his Family* by Johann Valentin Tischbein (1715-1769), painted around 1750 reflects in the room and in the figures a rather empty formalism. The room, decorated with elegant panels, is quite naked as far as ornaments are concerned, except for the painting set on the table in the corner at the left, which seems to commemorate the premature loss of a little son. Along the dado of the bare walls chairs are lined up in a stiff row. We glimpse a row of other rooms which one imagines equally sparsely furnished. Around the table, on which the coffee is served, four prim figures, father, mother, and two young girls, the younger one particularly haughty, carrying without any enthusiasm a basket of flowers. A certain distance seems to exist among the people, and in the same way, the room also lacks any warmth. This chilly air, of rooms that have only just been assigned to the people who are to live in them, is found again throughout the first period of German Neoclassicism.

Barely more animated are the English conversation pieces where, if the adults have the stylized hauteur of fish in brilliant livery, the little ones of the family, arrested by the painter in playful or lighthearted movements, suggest the image of darting minnows among the motionless, intent, mature fish. And these aquariums are lighted by that 18th century sun, which seemed never fated to set: the sun of the enlightenment, of the age of reason. But at least one of those painters of conversation pieces, a foreigner in England, John Zoffany (1733-1810), was able to transfer on to canvas the warmth of that sun, making it almost audible—Apollo's golden lyre—like a symphony by his contemporary Franz Joseph Haydn (1732-1809). Thanks to Zoffany, that sun has been fixed in his canvases. It is as if a game of robots, when the mechanism had run down, had been caught forever in essential gestures, as the music which marked its rhythm continued to hum in our ears.

Zoffany's portrait of *Sir Lawrence Dundas and his Grandson* represents an interior of the house of Sir Lawrence at 19 Arlington Street, London. The paintings such as the marine by van der Capelle over the mantelpiece document the taste for works of the Dutch School, while the bronzes on the mantelpiece show the interest in classical antiquity. The 18th century is the period in which the great English private collections were formed. English agents and dealers in Italy, among whom Thomas Jenkins was a leader, sent to England the prized pieces from the noble Italian collections then being sold. This room radiates the refined collector's taste, and yet it is not without its domestic intimacy: the little child affectionately clasps his grandfather's arm, as the older man interrupts his correspondence to indulge in family affections. The atmosphere is quite different from the rigid formalism in the Tischbein

111: Johann Valentin Tischbein. *Count Vries and his Family.* KUNSTMUSEUM, DÜSSELDORF.

family group. Zoffany's picture can be dated around 1770 (the child was born in 1766).

A little earlier is the painting which shows Queen Charlotte in her boudoir at Buckingham Palace with George Augustus, Prince of Wales (born in 1762, later Prince Regent and George IV) in the costume of a Roman warrior, and Frederick, Duke of York and Albany (born 1763) in Oriental costume (unless this is the Princess Royal, born in 1766). The bright colors of the painting: the red of the Oriental rug, the green of the hangings, the white of the Queen's dress and the lace of the dressing-table with touches of pink, give the scene a festive air, which is enhanced by the exotic note of the children's costumes and the Chinese statuettes around the mirror behind the Queen. Thanks to a charming device the Queen's profile is framed in the small mirror of the dressing-table. The room reflects the refined taste of George III's consort, who liked to surround herself with works of art and every kind of curiosity. As Mrs. Philip Lybbe Powys recalled in her diary, under the date of March 23rd, 1767: "The Queen's apartments are ornamented . . . with curiosities from every nation that can deserve her notice. The most capital pictures, the finest Dresden and other china; cabinets of more minute curiosities. . . The floors are all inlaid in a most expensive manner, and tho' but in March, every room was full of roses, carnations, hyacinths, &c. dispersed in the prettiest manner imaginable in jars and different flower pots on stands. On her toilet . . . the gilt plate. . . ." The gilt furniture in the picture dates from about 1750.[26]

112: John Zoffany. *Sir Lawrence Dundas with his Grandson,* c. 1770.
THE MARQUESS OF ZETLAND COLLECTION, RICHMOND, YORKSHIRE.

113: John Zoffany. *Queen Charlotte with her Two Older Children,* c. 1768.
WINDSOR CASTLE. (Reproduced by the gracious permission of H. M. the Queen)

114: The Gallery of Strawberry Hill. Engraving by J. C. Stadler, c. 1760.

The revival of the taste for the Gothic is most often attributed to the "dilettante" Horace Walpole (1717–1797) in the decoration of his house at Strawberry Hill (to the west of London, on the Thames) in 1747 and the years following. But his was not the first revival of an archeological nature in English decoration. Already at the beginning of the 17th century, John Smythson had drawn on Gothic inspiration in the reconstruction of Bolsover Castle in Derbyshire, and other precursors of the Gothic revival were the architects John Vanbrugh and William Kent.[27] The Gothic of Strawberry Hill was not, after all, very different from that amateurish Gothic ornamentation ("carpenter's Gothic") which was being diffused in England; to our modern eyes it betrays the period in which it was brought into fashion, the Rococo age. The fan tracery of the ceiling and the pendants in the gallery Strawberry Hill, though they imitate those of the famous chapels at Westminster Abbey and King's College, Cambric seem a tasteful variation on Rococo style, an example of tha hybridization which then was prevalent. In fact, the Chines style was also grafted on to the Gothic, and in 1754, a contributor to *The World* observed: "It has not escaped your notice how much of late we are improved in architectu not merely by the adoption of what we call Chinese, not by the restoration of what we call Gothic, but by a happy

115: Arthur Davis. *Sir Roger Newdigate in his Library.* F.H.M. FITZROY NEWDIGATE COLLECTION.

ixture of both." In the preface to his *Description of Strawberry Hill,* Walpole observed that his house was a very proper habitation for the author of the *Castle of Otranto:* that novel, which was to begin the series of tales of terror, whose taste for complicated plots and cruel, macabre episodes, persecuted maidens, horrible dungeons, grim bandits, etc., has a curious affinity with the works of the Marquis de Sade. As to the sources of Walpole's Gothic, he did what was also done at the end of the 18th and the beginning of the 19th century by the designers of Empire furniture: not finding in the past the models for all the objects required for modern use, they adapted ancient forms to functions different from

their original ones. For the French cabinet-makers, the moulding of an antique stele could become the cornice of a bookcase or the back of a chair. So Walpole copied the tomb of Archbishop Warham at Canterbury for a fireplace in his Great Parlour at Strawberry Hill.

Almost at the same time Sir Roger Newdegate (1719 1806), collector of ancient sculpture and founder of the Oxford poetry prize bearing his name, had his library done over in Gothic style. The painting by Arthur Davis (1708 1787) shows us the nobleman sitting on a Chippendale chair in a room which need not envy Strawberry Hill.

116: The Study of the Duc de Choiseul, 1757. Miniature by Blarenberghe, painted on a snuffbox by A. Leferre. LOUVRE, PARIS. (Photo Bulloz)

The *Study of the Duc de Choiseul,* reproduced in two miniatures by Blarenberghe painted on a snuffbox by A. Leferre, illustrates what we said in the Introduction about the changes of taste in proportions and furnishing of apartments which began in the 18th century in the France of Louis XV. Instead of the impressive suite of grandiose rooms, smaller, more intimate rooms were now preferred, with furnishing highly specialized for various uses. Varied also were the rare woods employed in the inlay work. It has often been observed that these innovations have an exquisitely feminine touch, and that this style is well named Louis XV, that king of whom it was said "jolie figure de fille, insensible et glacée." Conqueror of women, not of empires, Louis XV has given his name to a kind of furnishing that has always enjoyed the favor of refined collectors and the newly rich. His arch of triumph was the canopy of a bed, his nickname was "le Bien-Aimé." But he is not to be smiled at: his reign witnessed many inventions in tasteful furniture; his was indeed an age which attended to the comforts of a life of pleasure, but what are the sums squandered by that king on his luxuries, compared to the unspeakably huge amounts we spend on murderous experiments?

It was during this period that the distribution of apartments was set in an arrangement which lasts today: bedroom, living room (one no longer received in the bedroom), antechamber, little rooms like the boudoir and the study *(cabinet de travail).* Around 1750 the dining room appeared, with appropriate furniture. In almost every apartment a dressing room was found, and in some cases a bathroom. The rooms were smaller than in the past, better heated, more sensibly arranged. Paneled with wood, they were decorated with lively paintings over the doors, with furniture that was often fused with the decoration of the room (like the *trumeau,* and the *console),* and some armchairs with fixed places along the wall *(fauteuils meublants)* and other movable chairs *(fauteuils cabriolets* or *courants)* used to form a more intimate circle. These suites assume an air that we might call coquettish today. Rigid lines, sharp corners were avoided, on every side there was a

117: The Study of the Duc de Choiseul, 1757. Miniature by Blarenberghe, painted
on a snuffbox by A. Leferre. LOUVRE, PARIS. (Photo Bulloz)

smiling curve: the eye followed the outline of a piece
of furniture as if it were the sinuous line of a woman's
body. The armchair embraced the form of the person
who sat in it, and allowed ladies' dresses to be
comfortably arranged. Thus in decorations, furniture,
dress and manners, a harmony reigned such as was
probably never seen before (except perhaps in the
Italian Renaissance, though in that case the accent was
not chiefly on interior decoration); and France
deservedly became the arbiter of taste for the whole
Western World. Refinement went so far as to devise
forms of sofas suited to every kind of repose, to
make distinctions between winter and summer
furniture. And as furniture thus acquired a greater
personality, the artists who depicted it in their
paintings and prints treated pieces of furniture like
people, no longer summarily as mere accessories.
And thus the figurative documentation of rooms
becomes more abundant and precise.[28]

The miniatures of the *Study of the Duc de Choiseul*
date from 1757. In 1772 the Duke, fallen upon evil
times, was forced to sell most of his collection

of paintings in a sale that has remained famous.[29]
Here in the study we find the bed which, as we have
observed, at this time was usually set in a room to
itself, but it should be said that the two miniatures
actually represent two different rooms which were
probably communicating. The fireplace has assumed
far smaller proportions. The mirror is surmounted
by the profile of Louis XV in *silhouette*. It was in fact
in the 18th century that the fashion for these shadow-
profiles became widespread, taking its name from
Etienne de Silhouette, Louis XV's minister of finance,
who cultivated this hobby on his retirement from
public life.[30] The pictures on the walls are reproduced
with such precision that it is possible to identify
nearly all of them: paintings of Greuze, Fragonard,
Teniers, Potter, Terborch, etc. The statuette on the
bookcase is of a Greek priestess burning perfumes in
a tripod. The antique tripod inspired a piece of
furniture, popular in the last quarter of the 18th
century, known as an *athénienne,* which served such
various uses as brazier for perfumes, flowerstand,
dishwarmer, washstand etc.[31]

This painting of a *Room in the Prinz-Max-Palais in Dresden*, painted in 1776, is a rare 18th century example of an interior painted for its own sake, without people: it is one of the first, if not the first, of a genre which was to have an enormous success in the course of the 19th century. It is a bed–and work-room, with a little domestic altar to the left of the bed, and an arrangement of pictures on the walls and in the embrasures of the windows, a decorative notion which was to become very common in the Biedermeier period. The room is hung with green material; green also are the bed's cover and canopy

and the upholstery of the chairs, the table at the
right, the screen and the firescreen, so that the
impression of the room—with the green accentuated
by the brown floor and wood of the furniture, and
the gold and white of the doors and window
embrasures—is restful, almost sylvan.

118: Anonymous. *Room in the Prinz-Max-Palais in Dresden,*
1776. Formerly HABERSTOCK COLLECTION, BERLIN.

119: Bernard Lépicié. *Children's Game.* Engraving after a painting by Charles Coypel.

Michelet wrote that the Louis XV style was a return to a feeling
of life and humanity. In the vivacious genre painting of the epoch,
rooms were enlivened with figures, as if incarnating in these figures
the spirits of gay and serene décors. And never was this more
faithfully achieved than in this engraving of a *Children's Game*
by Bernard Lépicié (1698–1755) after a painting by Charles Coypel
(1694–1752). It suggests that passage from Pope's *The Rape of
the Lock* in which the sylphs are described in their various duties
of guarding and taking care of all the things which a lovely lady
makes use of during a day:

120: François Boucher. *The Breakfast.* LOUVRE, PARIS.

"Haste then, ye spirits! to your charge repair:
The flutt'ring fan be Zephyretta's care;
The drops to thee, Brillante, we consign;
And, Momentilla, let the watch be thine;
Do thou, Crispissa, tend her fav'rite Lock;
Ariel himself shall be the guard of Shock.
To fifty chosen Sylphs, of special note,
We trust th' important charge, the Petticoat;
Oft have we known that seven-fold fence to fail,
Tho' stiff with hoops, and arm'd with ribs of whale;

Form a strong line about the silver bound,
And guard the wide circumference around.
Whatever spirit, careless of his charge,
His post neglects, or leaves the fair at large,
Shall feel sharp vengeance soon o'ertake his sins,
Be stopp'd in vials, or transfix'd with pins...
He spoke the spirits from the sails descend;
Some, orb in orb, around the nymph extend;
Some thrid the many ringlets of her hair;
Some hang upon the pendants of her ear..."

121: Jean-Michel Moreau le Jeune. *The Elegant Supper*, engraving.

22: Daniel Chodowiecki. *Family Scene.* KAISER-FRIEDRICH MUSEUM, Berlin.

The gay and slightly lascivious masquerade of Coypel in which the plump children play with the skirt (similar to the one described by Pope), the dressing gown, the rouge and the box of beauty-spots in the bedroom of the absent beauty breathes the same air of fantastic and gallant parody that animates Pope's poem.

Not long thereafter, the publication of the *Antichità di Ercolano* was to make widely known those paintings brought to light in which cupids drive coaches drawn by swans, dolphins or griffins, or in which winged genii dance, make music, play childish games, or apply themselves to various arts, or carry symbols and instruments, discs, thyrsi, baskets or basins. Groups very similar to these had been created by the illustrators of emblem books of the 17th century, above all by the Dutch ones like Heinsius, Vaenius, Hooft, Crispin de Passe. The nest of Cupids, the sale of Cupids, Cupid in a cage, were Hellenistic motifs which Europe had already known through other sources and had exploited since the Humanists. Now it rediscovered them with delighted surprise in the lively paintings of Herculaneum. The discovery gave new nourishment to a fashion which already had deep roots, and the little Cupids and winged genii were later to play a predominating role in Neoclassical decoration.

Alongside this mannered mythology the faithful rendering of daily life in its bourgeois or even lower-class aspects continued to prosper, inspired by a human curiosity with a vein of tenderness and humor which, in the case of Chardin, meant something more than just giving artistic expression to the "Third Estate." With Chardin realistic observation was sublimated into poetry. The sense of an intimate, warm corner of the house is rendered with delicate sensitivity by François Boucher (1703–1770) in his *Breakfast* (*Fig.* 120): the sun which floods the room from the window brings out the pale green lacquer of the mirror's frame and makes the mother's red tippet glow, as she turns to the little girl laden with toys. The room is still aristocratic, but the sentiment is bourgeois. In *the Elegant Supper* by Jean-Michel Moreau le Jeune (1741–1814), the most famous vignettist of the French 18th century, two couples of lovers are dallying at a supper table. Here too we have the impression of a secluded corner, only a step from the bed. Furnishing and dress are of the 1770's, while the epergne on the table already anticipates Empire style. In the *Family Scene* by Daniel Chodowiecki (1726–1801), the furnishings are of slightly different epochs: the chair at left dates from the first half of the 18th century and so does the clock surmounted by Saturn with his scythe on the table at the right, whereas the stove has a curving Rococo line. A sentimental note is insinuated into this realistic representation. Born of a Polish father and a French mother, Chodowiecki, who lived in Berlin, reflects the double influence of Hogarth and Greuze. The scene reproduced here seems to belong to the same type as the 19th century Russian genre painting (Fedotov).

123: Hubert Robert. *The Breakfast of Madame Jeoffrin.*
VEIL PICART COLLECTION. (Photo Bulloz)

The taste for classical antiquity (strongly influenced by publication of the Herculaneum excavations), combined with the influence of English taste (Anglomania was a common phenomenon on the Continent in the 18th century), to first temper and then eliminate the domination of the Rococo curved line. Gilding was minimized and these influences led, in short, to that elegant sobriety so typical of Louis XVI style. The unbridled fantasy of Rococo ornaments, impregnated with exoticism (including the enchanting chinoiserie),[32] was replaced by the somewhat monotonous symmetry of decorative garlands and geometric patterns. Cupids in delicate sculpture or *grisailles* over doorways, allegorical statues and their symbolic attributes; fluting in pilasters and in table legs once again became rigid. Classically derived architectonic inspiration again was dominant. Furniture was no longer fused with wall decoration but regained an independence that soon led to virtual isolation. Visual allusions to the arts (exemplified by the lyre appearing in the back of a chair) and to pastoral life (motifs such as rakes, bagpipes) give this mild Neoclassicism an aura perfectly attuned to the romance of Daphnis and Chloe.

All of these elements are well illustrated in two etchings by François Dequevauviller (1745-1807), *The Conversation in the Drawing Room (L'Assemblée au Salon)* and *The Musicale (L'Assemblée au concert)*. These etchings were made from paintings by Nicolas Lavreince (1737-1807), a Swede who spent some twenty years, at various intervals, in France. The etching of *Conversation in the Drawing Room* was especially praised in the journals of the time for its ability to "depict very well just what takes place in the best homes." The scene is believed to represent the salon of the Duc de Luynes et de Chevreuse, to whom it is dedicated. The theme had been handled twenty years earlier by Antoine-Jean Duclos in prints derived from paintings of Augustin de Saint-Aubin which depicted similar entertainments towards the end of Louis XV's reign. The contrast between the prints of Dequevauviller and Duclos is not so much in the rooms depicted as in the technique of the two artists: the older one's is soft and light, whereas the more modern one is precise to the point of dryness. This was in conformity with the trend of taste reflected in both the major and minor arts.

In *The Breakfast of Madame Jeoffrin* by Hubert Robert (1733-1808), the painter gives us an intimate view of one of those ladies who shone in contemporary salons, for Madame Jeoffrin's salon was frequented by distinguished artists and men of letters. Unlike Thackeray who, in his *Meditations at Versailles* of the

124: François Dequevauviller. *Conversation in the Drawing Room*, 1784. Etching after N. Lavreince.

125: François Dequevauviller. *The Musicale*, 1784. Etching after N. Lavreince.

following century, represented the Sun-King in cruel *déshabillé*. Robert's intention was not mercilessly satirical. Instead it was inspired more by genuine admiration for the simple and the everyday, a taste which was widespread in that aristocratic society whose doom was already sealed.

This love for simple bourgeois, or even humbler rooms also inspired the delightful little picture by Antoine Ruspal (1738–1811), *The Dressmaker's Shop in Arles*. Clearly, the enchanted realism here cannot possibly stem from the tradition of Velasquez (what a contrast to *The Spinning Women!*) or of Le Nain.

126: Antoine Ruspal.
The Dressmaker's Shop in Arles,
late 18th century.
MUSÉE REATTU, ARLES.

127: Maurice Blot. *The Contract,* 1792. Etching after J.-B. Honoré Fragonard.

The same sentiment also inspired a quantity of paintings and prints like *The Unforeseen Accident (L'Accident imprévu)* by Louis Darcis (date of birth unknown). Here the scene is a simply furnished garret, the walls covered with common paper of alternating dark and light stripes. One must not imagine that the bust on the armoire is one of the usual classical decorations, for it is really a milliner's mannikin which here seems to parody that kind of ornament in the rooms of the rich. The milliner has dropped her work to read the letter, no doubt an amorous note, brought by a little messenger-boy; the iron emits a cloud of smoke which is not that of an incense-brazier before an altar of Venus.

Such amorous subjects were then very fashionable. *The Contract,* an etching by Maurice Blot (b. 1750)

after a painting by Honoré Fragonard (1732–1806), is worthy of attention particularly because of the increasing importance of interior accessories in the painter's eyes. Eventually, these were given the same visual authority as the figure. Thus, both the divan and the writing desk in the foreground are extremely elegant, in contrast to the chest of drawers in the background and the humble pewter ewer and basin.

The writing desk especially is imposing, with its classically inspired *ormolu* decorations: the Pompeiian motif of *putti* playing with a she-goat; and the draped caryatids at the corners. This desk is certainly a signed piece, perhaps by Riesener who specialized in making mahogany furniture (particularly writing desks, commodes, and elbow-high pieces), soberly decorated with magnificent bronzes.

128: Louis Darcis. *The Unforeseen Accident*, 1801. Mezzotint after a painting by Nicolas Lavreince.

129: Marguérite Gérard. *Reading the Letter.* Present whereabouts unknown.

There is little variety in the background interiors illustrated by genre painting of the *petits maîtres* who abounded in France at the end of the 18th century. Consider, for example, the elegant little paintings of Louis-Leopold Boilly (1761–1845), in which walls are divided by rectilinear frames against which some shadowed painting or piece of furniture can be glimpsed. The foreground is usually marked off by a screen or a hanging and frequently includes a table, a toilette with a still life of objects, and a chair covered with disordered clothing. People and objects are all reproduced with the same meticulous care. These observations also apply to the genre paintings of Marguérite Gérard (1762–1830), Fragonard's pupil and sister-in-law. (She is known to have collaborated with both Fragonard and Boilly.) In the picture *Reading the Letter,* Mlle. Gérard renders the furniture with such precision that we are able to recognize pieces that still exist. Thus the Jacob chair, with arms supported by sphinxes, is very similar to a chair found today in a French collection, except that the latter has a palm-leaf decoration instead of the typical Louis XVI triglyphs around the fascia of the seat.[33] The chair probably dates from the 18th century,

130: J. B. Mallet. *The Petit-point Cupid.* MUSÉE COGNACQ-JAY, PARIS.

for indeed the works of George Jacob (1739–1814) foreshadowed Empire furniture by a number of years and it was he who executed the "antique" furniture designed by David. In *Reading the Letter,* the room is still late 18th century, although the dress of the two women is early 19th century.[34]

Similar rooms are found in the works of J. B. Mallet (1759–1835). *An Animated Salon (L'Assemblée au complet),* for example, is decorated with grotesques of the kind made popular by Reveillon which adorn the wall panels (*Fig.* 132). In the *Petit-point Cupid,* we see on the fireplace documentation of the fashion for

chinoiserie and in the embroidery itself, being shown to the seated lady, we see the new fashion for Pompeiian cupids.

The interior shown by Georg Karl Urlaub (1749–1809) in *Checking the Accounts* (*Fig.* 131) illustrates that taste for modest interiors and humble domestic tasks which, with quite another accent, Chardin had also depicted. The theme of Urlaub's painting had already been introduced in an engraving for the *Genealogischer Kalendar auf das Jahr 1781,* made by Chodowiecki, who was indeed responsible for introducing scenes of everyday Berlin life into German art.

132: J. B. Mallet. *An Animated Salon,* c. 1790. VEIL PICART COLLECTION.

31: G. K. Urlaub. *Checking the Accounts,* 1798
TÄDELSCHES KUNSTINSTITUT, FRANKFURT.

133: Anonymous. *Late Eighteenth Century Interior.* GIORGIO ALBERTAZZI COLLECTION, ROME.

The Neoclassical room which we see in the *Late 18th Century Interior* by an unknown painter can be considered typical of the period. The carved and gilded console is supported by rigid, inverted-obelisk legs, between which carved and gilded festoons are draped. The rigid valances over the windows are surmounted by vases from which more festoons fall, and a Greek key pattern decorates the wall under the mirror. Only in the corners of the room, just under the ceiling, and in the panel above the mirror are we still able to see surviving Rococo motifs. This interior is a background to a·theatrical scene and it is probably an imaginary interior, a generalization of the taste of the period. In contrast, there is nothing imaginary about the room in the *Portrait of Marchesa Gentili-Boccapadule*, by Lorenzo Pécheux (1729–1821), first painter of the King of Sardinia and Director of the School of the Nude from 1777 to his death. The Marchesa is painted in her private museum of natural history as, with one hand, she raises the curtain to display her magnificent collection of butterflies and holds a twig in her other hand. The handsome console is supported by two Egyptian telamones while its top is made of various samples of semi-precious stones and the fascia is decorated with Egyptian hieroglyphics. This piece already utilizes forms which later became current in the Empire style. This can also be said of the stool supported by winged griffons on which an instrument for electrical experiments is placed, next to some small shells. More shells, corals, madrepores, fossils, Etruscan black ware and a stuffed bird adorn the various shelves of the *étagère* whose base is formed by monopode goats joined by festoons. In an elaborate basin, there are some fish, probably preserved in alcohol. A classical statue standing in the rear niche, a model of a hairy barbarian in the side niche, and a laurel-crowned bust on a low pedestal give the room the archeological air then in fashion.

134: Lorenzo Pécheux. *Portrait of Marchesa Gentili-Boccapadule*, 1776. PRIVATE COLLECTION, TURIN

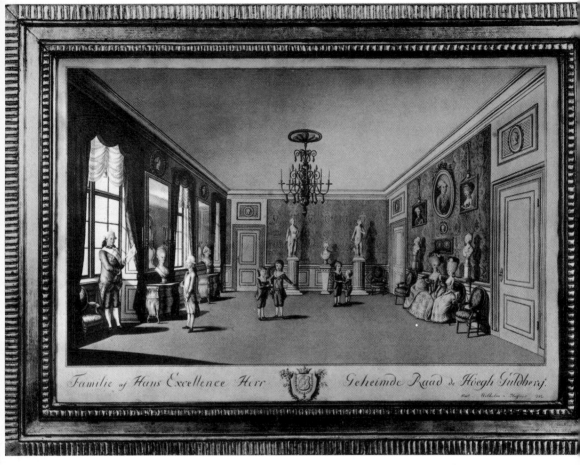

135: Wilhelm Haffner. *Family of the Prime Minister Hoegh Guldberg,* engraving, 1782.
DANSK FOLKEMUSEUM, COPENHAGEN.

Classical statues and busts as well as medallions, coins and gems were virtually a mania of the age. We find them all around the ground floor drawing room where the *Family of Prime Minister Hoegh Guldberg* is portrayed by Wilhelm Haffner.[35] The furniture—the commodes and chairs and sofa—is still Rococo, but each chair is placed with strict symmetry, as are the busts, the statues, and even the paintings on the wall. The pedestals of the statues, formed by short Ionic columns, are rigid, and this room has the empty, somewhat icy and museum-like atmosphere which is so very characteristic of early Neoclassical interiors.

136: J. F. Martin. *Family of Gustavus III,* drypoint, c. 1785, after a drawing by Cornelius Hoget.
ROYAL COLLECTIONS, ROSENBORG CASTLE, COPENHAGEN.

Similar truncated Ionic columns supporting two classical statues are found in the room of the *Family of Gustavus III* by J. F. Martin (1755–1816). Gustavus III and Queen Sofia Madeleine seem to be giving the little Crown Prince Gustavus Adolphus a geography lesson. The other couples are Duke Frederick Adolphus with Sofia Albertina and Duke Charles with Edvige Eliszbetta Carlotta. The two tables are characteristic of English furniture of the period. The principal activity, centering as it does about the globe, witnesses the scientific interest and archeological taste of the age. Here too there is a rigidity and sparsness of décor.

137: Anonymous. *Interior of the Antiquary's Shop, Naples,* 1798. M. GOFFI COLLECTION, ROME.

"The owner of the hat painted Naples 1798," is the bizarre signature in the left-hand corner of the strange *Interior of the Antiquary's Shop.* In the tradition of Pier Leone Ghezzi (1674–1755) and of the *Parody of the School of Athens* by Reynolds (1720–1792) the people are portrayed with a spirit close to caricature. The central figure is evidently a foreigner of the kind who were always searching for antiquities.[36] The shelves are lined with Greek vases as well as with some paintings, mostly common tempera views of

Naples and Pompeii which foreigners then bought in much the same way as they buy postal cards today.

In its furnishing and dedication to scientific ideals, the curious pen drawing signed Crussaïre is still 18th century. Views of Rome hang above the fireplace (easily recognized is the basilica and square of Saint Peter's) and below one window. The plan of a villa and a garden near a river (also probably related to a Roman locale) is held to the floor by two weights and various kinds of terrain and cultivation, each with its identi-

138: Crussaïre. *The Genius of Science and Invention,* pen drawing, 1814. PRIVATE COLLECTION, ROME.

fication, flank the fireplace. Above is the legend:
Etude du Genie des Sciences et des Arts d'Invention,
all of which establish the interests of the owner, who
concentrates on an open book and another plan
unrolled before him. Painted in the vault of the room,
over the inscription, is an emblem flanked with wings,
surmounted by a little flame and set against a starry
sky. All these objects and decorations seem to emanate
mysterious allusive spells, in an atmosphere reminiscent of the *Magic Flute.*

The little picture, *The Chess Club of Hereford,* by
T. Leeming (a London miniaturist who from 1811 to
1822 showed at the Royal Academy), also documents
the tastes of the period. Classical motifs appear in the
large amphoras in background niches and the Oriental
taste is displayed in two vases on the mantelpiece.
The furniture is still 18th century in style but the dress
is early 19th century. Above the fireplace is a view
of Hereford Cathedral and to the right is a Saint
Sebastian of the Venetian school. (See next page.)

139: T. Leeming. *The Chess Club of
Hereford*, early 19th century.
IAN GREENLEES COLLECTION, FLORENCE.

Coupe du SALON, fur les Croifés ét leur vis-a-vis.

140: Attributed to Couvet. *Project for a Room,* watercolor, c. 1780. O. LEFUEL COLLECTION, PARIS.

The evolution of taste from a Neoclassicism still rich in Baroque elements to a more literal archeological or "pedantic" Neoclassicism, is seen by studying late 18th century projects for the decoration of interiors. The criterion of symmetry applied during the Renaissance and Baroque periods was generally limited to the exterior, while interiors followed no strict rules as to furnishing, since the practical considerations of the preceding centuries still prevailed. But with Neoclassicism, symmetry permeated the interior to such an extent that the merely useful piece of furniture (like the clothes wardrobe, which completely disappeared) was whenever possible concealed, to be replaced by the less useful but more architectonically beautiful piece, such as the console. Carpet design and color became counterparts of the architectonic lines and colors of a room, thus banishing Oriental rugs which

could not reflect the style of the whole. In short, with Neoclassicism the basis of a proper syntax of interior decoration was established and solecisms were no longer tolerated.[37] In the *Project for a Room* attributed to Couvet there is still an echo of Caracci's bland classicism. (In the Galleria of the Palazzo Farnese Caracci designed sphinxes with high baskets on their heads, while here the sphinxes recur in the lunettes and the tall basket is seen on the head of the central torch-bearer.) A medallion showing a female faun playing with her little one is set between the two Ionic columns, whose bases are decorated with similar bas-reliefs. These motifs, like other decorations such as the fountain to the left (which balances the fireplace on the right), are freely drawn from the antiquities at Herculaneum but are also handled in the spirit of that style known as Louis XVI, typified by the garlands

141: Project for the Decoration of a Room, late 18th century.
(From the *Magazzino di Mobili,* no. 2, Florence, March 1797, Plate IX.)

falling from large masks over the lunettes.

In the *Project for the Decoration of a Room,* taken from the *Magazzino di mobili,* decorations inspired by the antiquities at Herculaneum are inserted into an architectonic scheme which is orthodox according to the ancient canons. It is only in the *grisaille* over the central panel that we note a certain freedom of interpretation still 18th century in manner. The accompanying text read: "The Plate represents a decoration, to be carried out in painting, suitable for a *Sala,* a room ordinarily used for balls and for conversation and for dining. We have therefore chosen an appropriate kind of ornamentation. In it we have been careful to avoid what we consider the frequent defects resulting from work based only on rule of thumb rather than good theories or reflections prompted by artists of genius who have formulated

and practiced the best rules of this kind. In this design, it has been our first concern to observe a primary law, that of achieving unity and uniformity of the whole. Apart from the merits of harmony and agreement of colors, this must be the principal aim of all compositions, including those of painting and relief. An intercolonium of composite pilasters supports a simple architrave which serves as a base for the ceiling. In the inter-columnar spaces closest to the room's corners are two well-proportioned arches set apart by a simple fascia which encircles the room, thus simultaneously unifying it and dividing its height into two parts. Beneath these arches are doors which terminate in a simple cornice. All background ornamentations are analogous to the uses of a *Sala,* and they can be varied according to the use for which the room is destined."[38]

142: Percier and Fontaine. *Project for a Bedchamber,* watercolor, early 18th century. O. LEFUEL COLLECTION, PARIS.

"One tries in vain to find forms better than those we have inherited from Antiquity," we read in the preface to the famous *Recueil de décorations intérieures* by Charles Percier (1764–1838) and Pierre-Leonard Fontaine (1762–1853). This book, published in 1812 (though plates had begun to appear in installments in 1801) was the Bible of the Empire style. Percier and Fontaine began with Pompeiian decorations (they called them "Etruscan") and they adopted a range of colors suggestive of the delicate shades of Wedgewood china, then very popular.[39] The rather austere *Project for a Bedchamber,* above, is a Pompeiian interior, adorned with a few bronzes (the wealth of bronzes comes in a later period) and furnished only with a bed and a mahogany commode of ancient inspiration.

The effect is that of an archeological reconstruction, for the only imaginative detail is the canopy of the bed, suggesting cage of fluttering birds—but prototypes for this, too, are fo in Pompeiian frescoes.[40] In the second Project reproduced here, the sense of pure archeological reconstruction is alleviated in several ways: wall paintings are reduced to a runn frieze above the upper walls, which are draped with fabric. The drapery lends a softness that is new, as if a lovely *chlan* had been arranged on an ancient marble statue. Furniture i more abundant and more varied and the monopode-sphinx flowerstands, though inspired by the celebrated Pompeiian tripod, no longer seem directly imitative. Furthermore, the back wall of the bed is formed by a mirror. In its general

143: Percier and Fontaine. *Project for a Bedchamber,* watercolor, 1799-1804. O. LEFUEL COLLECTION, PARIS.

144: *Elevation Studies for the Bedchamber of Madame G.,* watercolor, c. 1800. O. LEFUEL COLLECTION, PARIS.

appearance, this room is similar to one decorated for Madame Recamier. The third Project, illustrated by three elevations, was later reproduced with variants, as Plate 37 of the *Recueil.* "The trompe-l'oeil wall hangings suspended from a simulated cornice" are delicate grotesques in the style of Reveillon.[41]

The antiquity of the Consolate style had its own Alexandrine delicacy but, as Philippe Jullian has shrewdly written (in a text which despite its parodying tone contains some truths): "Quickly the Imperial and virile style transformed into bronze the cupids which had been painted on wooden panels, graces became victories, delicate rosettes became shields. The Directoire came from Egypt, making a stop at Lesbos, the Egyptian taste having come from Piranesi, who was the Magic Flute. Egypt is the China of Neoclassicism."[42]

A translation of the *Recueil* appeared in Italy at the late date of 1843,[43] proving that the Empire style, despite changes in fashion, still had a following. In fact, Italian cabinet-makers continued to make furniture either in Empire style or, at least, using Empire motifs—especially for the decoration of state rooms. This practice was widespread and occurred in Germany, for example, with the designs of Klenze and Schinkel around 1830. Empire became the official style of courts from Russia to Brazil, just as Baroque had so identified itself with the church in Piedmont that Baroque churches continued to be built in that region as late as the end of the 18th century.[44]

145: Percier and Fontaine. *Bedchamber Designed for Monsieur G., Paris.* (From the French serial reproductions of 1801.)

The *Bedchamber Designed for Monsieur G., Paris,* is thus described in the Italian edition of *Recueil:* "The decoration of this room, one of the least rich in the present collection, is distinguished by the adaptation of its fireplace, formed by paired pilasters on either side, which support an arch over it. The spaces between each pair of narrow pilasters have been arranged to serve as bookshelves. The rest of the wall space is draped with flowing fabric over which valuable paintings are hung. Painted on the rear wall, there

behind the bed, and bounded by a circle of stars, is a representation of a chariot bearing Diana with outspread wings, covering the earth with her veil." Since in this period symbolic decorations were chosen according to the character of the room's inhabitant, the presence of the goddess of chastity in Monsieur G's bedroom might indicate his sober behavior, but it is possible that the subject was chosen because Diana, as the moon goddess, also signified Night in general. Another Hippolytus must have been the inhabitant of

146: Percier and Fontaine. *Bedchamber Designed for Monsieur O., Paris.* (From the French serial reproductions of 1801.)

the *Bedchamber Designed for Monsieur O., Paris,* except that Diana is here presented in loving guise: "The small dimensions of the room to be decorated and its length, far greater than its width, suggested that the bed be decorated as a little temple to Diana, its light covering supported by four columns set on pedestals. The compartments of the bed's canopy, the divisions of the cornice, the frieze, all are covered with emblems and attributes of Diana. A bas-relief placed above the bed represents the goddess guided by Love to the arms of Endymion. The herms set at the front corners of the bed's platform represent Silence and Night, and curtains, at right and left of the forward columns, conceal the entrances to dressing-rooms. The ceiling of the room follows the peaked line of the bed canopy and seems to be supported by free pilasters and colonnettes which permit a glimpse of painted foliage —the trees among which the little temple is presumed to stand."

147: Percier and Fontaine. *Studio of Citizen I., Paris.* (From the French serial reproductions of 1801.)

148: Percier and Fontaine. *Bed Designed for Monsieur T., Paris.* (From the French serial reproductions of 1801.)

The interior decoration of the *Studio of Citizen I., Paris* was reproduced in five plates of the *Recueil,* including decorative details, a cross-section, and a view of the ceiling. (Citizen I. is the famous miniaturist Jean-Baptiste Isabey.[45] The interior view is described thus in the *Recueil:* "This room, whose background is occupied by a bed set on a platform, serves both as a work room and a room for sleeping. Wooden pilasters form the divisions of the wall panels, over which we see represented, in Etruscan style and against brown backgrounds, allegorical figures of Painting, Sculpture, Architecture, and Engraving. Above is a bas-relief frieze, composed of figures of Fame and garland-supporting torches which frame medallion portraits of famous painters, identified with their names, countries and dates of birth and death. [In engraving the line drawing, the printers of the *Recueil* evidently forgot the inevitable inversion, so that the inscriptions under the names of the painters can be read only from right to left.] The stove, set inside a marble and bronze faced terracotta pedestal, supports a

bust of Minerva. Chimeras' feet, in front of each
pilaster, form brackets for vases and utensils. On the
ceiling toward the windows, Apollo symbol of Day
is seen, and toward the bed and inner wall is Diana,
symbol of Night. Everywhere, the ornaments which
form details of the room refer to the arts associated
with drawing, identifying the inclinations and talents
of the eminent artist for whom they were executed."
The *torchère* bears an Argand lamp as was then the
custom.[46] Under the bust of Minerva (not seen in this
plate) there was a genie bearing crowns of victory and
a caduceus flanked by cornucopias, old emblem
of Alciati with the words "Virtuti fortuna comes,"
already adopted as a motto by various printers.[47]

The *Bed Designed for Monsieur T., Paris* is described:
"The form, the arrangement, and the unity of the
accessories clearly indicate that it was made for a
warrior and a great hunter. Arms of various kinds and
skins of wild animals serve as ornament. An arrow
and a bow attached to the ceiling sustain the draperies
which protect the occupant from air and insects during
the night. The painted bas-relief frieze in the background represents the hunting of animals."[48] The
"Platinum Room," a gallery designed for the King of
Spain, represents a "study of small dimensions,
entirely made in Paris with extreme care and precision
and transported to Spain. Mirrors in the compartments of the arches multiply the extension of the
vault and repeat, *ad infinitum*, the richness of the panels.
The walls are in mahogany and the ornaments are of·
platinum. Large paintings representing the Seasons
which fill the spaces between the pilasters and smaller
medallions of children playing have been painted by
Girodet. Little paintings, views of the most beautiful
known localities, are by Bidault and Thibault. This
room as a whole presents an extraordinary richness."

The line drawings of interior decorations by Percier
and Fontaine combine the inspiration of classical
antiquity with a Renaissance clarity. In this same
spirit Robert Adam in 1768-69 designed an icono-
stasis, or screen, for the King's College Chapel,
Cambridge, to replace an early 16th century one.
The affinity of his design with those of Percier and
Fontaine (who cannot have known it) shows a surprising agreement of results which evidently accept the
same premises.[49]

In 1881, when Empire style had not yet returned to
full favor, Ernest Chesneau made the following
observations, remarkably positive for the time in
which they were written: "Percier had not given
enough thought to the need of variety which is one
of the most fertile elements in our spiritual activity...
He drove reason to the point of abstraction, simplicity
of line to deficiency, purity of outline to dryness,
correctness of form to aridity. And despite this,
despite the absence of variety, the lack of agility and
fantasy, despite the poverty of imagination, despite
the abuse of elementary geometric patterns like the

149: Percier and Fontaine. *"The Platinum Room"*,
Casita del Labrador, Aranjuez.
(French 1812 edition of *Recueil*.)

perfect circle and the right angle, despite the constant
repetition of the same motifs—terms that were too
short or too long, rarely proportional, winged figures
of repellent stiffness, ill-conceived monsters, singular
chimeras' feet—despite the inelegance of certain forms,
their heaviness and the neglect of well-being and
comfort that they denote, despite the monotony of
invariable parallelism and absolute symmetry, one
must nevertheless admit that he created not only a
style, but also *style* in the absolute sense: style through
the logical character, clearly distinguished, of form in
agreement with function, and through the perfect
harmony of details and the whole. This style, even
though of a specific date, nevertheless lasts because of
the solidity of the materials used and the scrupulous
care shown in the execution. Ignoring the anathemas
hurled at it by triumphant Romanticism, amateurs
and artists are today pleased to rehabilitate this period,
as if to protest against voluptuous overstuffing and
the pleasant bric-a-brac of contemporary furnishing,
art of modistes and upholsterers, an enchanting art,
but one with no future and with no kind of style."[50]

150 (top): T. Hope. *Drawing Room with Oriental Landscapes.*
(Household Furniture, 1807.)

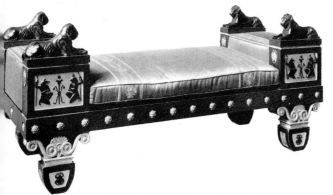

151 (center): T. Hope. *Egyptian Sofa.* VICTORIA
AND ALBERT MUSEUM, LONDON.

152 : T. Hope, *Egyptian Room. (Household Furniture,* 1807.)

The rigorous archeological trends in England were
best personified by Thomas Hope (1769–1831), a
curious figure descended from Scots bankers who
immigrated to Holland, then returned to England at
the time of the Napoleonic wars. Hope was the auth
of an exotic novel *Anastasius,* which his contemporaries hailed as "a *Don Juan* in prose," a work
which Bryon might gladly have written. In *Househo
Furniture and Interior Decoration* (1807).[51] Hope mea
to provide an English equivalent of the *Recueil de
décorations intérieures* of Percier and Fontaine, and
Modern Costume, the ideas of which were suggested
to its author draughtsman Henry Moses by Hope,
fashion was to be reformed according to a strict and
archeological "Greekness." To the English, Hope
used France as an example: "While the French are
beginning to make most rapid strides toward the
purest style of the antique, shall we obstinately lag
behind because of an irrational adherence to a vitiate
and corrupt style?" He reacted against the picturesqu
garden on the grounds that a garden should surrour
the house, continue it and form the transition betwee
architecture and wild nature. He praised the hanging
gardens of Genoa and those of Roman villas for if
symmetry is pleasing in buildings, why shouldn't it
please in gardens too? If we like columns placed at
regular intervals, why should we object to evenly
spaced trees? All nature tends towards symmetry.

But was Hope correct in boasting of himself as
the champion of Greek purity? Judging by Maria
Edgeworth's description of *Deepdene,* Hope's villa,
it would seem not: "This house is magnificently
furnished but to my taste much too fine for a countr
house, even making the idea of comfort improbable.
There is too much Egyptian ornament, Egyptian
hieroglyphical figures, bronze and gilt, but all hideou
... In every passage and hall there are collections of
frightful monsters in bronze or stone or plaster."[52]
We have seen some of the Egyptian pieces made on
Hope's designs; those reproduced here, the *Egyptian
Sofa* and *Egyptian Side Chair,* were meant for the
Egyptian Room whose plan is illustrated in *Househo
Furniture.* To some extent, these pieces illustrate the
flaw in all Regency furnishing for, excepting only the
excellence of craftsmanship, they look as if they had
been made for the stage. Imitating any variety of styl
(Greek, Egyptian, Gothic, Indian, Chinese), Hope's
rooms were a "masquerade." They are all different,
Miss Mitford observed after a visit to Rosedale Cottage: "the saloon Chinese, full of jars and mandarins
and pagodas; the Library Egyptian, all covered with
hieroglyphics, and swarming with furniture crocodile
and sphinxes. Only think of a crocodile couch and a
sphinx sofa! They sleep in Turkish tents, and dine in
Gothic chapel."[53] Had the pieces been shifted from
one room to another, a mixture of heterogeneous
elements would have resulted, as it did in feminine
costume. On this last point Anne M. Buck observes
that "between 1800 and 1810 such unclassical details
vandyked ornament, an antique stomacher, and
Elizabethan ruff appear within the classical form."[54]

153: T. Hope. *Room with Statuary Group by John Flaxman.* (From *Household Furniture,* 1807 edition.)

In classically inspired silverware there was also a strong Rococo element and some silversmiths even went so far as to make replicas of famous works by French 18th century artists. In fact, Louis XIV and Louis XV styles were still considered the expression of regal taste, (as in the Waterloo Chamber of Apsley House (1828) and the Elizabeth Saloon at Belvoir Castle), thus foreshadowing the Neo-Rococo style of the continent which triumphed toward the middle of the 19th century. The spread of the "picturesque" point of view caused English taste to develop rapidly toward that eclecticism which in the course of the 19th century was eventually to bring about the dissolution and liquidation of all historic styles throughout Europe. Thomas Hope's *Drawing Room with Oriental Landscapes* shows furniture similar to that designed by Percier and Fontaine, embellished with picturesque decoration (Oriental scenes, Persian winged lions, peacock feathers in the lunette). This furniture reveals, however, a greater sense of volume and a lesser affectation of ornament than its French counterpart. Hope's *Room with Statuary Group by John Flaxman,* shows a unique play of mirrors which are arranged to reflect the sculpture of *Aurora and Cephalus* in the draped arches around the room.

154: T. Hope. *Egyptian Side Chair.*
VICTORIA AND ALBERT MUSEUM, LONDON.

179

155: H. C. Loeillot. *Napoleon in his Library at Malmaison,* drawing, c. 1824-41. MUSÉE MARMOTTAN, PARIS.

Napoleon's Library at Malmaison was described in the *Recueil* as follows: "The site chosen for this library required its division into three parts which resulted in the arrangement of free-standing Doric columns supporting arches. The two circular bays which close the rectangle to east and west, incorporate in one case a glass door opening on to the allée in the garden, and in the other a fireplace and a mirror without foil which looks towards the countryside. The main subject of the ceiling represents Apollo and Minerva while portrait medallions of the most famous ancient authors and the names of their works, surrounded by laurel, occupy other sections of the vaults." The paneling is of a pale mahogany. The writing desk seen in the drawing by Henri-Charles Loeillot (Karl Loeillot-Hartwig, born at Stettin in 1798) is not of the period, nor is the Napoleon sitting at it painted from life, as we can easily calculate from the dates of this water-colorist.[55] The *Napoleon in His Study at the Tuileries* by Isabey, however, dates from Napoleonic times and

156: J.-B. Isabey. *Napoleon in His Study at the Tuileries,* c. 1806. Formerly HUGO FINALY COLLECTION.

is a variation on the well known David portrait (one version of which is now in the National Gallery, Washington). The writing desk reproduced here is now conserved at Fontainebleau.[56] The fashion of decorating a study or library with the names of illustrious writers (at Malmaison we see portrait medallions of Homer, Virgil, Dante, Voltaire, Terence, Ossian and, within garlands, the names of Pindar, Euripides, Cicero, etc.) as well as with appropriate divinities, such as the Apollo and Minerva seen here, was very common. The same principle of rationally appropriate attributes prompted Percier and Fontaine to conceive the council chamber at Malmaison "in the form of a tent, supported by pikes, *fasci,* and insignia, among which groups of arms are hanging, recalling those of the most famous warrior peoples of the world." Also in tent-form is the room of the Empress Josephine at Malmaison, where Loeillot, in a watercolor of 1826, has set Queen Hortense and Prince Eugène in reverent attitudes at their mother's death-bed.[57]

157: A. Garnerey. *The Music Room of Malmaison* (formerly the "Little Gallery"),
watercolor, 1812–32. CHÂTEAU DE MALMAISON.

At Malmaison is conserved a very beautiful watercolor
of the "Little Gallery," today known as *The Music
Room of Malmaison.* The watercolor was begun in 1812
by Auguste Garnerey (1785–1824) and finished
in 1832 by his sister, as we learn from the writing in
the lefthand corner of the work. The black-patterned
red draperies stand out against the pale green of the
walls and the upholstery of the sofas and chairs is of
the same red with black trimming. Garnerey's art is
so precise that we can even identify the pictures and
the sculptures: the large picture to the left is *Stella
Drawing on the Wall of His Prison* by François Marius

Granet, opposite *The Death of Raphael* by Pierre N.
Bergeret. Below the latter are works by Richard in
Troubadour style (*Valentina of Milan Dreaming of her
Husband, Charles VII engraving his farewells to Agnes
Sorel* and, between these two canvases, *Saint Louis
surprised by his Mother at the Sickbed of Queen
Marguerite of Provence*).[57a] Toward the rear is *Venus
crouching with Love in her Arms*, by P.-P. Prud'hon,
and at the entrance to the great gallery we can make
out Canova's *Dancing Girl*, now owned by the
Hermitage.[58] In the Garnerey watercolor, the armchair
in the center of the room holds a large cashmere

158: J.-B. Isabey. *Napoleon Placing his Son in the Arms of Marie-Louise after his Baptism,* watercolor, 1811. Formerly PRINCE OF MONTENUOVO COLLECTION.

shawl, left there by the person who had been sitting in it. That sitter had left it there in 1812, but we see her seated there in an earlier watercolor by Garnerey, made in 1807, now in the collection of Prince Napoleon. She was, of course, the Empress Josephine.

In a watercolor by Isabey, *Napoleon Placing His Son in the Arms of Marie-Louise after His Baptism,* the other Empress, Marie-Louise, can be seen sitting in a bed reaching toward Napoleon and their son. The furnishings to the left are a toilet-table and washstand designed by Prud'hon in 1811. A description of the toilet-table underlines the allegorical taste of the era:

"A garland of flowers, supported by two candelabra, forms the frame of the mirror. The figure of Pleasure, turning in the lower part, joins the two ends of the garland . . . The Spirits of Trade, Industry, Taste and Harmony surround the young Flora and offer her the tribute of their hearts and the fruit of their toil. The Spirits of Science and the Fine Arts, set on the candelabra, hasten towards the Goddess and place their homage at her feet." The wash stand is naturally an *athénienne* in the form of a tripod. It "supports a pitcher *(aiguière)* on which is seen the Nymph of the Seine lying on some reeds, surrounded by Cupids and by Zephyrs."

159: Empress Marie-Louise (under the guidance of J.-B. Isabey). *The Empress Visiting the Maréchale,* watercolor, 1813. DUCHESSE DE MONTEBELLO COLLECTION, BIARRITZ.

In another watercolor, *The Empress Visiting the Maréchale,* which bears the words "Drawn by Marie-Louise for her Friend the Duchesse de Montebello" we see a lady in bed with a note in her hand, and another lady visiting her. In a copy of the watercolor now in the Museo Lombardi, Parma, the lady in bed is identified as Marie-Louise herself, but in fact the *visitor* is Marie-Louise, who is calling on the Maréchale in her apartment at the Tuileries. Marie-Louise sought the assistance of

her drawing-master Isabey, whose collaboration gives the picture its charm. The person standing near the *secrétaire* is Corvisart, who holds a little bronze bust of the King of Ro The furniture is still in Louis XVI or Directoire style, as is drapery of the alcove. As to the relationship between Mar Louise and the Duchesse de Montebello, her lady-in-waiti we read in the *Mémoires* of Queen Hortense that: "She (Marie-Louise) was intimate only with her lady-in-waiting

160: A. Garnerey. *Princess Schwarzenberg Reading in the Austrian Embassy, Paris,* watercolor, 1812. CASTLE OF ORLIK, CZECHOSLOVAKIA. (Photo Courtesy of Prince Schwarzenberg Archives)

vas a type of fondness that most people found difficult to ⅃derstand, but is easily explained by those who know how to d the inner recesses of the heart. A princess from birth is ⸴rounded by respect and care. To her, people devoted great ⸴rts, studied her tastes, anticipated her slightest wishes. ▌ those who served her looked at everything with her eyes, :h the same pleasure or boredom, almost with her very ⸴otion. But if somebody close to her seemed to have other ⸴rests, other pleasures than her own—like those coquettes ⸴o, always sure of their attractions, only notice those who ⸴ indifferent—so a princess, object of all adoration, would astonished and struck by such a novelty. Whoever wanted withdraw from her presence was allowed to fear neither ⸴rigue nor flattery. The desire to bring such a one back, to ⸴gage her again, became the primary concern, even if the fact departure was born of necessary causes. Such was the ⸴sition of the Empress and the Duchess of Montebello... ⸴hen she withdrew—even for an instant—the Empress wrote ⸴tes to her. In her absence, she could make nothing happen. I have heard (Napoleon) say to the Empress several times ⸴u are fooling yourself thoroughly if you believe that your ⸴chess has any love for you. She loves only herself and her ⸴ildren. You are a dupe to be so fond of her.'"[59]

Two little watercolors by Auguste Garnerey have preserved vivid glimpses of palace life under the Empire. (The property of the Schwarzenberg princes, they are now beyond the Iron Curtain in the confiscated castle of Orlik near Vltavou, Czechoslovakia.) Both watercolors show us two interiors of the Austrian Embassy in Rue de la Chaussée d'Antin, Paris. In *Princess Schwarzenberg Reading* we see Anna, born Countess Hohenfeld, the wife of the Ambassador Field Marshal Prince Karl Schwarzenberg, reading in an ample armchair, near the writing desk. The simple room, on whose walls some little pictures and two large maps are hanging, as in a Dutch interior, speaks to us through living things, caught in their everyday existence. The lady seated with such assurance in the chair sheathed in its *housse* with symmetrical laces, the dog curled up in the other chair, the firescreen set askew as if someone had just moved it, the engineer's drawing-board to the right with two sheets of white paper ready to be used—all these things are not so much examples of decoration as they are elements of a life that is still warm. One cannot help but feel that this document of a period (see the signature and date on the hearth rug) is as vivid and immediate as a page of *War and Peace.* Perhaps the magic is produced by the candor of the central figure: lady and armchair seem carved in soft marble.

161: A. Garnerey. *Bedchamber of the Austrian Embassy, Paris,*
watercolor, c. 1812. CASTLE OF ORLIK, CZECHOSLOVAKIA.
(Photo Courtesy of Prince Schwarzenberg Archives)

Figure 161, the *Bedchamber of the Austrian Embassy, Paris,* see a little boy caressing the same dog that we saw curled a chair in the first watercolor. Nearby is a bed under a tective canopy. Another child is playing diabolo, a game ch became very fashionable in France precisely in 1812.[60] ough the door we see into the next room where the mother hese two children and the young man (probably their older ther) are reading. Of the three youths, Friedrich. Karl and Edmund, Friedrich later wrote under the pseudonym of Lanzknecht and Edmund became a Field Marshal like his father. Seen here from her other profile, the Princess seems much less haughty than when she was posing in the stiff armchair. A plant on the windowsill lends an idyllic, bourgeois note to this aristocratic room. The columned fire-place, the clock with the Cupid, the *psyché,* the little round table supported by three columns are still to be found at Orlik.

162: A. Garnerey. *Queen Hortense in her Boudoir,* watercolor drawing, 1811. O. LEFUEL COLLECTION, PARIS.

Two sketches by Garnerey show us Queen Hortense in the Palace in rue Cerutti, Paris. In the first, *Queen Hortense in her Boudoir* (a study for the perfected watercolor in the collection of Prince Napoleon[61]), we see the Queen standing, bare-headed (in the finished work she is wearing a veil), leaning against the arm of a sofa. The room is draped in blue with a ceiling of pleated fabric in the form of a tent-roof, bordered with triangular festoons in medieval taste. In fact, Hortense had a weakness for the medieval-inspired *Troubador* style, as she showed in her book, *Douze romances mises en musique et dediées au Prince Eugène par sa soeur.*[62] This blueness, the Gothic note of the pavilion-like fretwork, the two Louis XVI cabinets on either side of the sofa, and the alabaster *veilleuse* that hangs from the ceiling (reflected in the mirror behind the sofa) make the style of this room a model for the Second Empire style which was later to flourish under the reign of the "pale son of Hortense." The two cabinets, or *serre-bijoux,* eventually found their way to Saint-Cloud, under Napoleon III. The *jardinière* seen at left is now in Malmaison, and the

bookcase reflected in the mirror can be seen today at the castle of Arenenberg, Thurgau, Switzerland.

The second little picture, *Queen Hortense in her Drawing Room,* shows walls almost hidden behind an array of small pictures, so scrupulously rendered that it is possible to identify them. For example, on the wall to the right of the fireplace, the tallest picture of the upper row is *The Interior of the Church of the Capucins in Rome* by F. Granet, a work distinguished by its superb treatment of light and shadow.[63] This taste for simultaneously displaying a vast quantity of art and objects anticipates the Biedermeier period, as we shall see. Note the quantity of knick-knacks on the writing-table, and the visiting-cards stuck in the mirror frame. On the righthand table, draped with a velvet cover, further knick-knacks include a lamp with a Gothic shade, a round cheval-glass supported by a little bronze Cupid and a crystal box, while on the bookcase against the right wall we note a hyacinth in a porcelain pot. Covering tables with such knick-knacks was a widespread custom during this period. With regard to decoration, Queen Hortense had

163: A. Garnerey. *Queen Hortense in her Drawing Room,* watercolor drawing. O. LEFUEL COLLECTION, PARIS.

very romantic taste. If we can believe her, she was the first to introduce into France the round table placed in the center of a drawing room: "I was the first in France who established, in the drawing room, a round table to be used for work or for evening entertainment, as is common in the countryside. Previously, French hostesses arranged groupings near the fireplace, all the ladies in a circle, with their gentlemen standing up in the center of their group. Sparkling conversation, in which each tried to show his wit, was the only occupation of an evening."[64] In her *Mémoires* Queen Hortense also gives an idea of the social life of the time: "In the morning, nobody was allowed to visit me. I sketched with Adèle, I dined either alone or, occasionally, with her and in the evening, surrounded by my children, I was at home (at eight o'clock) to people on my visiting list. We performed music, we played billiards or we sat at a large table which enabled everyone to do what most pleased him. The ladies worked or chatted. Tea was served at ten o'clock and about midnight, or one o'clock in the morning we stopped the animated conversation which might

easily have lasted well into the night, except for the delicate health of the hostess. I went to great trouble to persuade my officers not to remain standing as if they were carrying weapons but, instead, to take part in the conviviality. I wanted my home to be like a family gathering where the good always reigned and where a pleasing gaiety did not exclude respect for the hostess."

Madame d'Abrantès also speaks of these gatherings in her *Mémoires:*[65] "What pleasant hours we spent at her home! How sweetly they flew! It was then (at one of them) that she composed *Partant pour la Syrie! Reposez-vous, bons chevaliers,* and many other romances that we are all familar with and still sing... Other times we all sat at the round table: Gérard with his immortal pencil, Isabey whose talent was often imitated but never equalled. Garnerey, having worked a long time on a pretty drawing for an album, finished the room in which we were with such charming detail that it was possible to see every rung of the chairs which were in it. Nothing was insignificant, yet all was blessed with the same detailed study."

189

164: Comte de Clarac. *Caroline Murat in the Royal Palace, Naples,* watercolor,
c. 1808–13. CONTE G. B. SPALLETTI-TRIVELLI COLLECTION, ROME.

Charles-Othon-Frédéric-Baptiste, Comte de Clarac
(1777–1847), was tutor to Murat's children and
director of the excavations at Pompeii. Though he
later became famous as an archeologist and curator
of antiquities at the Louvre (after 1818), de Clarac
perhaps deserves greater fame as a painter, since as
an archeologist his works seem principally of a
popularizing nature.[66] Indeed, the sketches he
brought back from a voyage to Brazil won the praises
of Alexander von Humboldt for having given the most
faithful reproduction of the luxuriant vegetation of
the New World (his *Virgin Forest in Brazil* was
engraved by Claude François Fortier). Generous when
it was a question of something that appealed to his
artistic sense, Clarac paid fifteen thousand francs for
a porphyry model of the temple of Paestum which
later went to the museum of Toulouse. It was this
circumstance which persuaded his first cousin,
Joséphine de la Millière, to reject his proposal of
marriage, for such wastefulness in a man of no

ortune looked dangerous to her, and she was right, because Clarac died burdened with debts.[67]

The oil painting of *Caroline Murat in the Royal Palace, Naples* (*Fig.* 16) was painted, as we said in the introduction, by Clarac. The same subject is also depicted by Clarac in a watercolor (*Fig.* 164) in which the Queen is wearing a feathered bonnet instead of being bareheaded as in the oil painting. The table with a green velvet cover is laden with knick-knacks, identical both in the oil and in the watercolor. In the watercolor one can see that the ceiling is decorated with medallions of illustrious women whose names are visible above the cornice: Madame de Sévigné, Clotilde de Suzville, Madame du Châtelet, Maria Theresa. The miniature by F. MacDonald (morganatic husband of Caroline Murat) reproduces the same scene, but shows a number of variants. The decoration of the ceiling is here a row of female figures holding hands as if in a dance; objects about the room have been altered; the rug has been simplified; and instead of the drawing-case there is a waste-paper basket. From a visit to the Royal Palace in Naples today we cannot discover what the ceiling of this room was really like, because after a fire in 1837 the decoration of the room was changed and the present heavy frieze of gilded stucco on a white ground was added.[68] The watercolor of the same room by Elie-Honoré Montagny (*Fig.* 17) illustrates a number of objects cluttering the console and flowers under glass bells; one would say that Biedermeier taste was already at work.[69] The Biedermeier metamorphosis of this corner of the Naples Palace is further documented by an oil painting (*Fig.* 166) which seems to catch this same room in a twilight atmosphere as opposed to the bright sunshine of the pictures of the Murat period. Even the landscape, the view of Vesuvius from the window, seems to share in this twilight mood; it is a neat, flat landscape, with no magic. The clear colors of the Empire are gone; at the window hang two heavy curtains, one violet, the other yellowish. The little sofa at the left, a *méridienne*, is still in its place and the table-cover and the rug seem unchanged, but all the charming knick-knacks have vanished from the table, as have the Cupid-supported mirrors and the Graces dancing around a candelabra. On the table now there is only a bell, next to the book, probably a prayer-book, into which the lady has thrust her fingers. The lady is certainly a member of the Bourbon family, for she has the nose of "Re Nasone" (King "Big Nose") and the slightly goatish Bourbon features. She is dressed in a high-necked dress with a train, with a black gorget rising to her chin and cuffs of black lace extending over her hands— a far cry from Caroline's light, white dress which exposed her arms and shoulders! On her head this lady has a great black plume, like those of the horses that pull hearses. She is possibly in mourning for Maria Carolina, who died in 1814, and she might be Maria Amelia, daughter of the deceased and wife of the Duc d'Orléans, later Louis-Philippe. The great-grandfather of Count di Gropello apparently bought this picture at Terlizzi, in Apulia, around 1850.

165: F. MacDonald. *Caroline Murat in the Royal Palace, Naples*. Miniature after a painting by the Comte de Clarac. Formerly COMTESSE MURAT COLLECTION.

Portrait of a Bourbon Princess in the Royal Palace, Naples. NTE GIANNI DI GROPPELLO FIGAROLO COLLECTION, ROME.

167: J.-F. (?) Garnerey. *The Duchesse de Berry in her Boudoir, Pavillon de Marsan, Tuileries, Paris,* watercolor.
CONTE LODOVICO LUCCHESI-PALLI COLLECTION, BRUNNSEE CASTLE, AUSTRIA.

Three enchanting watercolors of interiors inhabited by the Duchesse de Berry[70] were made by a Garnerey, not by Auguste (who died in 1824) but perhaps by his father Jean-François (1755–1837), also a distinguished miniaturist. In the *Room where the Duchesse de Berry was born in the Royal Palace at Casserta* (*Fig.* 18) we see a blue room with 18th century furniture. In the second we see *The Duchesse de Berry in Her Boudoir* at the Pavillon de Marsan in the Château of the Tuileries, Paris. The Duchesse is seated, reading, while near her are playing her two children, Louise Isabelle d'Artois ("Mademoiselle"), born in 1817, and the Duc de Bordeaux, born in 1820. This meticulous painting again allows the identification of pictures and objects, and we note the growing importance of flowerstands with fresh flowers which bring nature into the interior of the room, even though nature is otherwise sternly excluded by curtains and hangings. In *The Duchesse de Berry's Drawing Room* we see the Duchesse in the company of her father,

168: J.-F. (?) Garnerey. *The Duchesse de Berry's Drawing Room, Pavillon de Marsan, Tuileries, Paris,* watercolor, 1829.
CONTE LODOVICO LUCCHESI-PALLI COLLECTION, BRUNNSEE CASTLE, AUSTRIA.

Francesco I of Naples, who is reading, and her step-mother Queen Isabella, sitting at the writing-table. The furniture is still in Empire style, for such furniture continued to be made until 1830 and even afterwards,[71] popularized by La Mésangère (king of pinchbeck Percier and Fontaine) who nevertheless contributed to the resolution of Empire into Biedermeier. His romanticism of complex and bizarre hangings and his taste for flowers—even artificial ones—doubtless hastened the process. However, the language of Biedermeier can already be read in Garnerey's watercolor of 1829. Flowers are everywhere (even on the chandelier) and the profusion of objects—little beaded screens, porcelains in glass cases, the cage hung between the curtains and the larger one holding a parrot, the pictures neatly lined up around the convex mirror, the great flaring basket for waste-paper, the embroidery table (decorated with flowers at its base), the bronzes under glass on the highboy,—is all fully articulated Biedermeier.

1816   J. Isabey.

la Musique et le Thé.

le Réveil

We read in Queen Hortense's *Mémoires* (see p. 197) about those evening gatherings where everyone enjoyed such pleasant pastimes that a *soiré* lasted well into the night. Among a series of watercolors with which J.-B. Isabey represented the occupations of the various hours of the day we see *(From Eleven to One AM, Music and Tea)* just such a gathering. These watercolors are all that is left us of the project for the decoration of a Sèvres china service, whose theme was the life of a man of the world. A. Brongniart, who from 1800 was the director of the Sèvres factory, had suggested it to Isabey but it was never carried out.[72] The twelve subjects were to have been: from one to three AM, dancing and gaming; from three to five AM, sleep; from five to seven AM, awakening; from seven to nine AM, work in the study; from nine to eleven AM, breakfast; from eleven AM to one PM, receiving; from one to three PM, *toilette*; from three to five PM, promenade; from five to seven PM, dinner; from seven to nine PM, guests in the drawing room; from nine to eleven PM, the theater; and from eleven PM to one AM, music and tea. In *From Eleven to One AM, Music and Tea*, we see that the room is in a palace. A long sofa occupies the lower part of the wall in the background while, toward the center of the room on a round table supported by monopode winged lions, a samovar is steaming and tea is being served. To the left, another group of people is listening to the performance of a pianist. Other drawings concern the following hours: *From Three to Five AM, Sleep; From Five to Seven AM, Awakening;* and *From Seven to Nine AM, Work in the Study.* The thing which most strikes a modern eye in looking at these little scenes of everyday life is not solely the interior decoration (when this is not the specific subject of a picture, it rarely possesses that enchanted, magic quality of distant time and atmosphere). Instead, we are most likely to notice certain details of comfort, or discomfort. The weak illumination of the evening party, for example, must have left large areas of the drawing room in shadow. In the awakening scene, the man-servant who blows on the newly lighted fire reminds us that today fireplaces are no longer necessities and there are no servants (or almost none). We are so used to light and warmth (we build houses of glass and fill them with electric light or even neon, over-heating everything) that these 19th century rooms, rather than seeming cozy, would have seemed intolerably stuffy and depressing to us. As to the decoration, the study reveals details reminiscent of an age when learning was still encyclopedic and natural sciences went hand in hand with letters and the arts, for on the bookcase, among the busts of admired men, are a dog's skeleton and other zoological and archeological finds.

169–172: J.-B. Isabey. Project for a Sèvres Service, 1816. B. HOUTHAKKER COLLECTION, AMSTERDAM.
upper left: *From Eleven to One AM, Music and Tea.*
upper right: *From Three to Five AM, Sleep.*
lower left: *From Five to Seven AM, Awakening.*
lower right: *From Seven to Nine AM, Work in the Study.*

173: Tommaso Minardi. *Self-Portrait of the Artist in his Garret,* 1807. GALLERIA D'ARTE MODERNA, FLORENCE.

The more humble the room, the more it is furnished with bare necessities, the less dated it seems to our eyes. Thus, the garret where Tommaso Minardi (1787-1871) painted his self-portrait would be time-less, if it were not for the washstand, the skull (tribute to a conventional Romantic notion of melancholy) and the Neoclassic painting hanging in the background (also conventional with its contrast between standing figures and a figure seated in a

curule chair). Minardi, a purist follower of the Nazarenes, thought he was imitating the *Quattrocentisti.* What little originality he possessed was put into this painting, a *Self-portrait of the Artist in his Garret.* As Guglielmo De Sanctis tells us: "He spent a few months with his family in Faenza and there painted several pictures, in one of which he portrayed himself in his studio seated on a mattress. This painting was very popular and seemed to

174: Jean Alaux. *M. and Mme. Ingres in Rome,* 1818. MUSÉE INGRES, MONTAUBAN.

recall the Flemish manner.''[73] In the portrait of *M. et Mme. Ingres in Rome,* painted by a *pensionnaire* of the French Academy in Rome, Jean Alaux (1786–1864), the furniture and the almost non-existent decoration of the house are also timeless. Ingres, putting down his violin, is looking at his wife in the next room as she leans on a chair. If it weren't for the dress of the two figures and Mme. Ingres' hat and cashmere shawl on the chest of drawers, the room might seem modern, with its bare partition which divides the rear room. The Spanish picture just behind Mme. Ingres was bought by Ingres and is now in the museum at Montauban. Although it does not reach the heights of a Vermeer, this interior, as Henri Lapauze has rightly remarked, breathes a humble and moving intimacy.[74] The sunlight enters the rear room through the two windows at the left, and a fat cat bathes in its warmth by the open door.

176: G. F. Kersting. *Man Reading by the Light of an Argand Lamp,* c. 1814. SCHLOSSMUSEUM, WEIMAR.

Much closer to Vermeer was Georg Friedrich Kersting (1783–1847) who, in a series of scenes full of atmosphere, "paints the locale in which the man of his time moves, in which he is really at home."[75] The theme of Kersting's pictures is always the same, a single figure; a man at his desk, as in *Man Writing by a Window* (Fig. 177), or a girl at a mirror or at some quiet task as in *The Girl Embroidering.* The figure is presented in very simple surroundings, near a window which only rarely allows an exterior scene to be glimpsed. In general the figures are seen from behind, so that they do not attract the chief attention of the spectator. Thus our eyes are drawn first of all to the sparsely furnished room itself, and to the play of light and shade produced by the sun coming through the window or by a glowing lamp, as in *Man Reading by*

5: G. F. Kersting. *Girl Embroidering,* c. 1814. SCHLOSSMUSEUM, WEIMAR.

177: G. F. Kersting. *Man Writing by a Window*, 1811. SCHLOSSMUSEUM, WEIMAR.

the Light of an Argand Lamp (*Fig.* 176) and *Man Reading by the Light of a Bouillotte Lamp* (*Fig.* 178). What the painter wants to communicate is a feeling for the interior, for the "apartment" in the fullest meaning of that word. The half-turned figures are truly apart, detached from every external thing, absorbed in the atmosphere, in the *Stimmung,* of their personal activities. This approach is very different from that communicated by Romantic painters like

Caspar David Friedrich and Philipp Otto Runge, whose chief interest was the distance, the infinity of the surrounding world. In contrast, Kersting seems to concentrate on what is near.[76] Wordsworth in his *Ode to Duty* seems tired of an "unchartered freedom," seems to "long for a repose that is ever the same." This sense of a quiet harbor pervades Kersting's interiors, where the world that matters is found within four walls. These little paintings seem almost a reply

178: G. F. Kersting. *Man Reading by the Light of a Bouillotte Lamp,* 1814. OSKAR REINHART COLLECTION, WINTERTHUR.

to William Blake's words: "Hold Infinity in the palm of your hand,/ And Eternity in an hour." Why long for infinity when happiness is so close at hand? Why ask the spirit of the Wind to be transported like a swift cloud over the Universe, emulating her impetuous and tameless nature, when by staying at home one can feel the sovereignty of a world of familiar objects and find satisfaction in rehearsing its delightful inventory? In the quiet of the room, decked only with a drapery of white muslin over the window, longings of the human spirit are appeased. In the contemplation of a sober still life, a work-basket, a guitar, three flower pots, a world can be comprehended. The *Girl Embroidering,* is known to be Louise Seidler, also a painter, who posed for this picture in Dresden. Knowing of Kersting's precarious financial situation, she introduced him to Goethe, who took steps to have the painting bought by Duke Charles Augustus.

179: F.-L. Dejuinne. *Madame Récamier in her Apartment at l'Abbaye-aux-Bois,* 1826. PRIVATE COLLECTION, PARIS.

The quintessential intimacy of Kersting's paintings is certainly not found in the portraits of important people painted in their homes, a genre which was very popular in the 19th century. Until the end of the 17th century, portraits gave only the vaguest hints of background environment. With the 18th century, however, the spirit of the conversation piece, (medium-sized pictures of a gathering of relatives or friends in intimate surroundings), began to penetrate the individual portrait. The subject was picked up with all the paraphernalia of his *humus* and his *habitat*, just as the inaugurator of conversation pieces, van Eyck, had treated his subjects in the portrait of the Arnolfini couple.

Surely no one can say that there is much intimacy in the portrait of *Madame Récamier in her Apartment at l'Abbaye-aux-Bois* by François-Louis Dejuinne (1786–1844). The beautiful woman who had posed sitting on a sofa *à l'antique* for David, was transferred— with the necessary alterations in details of her dress— from the Neoclassic picture's vague room to the precise background of her "cell" in l'Abbaye-aux-

180: Franz Krüger. *Portrait of Prince August of Prussia.* KAISER-FRIEDRICH MUSEUM, BERLIN.

181: Joseph Schmeller. *Goethe Dictating in his Study,* 1831. LANDESBIBLIOTHEK, WEIMAR.

Bois. In the same Davidian pose, she sits here with her bookcase, harpsichord, harp and the great Sèvres vase on a round table. The mirror over the mantelpiece reflects the seraphic bed in a white alcove and we see the Baron François Gérard's painting of *Corinna at Cape Miseno* to the right of the window which, half-veiled by muslin curtains, shows a Gothic chapel among trees.[77] As in the David painting, Madame Récamier here looks at us, deliberately posing, and the charm of the neat, semi-cloistral room is considerably lessened by her artificial attitude.

The *Portrait of Prince August of Prussia,* painted by Franz Krüger (1797-1857), places its subject in front of another portrait of Madame Récamier, by Gérard,[78] and under a bronze chandelier in the exact center of a rigid and symmetrical Empire room. He is erect, stiff as a military mannikin, the chest thrown out, right knee bent forward. His left arm is on his hip to hold his sword, while his right arm is limply holding a great plumed, cocked hat. Sofa and chairs firmly stuffed and covered with printed silk are lined up against the walls, which are hung with damasked

silk with six-pointed stars at regular intervals, the whole crowned with a frieze of carved palmettos. On the table's dark cover are the plan of a fortress — also star-shaped — and the silhouette of a little bronze lamp surmounted by a winged *coephore.* A soft velvet-like cloak is thrown over a chair, and the only other soft thing in all this rigidity is Mme. Récamier herself, relaxing in an "antique-style" chair.

Like Prince August, Goethe is also looking towards the spectator in the painting *Goethe Dictating in his Study* by Joseph Schmeller. This room lacks intimacy because the artist has painted the picture crudely, in the arid and slightly childish style of an *ex-voto.* Here, also, there are two pots of plants in the window, but Schmeller isn't Kersting, and that window admits neither real magic nor light. The figures of Goethe and his amanuensis John are stiff puppets in an ordinary Biedermeier décor, with office furniture of the period. It is too bad that Louise Seidler's intro-duction of Kersting to Goethe didn't prompt the great man to have Kersting paint him in his study instead of this wretched Schmeller!

182: A. Garnerey. *Queen Hortense's Salon at Augsburg,* sepia drawing. BIBLIOTHÈQUE THIERS, PARIS.

183: Anonymous. *The Drawing Room of Queen Julie, Palazzo Serristori,* watercolor, c. 18
MARCHESE NAPOLEONE DEL GALLO DI ROCCAGIOVINE COLLECTION, RO

184: J.S. van den Abeele. *Princess Zenaïde and her Children in the Villa Paolina*, watercolor, c. 1840. MUSEO NAPOLEONICO, ROME.

Queen Hortense's large round table reappears in her drawing room at Augsburg, where the Queen settled in 1817 after her expulsion from France. She wrote in her *Mémoires:* "France had permanently exiled my family from her bosom. It was only under pain of death that any of us could ever again set foot on French soil. This decree broke my heart."[79] The Queen had reached that phase of life in which passions are stilled: "I had arrived at that state of peace which passion no longer could disrupt."[80] Although in the last chapter of her *Mémoires* the Queen describes her existence as tranquil and solitary, Auguste Garnerey's drawing of *Queen Hortense's Salon at Augsburg* shows her sitting at the keyboard of a typical Empire piano, (an Erard, with the capitals of its legs formed by Psyche heads) while an evening party is in progress. Some of the people are identified: Mademoiselle Louise Cochelet, the Queen's faithful friend, is next to Hortense, and sitting at the right near the bookcase is General Henri-François Delaborde. This bookcase, brought from Malmaison, and the Erard harp on the left, dated 1808, are now in Arenenberg castle. The walls are entirely covered with paintings, many of which are also at Arenenberg: on the back wall we recognize *The Birth of Henri IV of France*, and *Mary Stuart Receiving the Announcement of Her Death Sentence*, both attributed to J. B. Vermay.

The dispersion of the Bonapartes after the collapse of the Napoleonic empire linked their names to various Italian cities: Rome, Florence, Trieste. In Florence, Julie Clary, wife of Joseph Bonaparte, the former King of Naples and Spain, had taken beautiful apartments in the Palazzo Serristori in Via dei Renai: "a palace endowed with a vast and delightful garden

which Conte Averardo Serristori had created according to designs by the architect Manetti. It was on the left bank of the Arno and its green park extended as far as the old S. Niccolò gate. The garden, located between the palace and the river, had the appearance of a broad flower-filled terrace on which one could walk for a great length, just as today one strolls on the Lungarno Serristori which has taken its place."[81] "Queen Julie, because of her constitution and the ailments that afflicted her, was forced to spend her days on a *chaise longue*. From about 1827 on she enjoyed the company of her sister who, with her daughter Juliette, had come to live with her. This sister, Honorine Catherine Clary, was somewhat older and had married, in Marseilles, an officer of engineers, Henri Joseph Gabriel Blait de Villeneuve, who had left her a widow."[82] The *Drawing Room of Queen Julie, Palazzo Serristori*, shows a large room furnished with 18th century pieces. Its barren appearance is unusual for the period around 1830, but the taste of the era is revealed by the pots of flowers at the windows, the cross-stitched blue *housse* cushion on the sofa and the little screen placed on the round table. From the passage quoted above we may assume that the three ladies near the fireplace are Queen Julie with her sister and niece. Since this artist lacks the precision of a Garnerey, it is impossible to distinguish clearly the two pictures on either side of the fireplace, although they appear to be Tuscan primitives.[82a]

Another not very diligent painter was Jodocus Sebastiaen van den Abeele (1797–1855), the drawing master of Prince Louis Napoleon (later Napoleon III), who came to Italy in 1824. Around 1840 he made the watercolor of *Princess Zenaïde and Her children in the Villa Paolina*. Paolina Borghese in her will (1825) left the villa equally to Louis Napoleon, her nephew, and to his first wife Charlotte. In 1827, Charlotte and Louis Napoleon transferred the villa to their sister (and sister-in-law) Zenaïde, who came to live there with her husband Carlo Luciano, Principe di Canino.[83] The room, decorated with Neoclassic ornaments, has a vaulted ceiling from which an oil lamp is hanging. Its furnishings are not sumptuous, consisting mainly of a solid little Empire sofa with Aubusson upholstery, a few light Chiavari chairs and a very long wall bench on which a series of cross-stitched cushions are set.

185: F. MacDonald. *The Schoenwald Cottage at Frohsdorf,* watercolor, 1823. CONTE G. B. SPALLETTI-TRIVELLI COLLECTION, ROM▮

In 1818 Caroline Murat, who had taken the name of Contessa di Lipona (anagram of Napoli), moved from Hainburg to Frohsdorf, to a castle two leagues from Neustadt and eleven from Vienna, on the banks of the Danube. F. MacDonald (1777–1837), after a brilliant military and political career, stayed at Caroline's side and apparently—though documents are missing—became her morganatic husband. In 1823 MacDonald painted *The Schoenwald Cottage at Frohsdorf, (La Chaumière de Schoenwald à Frohsdorf),* in which the deliberately rustic quality of the room, with its log ceiling and walls, is made idyllic by the little hanging basket of roses and by the genteel arts practiced by the two girls, one busily drawing and the other playing the harp. Dressed in the peasant costumes of the region (a custom which still remains among the Austrian aristocracy), the girls are Letizia Maria Giuseppina Annunziata, born in 1802, (who in 1823 married Marchese Guido Taddeo Pepoli of Bologna) and Luisa Carolina Giulia, born in 1805, (who in 1825 married Conte Giulio Rasponi of Ravenna).

In MacDonald's enchanting *Interior of the Villa Paolina at Viareggio* of 1835, Letizia Pepoli is again playing the harp, and Luisa Rasponi is this time doing

F. MacDonald. *Interior of the Villa Paolina at Viareggio,* watercolor, 1835. CONTE G. B. SPALLETTI-TRIVELLI COLLECTION, ROME.

needlepoint on her embroidery frame. The artist is himself seen writing while Caroline is sewing.
During the summer Caroline, who normally lived in Florence in a palace in Borgo Ognissanti (where the Hotel Excelsior now stands), used to go to Viareggio, to the villa that still bears the name of Paolina. It had been built by Paolina in 1822, and left to Caroline in 1825: "I leave the villa and garden of Viareggio, with all the furnishings in it, to my sister Caroline Murat." The Viareggio of those days, on whose beach Shelley's body had been recovered a few years earlier, was quite different from the modern resort. Through the

windows of the villa in MacDonald's watercolor we see the deserted shore and sea. The decoration, rather Oriental in flavor, includes a frieze of Chinese hunting scenes crowning the walls, recalling a similar exotic taste in the more famous seaside building, the Brighton Pavilion. The festive decoration finds no response in the "furnishings," which couldn't be simpler or better suited to a summer house. The only bright note is provided by the flowerpots of *vernis Martin* on the mantel. The *housses* which cover the chairs and sofas suggest brief visits, so brief that it wasn't worthwhile to remove them.

187: Anonymous. *Lamartine's Drawing Room in Florence,* watercolor. MLLE. DE SENNEVIER COLLECTION.

Similarly, there is no sumptuous furniture in the bedroom seen in the painting of *The Borghese Family in their Palace of Borgo Pinti.* Instead there is an austere purity in the great white hangings on the walls and bed, and in the white marble fireplace, the hanging lamp of white opaline, and the white sofa. There is such simplicity in the decoration (on the mantel there is only a clock under glass and on the *toilette* we see none of the delightful knick-knacks listed by Pope in his famous passage from *The Rape of the Lock*), there is such sobriety in the furniture, that this room seems the ideal sanctuary for the expression of family affections. In fact, we see just such an intimate family scene: Princesse Adèle de la Rochefoucauld Borghese (1792–1877) surrounded by her three sons, Principe Marc' Antonio Borghese (1814–1886), Principe Camillo Aldobrandini (1816–1902), Don Scipione Salviati (1823–1892), and her daughter Maria Luisa (1812–1838).

During that same period (1825–1828) Alphonse de Lamartine was also in Florence, as secretary of legation to the Grand Duke of Tuscany. He and his English wife, Marianne Birch, had already been charmed by Florence during previous visits, and the poet's wife must have been his guide in appreciating the city's spell and the masterpieces of her museums. The magic of Florence, it must be remembered, had been discovered by the English before all other foreigners. In Florence, *salon de l'Europe,* Lamartine led the life of an elegant, witty gentleman of society. The first house where he lived was No. 126 Via dei Serragli, near the Torrigiani gardens. The locale could hardly have been more romantic, for the Marchese Torrigiani had built a tower in order to obtain a view over the cemetery which contained the grave of a person he had passionately loved in secret. From Marchese Niccolò Viviani in 1826 the poet bought some property opposite the Fortezza da Basso, between Via Valfonda and Via Faenza (today owned by Còntini Bonacossi), with a country house, garden, olive grove, vineyard, and three cows. Unfortunately Lamartine was anything but astute in business matters,

188: Anonymous. *The Borghese Family in their Palace of Borgo Pinti, Florence,* watercolor, c. 1828. MARIO PRAZ COLLECTION, ROME.

although this transaction seemed to be a solid one: "I wanted, when I would be old, to have a house just outside the city to retire to in winter, like the Russians and the English." As soon as he had begun the necessary renovation (which included, as fashion decreed, the Gothic decoration of the chapel), the transaction proved so disastrous that the poet decided that he himself could no longer afford the luxury of spending his final winters in Florence and that he would recoup the investment by renting the villa to some Russian or Englishman. In fact, he rented it to Princess Galitzin but finally resigned himself to selling the princely estate.[84] In Florence in addition to the French society of the Saint-Aulaires, the Castellanes, the Valences, and the Principessa Aldobrandini-Borghese, (née La Rochefoucauld, whose family is seen in *Fig.* 188) — "a Parisian club under a fairer sky" — Lamartine frequented Italian men of letters. He met Manzoni, who complimented him by saying that he (Lamartine) had achieved what was merely an intention in *I Promessi sposi.*

Lamartine also made friends with Florentine literary figures like Gino Capponi, G. B. Niccolini and Giuliano Frullani, and he later recalled with nostalgia the gatherings in the garden of Capponi's villa, Varramista. But the hours that most filled him with pride were those in which he was familiarly received by the young Grand Duke Leopold in the library of Palazzo Pitti, where they talked of politics, literature and art. At times the Grand Duchess was also present, with one of her children in her arms, like any ordinary mother. It is a pity that Giuseppe Bezzuoli, portraitist of that Florentine Biedermeier society, didn't paint such a scene of intimacy and affability, with the tower of the Palazzo Vecchio seen against a pale blue sky through a window half-covered by a heavy red curtain.[85] Instead, we have a mediocre watercolor of *Lamartine's Drawing Room in Florence* which shows quite ordinary furniture of the period. The harp and crucifix, however, are two objects which could be emblematic of the poet who wrote *Harmonies poétiques et réligieuses.*

During the 19th century, views of Italian court life were frequently painted, especially in Parma under Marie-Louise and in Naples under Francesco I and Ferdinando II. At the Neapolitan court the Biedermeier spirit triumphed. In the now restored Palace of Capodimonte in Naples can be seen paint-ings of family groups of the Bourbons, or medallion portraits which adorn tables, clocks, and decorative pieces. For example, the family of Francesco I paying homage to Ferdinando I can be seen painted on a pot-bellied porcelain vase. On the reverse of the vase are tender verses: "Behold us at thy feet, our

this floodtide of affectionate expressions within the domestic walls of sovereigns whom liberal propaganda was representing as monstrous tyrants (like the cozy tenderness of Charles Addams' monsters), is not without charm and appeal. The Bourbons represent a defunct but nevertheless somewhat glittering world which still held some reflections of the Golden Age. It is in this light, at least, that Harold Acton views them when he states that the reign of Ferdinando II was a time of flourishing commercial and economic growth, not a static period. With his witty, caressing pen, Acton enlivens little scenes of the bourgeois life at court, describing the loves of that Biedermeier Duchess of Malfi, Isabella, first the widow of Francesco I and then the bride of her own chamberlain, Del Balzo.[86]

It is Isabella whom we see in the plate *Queen Isabella in the Palace of Capodimonte,* probably by Carlo de Falco (1798–1882) who also painted the portrait of Maria Cristina, (*Fig.* 192). De Falco was a pupil of Costanzo Angelini (1760–1853), and at the exposition of 1826 he contributed a portrait of Queen Isabella. He was then named court painter, a position he held until the end of the Bourbon reign in 1860. In this picture we see every detail of the room's decoration scrupulously reproduced: the Aubusson rug of the restoration period, with the monogram of the Queen (an "I") under a crown at the corners; the sofa; the console; the chairs; the little circular table; and the maple work-table with black inlay—all Biedermeier pieces made in Naples. In addition, there are the footstool with sphinxes, books and miniatures, some in Gothic frames, on the round table, arrangements of artificial flowers under a glass bell and in alabaster vases on the two *guéridons* set one on either side of the sofa, the Alpine landscapes held up by spikes ending in gilded *paterae,* the oblong seascapes in heavy black frames, and, also in black frames, the miniatures flanking the console. Finally, through the door we see some of the bedroom furniture. This detailed décor forms an overwhelming frame for the little seated figure with a small red book in her hands. She is dressed in green and her chestnut hair is caught in a lace bonnet. Contrary to the 16th century portraits, where the surroundings were merely a generic background, this room is far more important than its occupant, who serves mainly to show that the room is meant for human habitation.

Sovereign-Father,/On this happy day of prospects fair,/To offer thee our hearts and further,/The profound love for thee we bear...." Arcadian sentiments among the artificial flowers and porcelains and furniture and knick-knacks (in which classicism is so diluted by the curved lines of bourgeois comfort),

190: D'Anna. *An Interior in the Palace of Capodimonte, Naples,* watercolor. N. SAPEGNO COLLECTION, ROME.

191: Raffaele D'Auria. *The Six Youngest Children of Francesco I,* 1831. MUSEO NAZIONALE DI SAN MARTINO, NAPLES.

Apparently the Palace of Capodimonte is also the setting for another *Interior* signed *"D'Anna dip"* on the base of the column at the left (*Fig.* 190). If it weren't for this signature, we would be tempted to attribute this watercolor to De Falco, for both artists show the same precise attention to the minutiae of the decoration. On the table, on the *étagère*, on the mantelpiece, on the *secrétaire*, the objects—many under glass bells—look almost like a collection of minerals. The curious pallet, with its coverlet gathered into knots at the corners, has a vaguely sinister look, like a bier. Here, too, there is an array of miniatures on the wall, and to the right of the fireplace a reproduction of Granet's painting, *Interior of the Church of the Capucins in Rome,* which we also noted in Queen Hortense's Paris drawing room. The decoration of the walls, a painted representation of drapery supported by lances, is still Empire, but

the decorative taste everywhere else is Biedermeier. If it weren't for the undeniable location of the room, established by the view of Vesuvius from the window, we might have imagined it in a German palace.

Biedermeier taste is again evident in the group of *The Six Youngest Children of Francesco I* painted by the Neapolitan Raffaele D'Auria in 1831. Francesco I actually had seven children by Maria Isabella of Spain but in this picture Antonio, Conte di Lecce, is missing. (Gino Doria, who explains that Antonio was fifteen in 1831 suggests that he may have been ill or abroad.) In the center of this group is the seventeen-year-old Maria Antonia, who two years later married Leopold of Tuscany. The plump little girl at the piano is the thirteen-year-old Maria Amalia, who the following year married Sebastian Gabriel, Infante of Spain. The second harpist is Maria Carolina, aged eleven, who married another

214

192: Carlo de Falco. *Portrait of Queen Maria Cristina.* ROYAL PALACE COLLECTION, CASERTA.

Spanish Infante, Francisco de Paula, but who died very young, in 1844. Next to her, the child with her feet on the stool, who has set down her embroidery to look towards us, is Teresa Cristina, who became Empress of Brazil in 1843. (The portrait reveals an extraordinary resemblance to her half-sister the Duchesse de Berry.) The boy with the sabre, at right, is Luigi, Conte d'Aquila, later chief of the Neapolitan Navy and husband of Maria Januaria, sister of Pedro II of Brazil. Finally, the little boy in *pantelettes,* whose left hand is on the mane of his hobby-horse, is Francesco di Paola, aged four, Conte di Trapani.[87] The symmetrical group, with the larger harp and the oldest daughter in the center and the smallest children at either end, is set against an equally symmetrical background: a pair of identically curtained windows, two paintings, and between them a clock under a glass bell. The taste of the age could not be

more precisely revealed!

The *Portrait of Queen Maria Cristina* by Carlo de Falco has characteristics similar to his portrait of Queen Isabella, (*Fig.* 189). Here, too, the Queen holds a book in her hand which, since she became a saint, we guess to be certainly a book of devotions. Among the decorative objects, the chandelier is the most conspicuous. Around the crystal globe was painted a Viennese landscape whose green tones gave the globe the appearance of a watermelon. It was bound by a hoop of mother-of-pearl with gilded applications and the little crystal dishes in which the candles are set were in the form of boats. They rested on *ormolu* arms, joined by festoons of ivory drops. It was an object which could be classified in that vast category of works in mother-of-pearl, *ormolu,* and micro-painting for which Vienna was famous during the Biedermeier period.[88]

193: Giuseppe Naudin. *Gold and White Room in the Palazzo Ducale at Parma,* watercolor, c. 1832. MUSEO GLAUCO LOMBARDI, PARMA.

At Marie-Louise's court in Parma Biedermeier was even more firmly established than in Naples. Imagine Marie-Louise against the background of "The Hundred Days" or of Saint Helena and she seems a goose in a covey of eagles. Set her by the death-bed of the King of Rome or next to a languishing, dying swan (for of the two winged symbols of the Empire, *l'Aiglon* reminds us more of a swan than an eaglet), and again she seems a goose. But if you set her among her embroidery and her paintbrushes, you recall the affectionate mother of Albertina and Guglielmo, the wife not of a dazzling hero like Napoleon, but of a fine, decaying officer like Neipperg (who, with that sad patch over his eye, does not have a head suitable for medals or cameos. Placed in her own personal world, she even can be seen as the wife of the honest chamberlain Bombelles. (Marie-Louise, like Maria Isabella of Naples, in her final marriage followed the footsteps of the Duchess of Malfi. One cannot see why the Duchess, immortalized by Bandello and Webster for marrying her chamberlain, should evoke our warmest understanding, if the wife of a Del Balzo or a Bombelles may not — unless it was the Duchess of Malfi's youth that makes her marriage seem more romantic. Thus, against her

Biedermeier background, even Marie-Louise acquires a respectable stature. In her Lilliputian surroundings (so vividly recalled by Marianna Prampolini[89]) Marie-Louise no longer arouses our indignation or our smiles. Hers was a doll's house court, and even physically there was something doll-like about Marie-Louise, her hands and feet were absurdly tiny). She was surrounded by her cross-stitching, chenille boxes, cases, slippers, cups, baskets and embroidery frames, samples of rugs, pom-poms, little bags, berets, writing paper with flowery letter-heads, and every kind of flower — natural ones in the gardens, cut ones in vases, painted ones in watercolors, embroidered in silk, cut in velvet, constructed from shells. If, we observe more closely these miniature human beings, these exquisite Lilliputians, overcoming our first impression of doll's house, and general china-like quality, we are surprised by the warm, often pathetic tone of their voices. This passage from a letter written to the Duchesse de Montebello by Marie-Louise in Vienna, November 1814, (at the beginning of her affair with Neipperg), has the tinkling sound of a toy music box: "I spend the rest of the time out riding or walking, or going into the city. We dine at seven, then play billiards. M. Meneval takes

194: Giuseppe Naudin. *Throne Room in the Palazzo Ducale at Parma,*
watercolor, c. 1832. MUSEO GLAUCO LOMBARDI, PARMA.

his ill-humor home, and Mme. Brignole and M.
Bausset play a game of piquet near my piano while I
make music with the General. I receive a few people
on Tuesdays and Saturdays, but it is already too
cold to have many people. The other days I see no one.
I shut my door when the General goes away."[90]
Other letters are full of passages in this same restful,
19th century tone. And when it comes to feminine
occupations! At times you would think that women
in those days did nothing but embroider letter-cases,
string beads on purses, and make slippers as presents
for their dear ones or acquaintances. But the Duchess,
from her clandestine union with Neipperg, also had
two children, Albertina and Guglielmo Montenovo,
and the correspondence between Marie-Louise and
Albertina shows us what tender, living flesh and
blood were concealed within the strange, glossy shell
of official life at that little court.

This life is admirably mirrored in the watercolors
of Giuseppe Naudin (1792–1872).[91] What surprises
us at first in these interiors is their relative nudity.
It is understandable that nothing must disturb
the purple solemnity of the *Throne Room in the
Palazzo Ducale at Parma,* so typically a throne room
that you would take it for a puppet-theatre set. That

there should not be a single picture on the pale blue
walls of the *Gold and White Room* or the *Red Room*
(*Fig.* 195) and that in the room shown in *Figure 7*
there should be on one wall a double row of prints
and on the other a single, isolated print, seems to
indicate a deliberate program of simplicity. This
simplicity is also characteristic of Biedermeier interiors
of the residences of German sovereigns. Marie-
Louise, as we have seen, was fond of embroidering,
of stringing beads, of painting, of all those arts
which ladies were taught in the 19th century and
which today seem so futile. These watercolors,
however, document only her interest in music, one
of the chief accomplishments of young ladies at that
time, who were instructed not only in instrumental
music but also in *bel canto,* which required a knowledge of Italian. In *The Red Room in the Palazzo
Ducale at Parma* (*Fig.* 195), we see a grand piano, a
typical Viennese instrument set on caryatid legs. In
the room shown in *Figure 7,* we see at the keyboard
the blond Albertina Montenovo, later Sanvitale
(the same blond woman who is sitting at the left
in the Red Room).

195: Giuseppe Naudin. *Red Room in the Palazzo Ducale at Parma,* watercolor, c. 1832. MUSEO GLAUCO LOMBARDI, PARMA.

196: D. A. Sequeira. *Family of Viscount di Santarém*, 1805-1810. MUSEO NACIONAL DE ARTE ANTIGUA, LISBON.

197: F. Schrank.
Family Portrait,
c. 1810.
WALLRAF-RICHARTZ
MUSEUM, COLOGNE.

198: Anonymous. *Drawing Room of the Palazzo Borromeo, Isola Bella,* watercolor, c. 1830. CONTE VITALIANO BORROMEO COLLECTION, ISOLA BELLA.

In Southern Europe, as we have seen, there was no lack of pictures reflecting daily domestic life or family joys, especially those provided by children at their favorite pastimes. It was in the North, however, that the sentiments of home and family received their most poetic expression. Compare the *Family of Viscount di Santarém* by the leading early 19th century Portuguese painter Domingos Antonio Sequeira with the *Family Portrait* by Franz Schrank (1747–1835), a Jesuit naturalist and draughtsman whose reputation as a painter is based only on this work which has the enchanting ingenuousness of a modern primitive). The Portuguese interior has nothing *gemütlich* about it. In a corner of the drawing room, living people are posing for a portrait while the people in the portrait over the fireplace are posing too. Two people are sitting stiffly at a circular table bearing a statuette of the sovereign. These men are the Viscount and probably his secretary, who have interrupted their work. If there is a certain nonchalance in the pose of the little boy at left (who acts as if he had been told to show his profile in order to bring some variety into the group), it is counteracted by the other children who hold hands in order to summon up their courage. They cluster close to their mother, who also seems to be striking a pose, and pretending to take a flower from a vase on the mantelpiece. The furniture is as stiff as the people: the columns of the large window and the fireplace are completely rigid, and the sofas along the wall are the kind that make you ache if you sit on them. In the German picture, things and people speak,

uttering a gentle elegy of bourgeois happiness. The window, with light muslin curtains drawn back to let the sun come in, must have been particularly dear to Northerners, to whom sunlight is so precious. The relaxed nursery atmosphere relegates the serious aspects of the decoration (the painting of Faith over the fireplace, the statue on the table to the right) to a secondary role. There is a wicker cradle and a baby's high chair, on which lies a rattle left by the little girl who sits on her mother's lap. Another girl is playing with a fruit-basket just in front of the teapot steaming on a little stove. The curly King Charles spaniel and the doll (who sits on a casually overturned chair) balance each other in the foreground and certainly seem more real and important than the allegorical painting of Faith, which is meant to indicate that such happiness is the deserved reward of a Christian family.

Expressions quite similar to Northern Biedermeier are found in those parts of Italy which were influenced by Austria. For instance, in the watercolor of the *Drawing Room of the Palazzo Borromeo, Isola Bella* (which today hangs in the very room it depicts), we find elements of the sentimental themes of the Biedermeier school of interior painting. The child playing on the floor, the dog curled on the chair, the man reading, the warmly crackling fire, all accentuate the *Gemütlichkeit* of the room. Even though it is aristocratic, this room is not very different from a bourgeois home. This is often true during the 19th century, when even the rooms of royal palaces, from Naples to Russia, were steeped in the bourgeois spirit.

199 (above): L.-P. Debucourt. *Interior of a Dining Room,* 1821. Etching after a painting by Martin Drolling.

The family dog, a kind of mascot of 19th century domestic bliss, appears again in the foreground of an etching which Louis-Philibert Debucourt (1755–1832) made after a painting by Martin Drolling: *Interior of a Dining Room.* This is a bourgeois interior with very little decorative pretension. Two antique vases are placed symmetrically to flank the door, which has a Medusa head plaque over it but, with several prints on the walls and a vase of flowers on the stove, the effect is not austere. The stove, a simulated classical column form with a capital, contrasts with the long pipe that crosses the ceiling, and brings to mind the locomotive which, later in the century, tries in vain to conceal its functional character behind a cloak of classical decoration. The man in slippers is breakfasting while the maidservant arranges crockery in a closet. Beyond the door, the lady of the house is playing the piano. This must be typical of any number of bourgeois interiors of the period, interiors which no other painter bothered to immortalize unless they could serve as background for a genre scene. Since in themselves they were of no interest, they were painted only to indicate the social condition of the people. Even Drolling's original painting is a genre scene, but it is also close to still life, for there is no action among the people. Set in banal, everyday reality they are only as important as the chairs placed against the wall or the flowers on the stove. This is not a family portrait, but merely typical bourgeois characters in bourgeois surroundings.

200: M.C.W. Rørbye. *View from the Artist's House at Amaliegade,* 1825. PRIVATE COLLECTION, COPENHAGEN.

201: Ida von Berstett. *Grandmother's Room,* watercolor, 1835. MARIO PRAZ COLLECTION, ROME.

202: Anonymous. *Bourgeois Interior,* watercolor, c. 1825. COOPER UNION MUSEUM, NEW YORK.

203a: Detail from *Family Tree* by Julius Oldach.　　　203b: Detail from *Family Tree* by Julius Oldach.

More pretentious is the *Bourgeois Interior* reproduced in an anonymous watercolor which can be
dated around 1825 by the dress of the two women.
We see Louis XVI furniture, a *toilette* and a fire-screen
in Empire style already translated into bourgeois
terms, two round Biedermeier tables, a *méridienne*
near the fireplace, the characteristic clock and vases
of artificial flowers under glass bells on the mantle-
piece and two commonplace rush-bottomed chairs.
On the little cover of the central table is the usual
collection of knick-knacks and on the commode is a
casket, probably containing a silver service. The panels
on the walls give the room a distinction that the
composite furnishing by itself would not provide.
The dog playing with its mistress' slipper adds a
note of domestic good-humor.

Unimportant families, if they did not allow themselves the luxury of summoning a painter, often
painted their own conversation pieces to remind their
grandchildren of the older generations. Thus, on the
little board backing the watercolor *Grandmother's
Room* is written (in German): "Room of my dear
Grandmother Amelie von Lilier, born von Esebeck,
painted by my dear Mama Ida von Berstett, born
von Lilier, in the year of her marriage in Munich, 1835.
On the sofa is seated my grandmother; my mother is
at the embroidery frame; and in the armchair is my
uncle Fritz von Esebeck, retired colonel of the Royal
French Army—Amelie von Holzing." In this room
even the rug seems home-made, a patchwork or
harlequin creation (although it is actually an Oriental
carpet of the geometric type). A figure in modern
Greek costume on a hand-embroidered sofa cushion
recalls the popularity of the Greek war of independence. The furniture is stiffly lined up along the walls
and includes the usual pieces: sofa, *secrétaire,* a low

cupboard surmounted by a mirror, a Muse on the
stove (as if to compensate for the ugly black pipe),
and the inevitable flowerpots on the windowsill.
Beyond the door, we see the *psyché* and a bit of the
muslin bed curtains.

The flowerpot in the window, that ever-present
accessory of Biedermeier domesticity, becomes a
dramatis persona in a picture entitled *View from the
Artist's House at Amaliegade* (*Fig.* 200), by the
Danish painter Martinus Christian Wesseltoft Rørbye
(1803–1848). The enchanting view of the port and the
ships is the voice of the outside world, of adventure,
of dreams, answered from the window by the domesticated flowers in the pots—hydrangeas, cactuses (one
protected by a glass tube)—and the tame bird in its
cage, the forever-stilled foot in the marble cast. The
view from the window is bounded below by a kind of
fence, and above by the fringe of the curtain, which
hints of a gentle prison with soft bars rather like the
two hands of a woman placed over your eyes. Perhaps
the painter only meant to paint a still life, but the
picture seems to signify a renunciation, tinged with
some regret, and a humble satisfaction in things that
are small and close at hand, the quiet happiness of
Biedermeier. This is why the picture is so poetic and
rich in meaning.

A painter from Hamburg, Julius Oldach (1804–
1830), has given us perhaps the fullest expression of
the Biedermeier spirit with the picture he painted on
the occasion of his parents' silver wedding anniversary. This *Family Tree* contains eleven portraits in
medallions. At the margins, above and below, are
various scenes of family life (eleven large and seven
small ones). The picture must be judged as a document
of customs rather than as a work of art, for it is
almost the equivalent of a souvenir photograph of a

204: Julius Oldach. *Family Tree,* 1828. KUNSTHALLE, HAMBURG.

high school class. Isabey, (as we have seen in *Figs.* 169–172) had already thought of depicting the hours of the day in a series of vignettes, but Oldach gives the family tree, with its fruit, its rhythm, the continuity of family life which is repeated every day like a dance of the hours. At the top, under the date February 17, 1803, is shown the wedding of his parents, and on either side a birth and a baptism. Then we see the painter working in his studio, the mother giving food to the children who are leaving for school, a visit to a sick woman, practice at the piano, children's games, business being transacted (in a shop where sacks are weighed), writing at the desk while the table is being laid, meetings and exchange of courtesies, the arrival of provisions, and finally, exactly corresponding to the scene of February 17, 1803 at the top, the anniversary feast at the bottom, with the date, February 17, 1828. Thus, as if in a magic circle, the life of a day is completed and corresponds with the cycle of twenty-five years, like the coordination of the hour hand and the tiny minute hand in a well-oiled watch. The domestic scenes pass before our eyes like the automatic figures of a clock-tower, those ingenious masterpieces of clockwork which in Nuremberg or Strasbourg or elsewhere enchant the crowds at noon. In his modest picture, Oldach has caught the law which unites the microcosm of man's life with the macrocosm of nature. He has unfolded before our eyes the humble daily round, governed by the sound of a carillon, muffled by the clock's glass bell, much as Schiller, in his famous *Lied von der Glocke* (1799) evoked, like the movements of a symphony, episodes of individual and social life which took place to the sound of the bell.

Oldach's picture interests us more for its message than for the details of furnishing that are glimpsed in the various scenes. The same sort of modest decoration is also found in a genre painting by Johann Baptist Pflug, known as Pflug von Biberach, after his native town (1785–1865). His painting *Baptismal Visit in the House of an Evangelical Pastor* illustrates the familiar muslin curtains, symmetrical arrangement of pictures, marble bust between two vases of flowers on the *secrétaire*, and a few chairs, still in 18th century style. A cradle in the foreground holds two hats, one of them similar to Napoleon's familiar head-covering. A grey cat crawls up the side of the cradle, as if after some delicacy. In this bourgeois setting, the hat seems to give the measure of the new age, which was anything but heroic.

205: J. B. Pflug. *Baptismal Visit in the House of an Evangelical Pastor*, 1828. STAATSGALERIE, STUTTGART.

206: A. Digerini. *Kitchen of the Palazzo Mozzi, Florence,* 1825. MARIO PRAZ COLLECTION, ROME.

The kitchens and little dining rooms of humble people have always been, even down to our own day, the most conservative among rooms. In them, the functional always prevails over the ornamental, and frequently one may even say that decoration does not really exist at all. Who has not seen in country kitchens before the last war those gleaming displays of copper utensils which can be discerned in the shadows of the *Kitchen of Palazzo Mozzi in Florence,* painted by a charming but otherwise unknown amateur, A. Digerini? The spacious hearth with the andirons and spit, the table with a still life of crockery and food near which the cook is preparing a stew, besieged by two cats on their hind legs, the china cupboard with the plates in neat array—these are things which, until yesterday, were timeless. But electrical appliances have transformed the dark, aromatic kitchen into a luminous and sterile laboratory. Beyond the open window, on whose sill there is a pot of red carnations. we see the silvery light of the Lungarno for the scene is the Piazza dei Mozzi, which faces north. There must not have been much noise in that corner of old Florence.

Today, interiors like those in the *House of French Peasants* (Normandy), and the *Evening Visit to the Betrothed* (*Der Kiltang,* a custom of the canton of Berne) by the Swiss painter Franz Niklaud König (1765-1832) can be seen only in folklore museums. All the utensils are in the open, clearly visible and a series of rustic natural still lifes cover the shelves. (In today's counterpart of such rooms, everything would be shut into cabinets.) The pets played on the floor, and the ticking of the grandfather clock marked the drowsy hours of a serene life.

208 (at right): F. N. König. *Evening Visit to the Betrothed,* colored aquatint. KUNSTMUSEUM, BERN

Humble rooms like the ones just discussed are difficult to date because they are seldom subject to shifts in taste and fashion, and even with regard to self-consciously decorated interiors it is sometimes hard to establish a date that is accurate even within a decade. Rooms with a coherent character, designed according to an over-all concept, are relatively few. We know them through designs such as those in the publications of Percier and Fontaine or Thomas Hope and through rooms which, because of their representative character, were retained unchanged by later generations. Normal rooms where people really live change gradually as new fashions lead the inhabitants to add this or that detail to an already existing decoration. In the 19th century owners rarely changed things completely from top to bottom, but often added piecemeal, as we will see in a series of Biedermeier rooms. These three types of rooms (pure design, preserved, and lived-in) can be seen in a comparison of three English rooms. Examine first the *Design for a Library*, a line drawing taken from P. F. Robinson's *Designs for Ornamental Villas*, 1827. Here everything is in harmony: the fireplace with classic amphorae, the statuary group on the neat bookcase, the classic decoration of the fireplace grate, the moulding of the mirror, the double fascia that frames the ceiling, the furniture. Such a project, if it was ever carried out, could not have retained the character it displays here, on paper, for more than a few years.

The *Interior of a New York House* was designed by the architect Arthur Jackson Davis (1803–1892). After youthful contact with Boston intellectual circles Davis was steeped in Classicism and designed some of the most impeccable Greek Rivival buildings in America (including Colonnade Row, 1832, a Corinthian colonnade which until a few years ago could still be admired near New York's Cooper Union, even though it had decayed considerably from its original splendor). In 1855 Davis introduced the Neo-Gothic castle to the picturesque Hudson Valley (often compared to the valley of the Rhine) when he constructed "Ericstan" for John J. Herrick at Tarrytown; and he also fostered the "Tuscan" style, a Renaissance imitation. This intelligent and precise experimenter was so gifted at absorbing the spirit of every style that, for example, the *Interior* which we reproduce here would probably have aroused the admiration of Thomas Hope. Hope's only objection might perhaps have been the eccentric position of the table in the first room, a position probably due to a desire to indicate the furnishings beyond the columns. The chairs are copied from those of the "Second room containing Greek vases" in Hope's *Household Furniture*, the table is a replica of the one Hope designed for Deepdene[92] and the sofa against the wall as well as the pole screen before the fireplace are both typical Regency pieces. This room, too, seems so cold in its impersonal Greekness that one can only imagine it in a club.

Dating from about 1840, a modest watercolor reproduces the *Drawing Room of Aldenham Park, Bridgnorth*, the ancestral home of the Acton family.

209 (above): P. F. Robinson. *Design for a Library*, line drawing, 1827. (From *Designs for Ornamental Villas*, 1827.)

210 (below): Drawing Room of Aldenham Park, Bridgnorth, watercolc c. 1840. E. SIOLI-LEGNANI COLLECTION, BUSSERO (MILAN).

The walls are divided by Tudor arches. We also see a Neoclassic ceiling, two Victory-candelabras remaining from a previous Regency décor, and the invasion of every kind of chair and table, a mixture typical of the later 19th century.

From a watercolor of the *Drawing Room at Field Place*, the house of Percy Bysshe Shelley's family, we can see what happens to normal lived-in rooms. An inscription on the back, written by Lady Shelley, wife of the poet's son Percy Florence, declares that the watercolor was painted in 1816 by Elizabeth Shelley, the poet's sister (1794–1831). The organ, the majority of the furnishings and the swags of the curtains at the windows are undoubtedly Regency. But what can we say about the two heavy armchairs protected by red and white striped *housses?* They are so similar to those of our own drawing rooms, these saddleback armchairs, that one wonders how Elizabeth Shelley, who died in 1831, could possibly have made this watercolor. In any case, its official date of 1816 is not very convincing. Those two chairs are probably among the first armchairs with springs, for springs were first used in the making of armchairs and sofas only in the 1830's.[93] After that, the shape of armchairs, sofas, divans became more corpulent and the military hardness of Empire seats was replaced by a comfortable softness which invited the body to assume positions previously not tolerated in society. The verb "to lounge" acquired its current meaning.

The apartment of a refined Englishman of the period, Thomas Griffiths Wainewright, (the hero of *Pen, Pencil and Poison*, by Oscar Wilde, who gave a *fin-de-siècle* interpretation to this historic figure of the artist-criminal) is described by J. Curling.[94] Wainewright's study was a large room, its floor covered by a Brussels carpet with garlands of flowers. At one end was the desk with a silver inkwell on it and among the other furnishings were a Tomkisson piano, a Grecian couch and a table laden with portfolios of prints. A Damascus sabre hung on one wall and on another was hung "a delicious, melting love-painting, by Fuseli." In one corner of the room there was "a fine *original* cast of the Venus de Medici." Some hothouse plants were lined up on a slab of white marble. On the shelves were books bound in old French morocco of rare quality. There was an elegantly gilded French lamp with a crystal globe painted with gay flowers and bright butterflies, and the chimney-piece was balanced by another large mirror on the opposite wall. Illuminated by that lamp, the room was steeped in a Correggio-like light. In the octagonal boudoir there was a Turkish ottoman, and at either side of the fireplace a *chiffonier* with a marble top. The crimson walls were partly hidden by a double row of prints gaily framed in rosewood or glossy oak. On the *chiffonier* was displayed Urbino majolica decorated with reproductions of Raphael paintings (especially a large plate with the *Marriage of Psyche and Cupid*), and other ceramics both *biscuit* and "green dragon." Foscolo's famous Digamma Cottage could never have achieved such refinement.

211 (above): Elizabeth Shelley. *Drawing Room at Field Place*, watercolor, 1816 (?). KEATS-SHELLEY MEMORIAL HOUSE, ROME.

212 (below): A. J. Davis. *Interior of a New York House*. NEW YORK HISTORICAL SOCIETY, NEW YORK.

The Brighton Pavilion was the supreme manifestation of the eclectic taste of the Regency period in England, which we have already seen documented in the Wainewright apartment. The Prince Regent, who had grown up in the shade of the Kew Gardens pagoda, soon became an enthusiast of that fashion for Chinese things which had been so prevalent all through the 18th century.[95] In 1790 the Prince commissioned the architect Henry Holland to create a Chinese drawing room in his London residence, Carlton House, and the result was a structure that had been inspired by classical canons camouflaged with exotic forms. As the work on Carlton House progressed, the Prince also commissioned Holland to transform his modest villa at Brighton. In 1802 a long gallery was built there to display a series of Chinese wallpapers and at the same time an exotic appearance was given the other rooms by introducing bamboo furniture and various Chinese accessories. Miss Mary Berry described it in her diary in 1811: "All is Chinese, quite overloaded with china of all sorts and of all possible forms, many beautiful in themselves but so overloaded one upon another, that the effect is more like an overflowing china shop than the abode of a Prince. All is gaudy without looking gay; and all is overcrowded with ornaments, without being magnificent." In 1803 Holland was succeeded as architect by William Porden, who designed a new pavilion entirely in the Chinese style. First of all, however, he built the stables, the riding-house, and the carriage-house in an Indian style, for he had become expert in this style when in collaboration with the architect Sir Charles Cockerell he designed Sezincote, the villa constructed in imitation of the buildings at Agra and Delhi. Shortly thereafter yet another artist appeared on the scene, one who had been even more profoundly concerned with Sezincote: Humphrey Repton. His opinion on the architectural style to be adopted for the new pavilion at Brighton is worth quoting, because it is a splendid illustration of the eclecticism of the period. He could not hesitate in agreeing that neither the Grecian nor the Gothic style could be made compatible with what had so much the character of Eastern building. "I therefore considered all the different styles of different countries from a conviction of the danger of attempting to invent anything entirely new. The Turkish was objectionable as being a corruption of the Grecian; the Moorish, as a bad model of the Gothic; the Egyptian was too unwieldy for the character of a villa; the Chinese too light and trifling for the exterior, however it may be applied to the interior; and the specimens from Ava were still more trifling and extravagant. Thus, if any known style were to be adopted, no alternative remained but to combine from the architecture of Hindûstan, such forms as might be rendered applicable to the purpose." Repton therefore presented a plan along these lines. The Prince found it perfect and ordered it carried out at once. Still financial difficulties ensued, and it was another architect, John

Nash who, to the great annoyance of Repton, began in 1815 the construction which we still see today: Hindu on the outside and Chinese on the inside. Completed in 1821, the Brighton Pavilion surpassed in splendor all the other exotic follies built in Europe, from the Haga Park pagoda in Scandinavia to the Casino della Favorita in Palermo. An almost sinister atmosphere was created, due to the abuse of the decorative motif of coiled serpents and dragons which wound around columns and furniture legs, or supported chandeliers like carnivorous plants.

A folio of drawings by the architect John Nash, *Views of the Royal Pavilion*, 1826, has preserved for us the image of these fabulous interiors which only in recent years have been restored to some semblance of their former splendor. Five solemn state rooms on the ground floor were joined by the long *Main Corridor* which is illuminated by a skylight painted with Chinese motifs. The walls were originally covered with Chinese paper with a pink ground and niches in it were occupied by Chinese statues. At either end a double ramp of stairs in cast-iron, simulating bamboo, led to the second floor, passing colored windows on which were represented Chinese figures in fluttering garments. In *The Banquet Room* the domed ceiling simulated the sky. It was partly covered by gigantic banana palm leaves from which

213: John Nash. *Main Corridor, Brighton Pavilion*, original decorative scheme, 1815. (From *Views of the Royal Pavilion*, 1826.)

214: John Nash. *Main Corridor, Brighton Pavilion*, final decorative scheme, 1822. (From *Views of the Royal Pavilion*, 1826.)

215: John Nash. *The Banquet Room, Brighton Pavilion*, 1822. (From *Views of the Royal Pavilion*, 1826.)

216: John Nash: *The Grand Saloon, Brighton Pavilion,* 1822. (From *Views of the Royal Pavilion,* 1826.)

hung a huge silver dragon, holding in his claws the chains of a vast chandelier composed of six smaller dragons, each supporting with its jaws a crystal cup in the form of a lotus flower. Four smaller chandeliers formed by dragons holding water-lilies (the chinese flower called *Lien-Hoa*) complemented the central chandelier, while on the walls large lamps of blue Spode porcelain mounted on dolphins and crowned with lotus flowers provided other sources of light.

After the Banquet Room, there came in a row the South Drawing Room, the Saloon, the North Drawing Room, and the Music Room. The two drawing rooms were relatively simple in appearance—the first with a pink ceiling and white walls crowned by a gilded Chinese fretwork design; the second with walls of a vivid yellow in a similar pattern, but lilac-colored, which provided a background for a series of Chinese paintings. *The Grand Saloon,* oval as in Holland's plan, was more ornate, with a magnificent gas chandelier (at that time a recent innovation), a cornice with bells, pilasters in the form of palm-trunks with serpents coiled around them, valances adorned with the usual dragon motif, enormous mirrors, and lacquered doors. Edward Brayley, the topographer, wrote enthusiastically of

217: John Nash. *The Music Room, Brighton Pavilion,* 1822. (From *Views of the Royal Pavilion,* 1826.)

The Music Room at the northern end of the Pavilion: "No verbal description, however elaborate, can convey to the mind or the imagination of the reader an appropriate idea of the magnificence of this apartment. Even the creative delineations of the pencil, combined with all the illusions of colour, would scarcely be adequate to such an undertaking. Yet luxuriously resplendent and costly as the adornments are, they are so intimately blended with the refinements of an elegant taste that everything appears in keeping and in harmony." From the domed ceiling hung nine gas chandeliers, rose-colored crystals in the water-lily and dragon motifs. The walls were decorated with Chinese landscapes in gold on a red ground, flanked by little pilasters coiled with serpents, and with blue panels on which a gilded fretwork pattern was set. Dragons belched flames menacingly near the paintings and other dragons held up the draperies. Between the windows were set important pagodas of Yung Chên porcelain echoed symmetrically across the room. It was here that George IV, accompanied by an orchestra of seventy musicians, entertained his guests after supper by singing in his baritone voice "Glorious Apollo" and "Mighty Conqueror." The floor was covered by an Axminster carpet, decorated with dragons, serpents, and large flowers on a blue ground.

218: John Nash. *Gallery of the Music Room, Brighton Pavilion,* 1821. (From *Views of the Royal Pavilion,* 1826.)

The other interiors of the Pavilion could not
compete in splendor with the state rooms, but none
was without its share of dragons, mandarins, exotic
birds, lotus flowers, water-lilies or serpents coiled
around columns. In the *Gallery of the Music Room* we
also notice little bells and banana palm leaves, the
leaves atop tall stem-like columns. This last theme
gives an even more astonishing aspect to *The Main
Kitchen* than it does to the other, richer rooms.
Robert Jones designed a large part of the furniture,
an exotic variety of Regency which, like the Pavilion
itself, has found its detractors as well as those who
sing its praises. Among the critics was William Hazlitt,

219: John Nash. *The Main Kitchen, Brighton Pavilion,* 1820. (From *Views of the Royal Pavilion,* 1826.)

who called the building "a collection of stone pump-
kins and pepper-boxes," while on the other side is
Osbert Sitwell, who went so far as to say that its
rooms really resembled the Oriental ones of the same
period, especially those in the palace of Hué, built
between 1790 and 1810 by the Emperor of Annam.[96]
The settings were quite different, however, for on
coming out of the palace of Hué, one was in the
midst of luxuriant, tropical nature, which continued
in living forms the artificial ones of the decorators,
whereas on coming out of the Brighton Pavilion one
saw only the pale gleam of the sea, shrouded from
time to time in fog.[97]

220: John Soane. *Dining Room and Library, 13, Lincolns Inn Fields.*
(From *The Residence of Sir John Soane,* 1835.)

Almost as startling as the Brighton Pavilion is another
English building decorated in the period of George IV:
the house and museum of the Neoclassical architect
Sir John Soane (1753–1837). An architect who
belonged to the innovating, revolutionary current of
Neoclassicism rather than to the academic school,
Sir John had some affinities with the bold French
architects of the 18th century, Ledoux and Boullée.
"In 1792," writes John Summerson, "when the style
arrived suddenly at maturity, there was not, anywhere
in Europe, an architecture as unconstrained by
classical loyalties, as free in the handling of proportion and as adventurous in structure and lighting as
that which Soane introduced at the Bank of England
in that year."[98] Between the end of the 18th and the
beginning of the 19th centuries Soane began to collect
the objects of art which he was later to arrange in his
museum, and at the same time (probably under the
influence of the theories of Payne Knight and Uvedale
Price concerning the picturesque) he introduced
picturesque effects in greater quantity into his
buildings. Illumination from above was one of the
most important of these effects. The arrangement of
Soane's House and Museum, a work of his last years,
expresses a certain ideal of archeological abundance,

21: John Soane. *The Painting Room, 13, Lincolns Inn Fields.*
(From *The Residence of Sir John Soane,* 1835.)

222: John Soane. *The Monk's Cell, 13, Lincolns Inn Fields.*
(From *The Residence of Sir John Soane*, 1835.)

an ideal already exemplified by Piranesi in his *Different Ways of Decorating Fireplaces*, 1769 (*Diverse maniere d'adornare i camini*) and by John Zoffany in pictures like *Charles Townley and His Friends in His Library* (1790) where the classical sculptures scattered in various parts of the house were assembled in the same room for the painting. Though Soane was rather unfortunate in his attempts at Gothic architecture, he greatly admired Gothic effects and tried to introduce some into his house. Speaking for example of the Breakfast Room, Soane says: "The views from this room into the Monument Court [a little court in the center of which Soane had erected an "Architectural Pasticcio," as he called it, formed of classical, Gothic, and even Indian fragments] and into the Museum, the mirrors in the ceiling, and the looking-glasses, combined with the variety of outline and general arrangement in the design and decoration of this limited space, present a succession of those fanciful effects which constitute the poetry of Architecture."[99] His virtuosity in uniting varied motifs can be seen in the combination of two semicircles and an arch-segment which divides the Dining Room from the Library. This tripartite arch recalls a section of the ceiling of Edward VII's chapel in Westminster Abbey.

The Sir John Soane Museum is the documentation of a taste and also of a failure. Soane had collected works of art to furnish his house, Pitzhanger Manor, which he had imagined as the ideal setting for the education of young architects, particularly of his sons, whom he meant to train for that career. But his sons were a disappointment to him, and in 1833 Soane, by a special act of Parliament, left his house and its contents to the nation, to become a public institution after his death. Since he had been unable to found a dynasty of architects, at least the Museum would enshrine his memory for posterity. The minute, loving description of his house and its treasures contains, in a sense, his spiritual testament and the expression of his pleasure in handsome furnishings, which he at times naïvely displayed, as in this passage on the *Dining Room and Library:* "The general effect of those rooms is admirable; they combine the characteristics of wealth and elegance, taste and comfort, with those especial riches which belong expressly to literature and art,—to the progressive proofs of human intellect and industry, given, from age to age, in those works which most decisively evince utility and power." Among the works in the Library was the Shakespeare that had once belonged to Garrick. In this room, as in the others of the house, there is no spot where the eye can light without finding a mass of things: books, statues, pictures, or objects, whose presence is multiplied by the round mirrors set here and there throughout the house. The eye cannot find repose from the windows, either, for the window of the Dining Room gives on the Monument Court, occupied by the "Architectural Pasticcio." The problem which Soane had to solve in making a Museum out of his house in Lincoln's Inn Fields was rather like the problem which faced Pietro da Cortona with the Piazza della Pace in Rome: to create space where there wasn't any. For this reason, in *The Painting Room*, Sir John arranged the paintings on movable panels which could be opened out like doors. "By this arrangement, the small space of thirteen feet eight inches in length, twelve feet four inches in breadth, and nineteen feet six inches in height, which are the actual dimensions of this room, is rendered capable of containing as many pictures as a gallery of the same height, twenty feet broad and forty-five feet long. Another advantage of this arrangement is, that the pictures may be seen under different angles of vision." The four ivory chairs had belonged to Tippoo Sahib, the Sultan of Mysore, whose territory fell under English domination in 1779. In this room there is Hogarth's *The Rake's Progress* series and the Nymph who can be seen in front of the window is a statue by R. Westmacott. *The Monk's Cell*, or *parlour* of Father Giovanni, whose statue stands on a chest of drawers in a niche opposite the fireplace, was decorated with fragments of architecture and religious sculpture meant to "impress the spectator with reverence for the Monk," while the Scriptural subjects on glass were "suited to the destination of the place, and increase its sombre character."

224: John Soane. *Gallery of the Belzoni Room, 13, Lincolns Inn Fields.*
(From *The Residence of Sir John Soane,* 1835.)

In the sepulchral chamber, the *Belzoni Room,* we see the sarcophagus that Giovanni Belzoni, an adventurer much talked about in England at the beginning of the century, had brought from Egypt and exhibited in the Egyptian Hall in Piccadilly.[100] Sir John Soane bought it for two thousand pounds. Like the *Monk's Cell,* this room, too, is so crammed with sculptures, vases, and fragments that its teeming appearance is extraordinarily Piranesian. In accordance with the principle of having a room's decoration follow its character, this room contains a death-mask of Parker the mutineer and a life-mask of Mrs. Siddons, one corner of her mouth a little distorted by the unpleasant sensation caused by the plaster's pressure. From the gallery under the cupola of the museum one can look down to see the sarcophagus. From this vantage point various other rooms can be seen as well. The play of arches, recesses, and depths among walls covered with a veritable eruption of carved stones follows the same principle which made Soane place mirrors here and there to multiply the views. Perhaps a psychoanalyst, more than a student of esthetics, could explain this obsession. In any case, these bizarre English constructions, the Brighton Pavilion and the Soane House-Museum, the first with its proliferation of serpents and dragons, the second with its profusion of carved stones scattered as in a cemetery, tend surely to make a sinister impression on the spirit of the visitor.[101]

223: John Soane. *The Belzoni Room and Sarcophagus, 13, Lincolns Inn Fields.*
(From *The Residence of Sir John Soane,* 1835.)

225: J. Kovatsch. *The Emperor Franz I in his Study in the Hofburg, Vienna.*
Etching, 1828, after a watercolor by J. S. Decker.

Not all monarchs were fond of posing, as George IV
was, against a background of exotic pomp. In fact, a
certain austerity was often the keynote, if not in the
courts, at least in the private rooms or studies of
royalty. Nothing could be more severe than the background of *The Emperor Franz I in His Study in
the Hofburg,* as we see it in an etching made by
Josef Kovatsch (1799–1839) from a watercolor by
Johann Stephan Decker (1784–1844).[102] The major
decoration is in the grain of the wood, lovely, silken
waves of polished mahogany surfaces. Everything else
seems as bald as the head of the Emperor, who is
seated at the table reading a report. Except for some
other papers, a clock and an inkwell, even the desk is
bare. More papers are on the draughtsman's table,
whose different grain is revealed by the etching and a
few books are on the shelf that runs under the cup-

226: G. F. Ziebland. *The Breakfast Room of Maximilian I,
Nymphenburg,* drawing, 1820. WITTELSBACH BIBLIOTHEK,
MUNICH.

227: Ludwig Schnell. *The Study of Friedrich Wilhelm III, in the Berlin Palace.*
Etching after a painting by L. Zielke. NATIONALBIBLIOTHEK, VIENNA.

board. If it weren't for the caged bird—as pensive as
the Emperor—and two potted plants in the window,
nature would be completely excluded from this rigidly
bureaucratic atmosphere.

Also very simple is *The Breakfast Room of Maximilian I, Nymphenburg,* (or Dressing Room), by Georg
Friedrich Ziebland (1800–1873), who also made a
watercolor showing the table laid for breakfast and
a caged bird on a little table by the window. In the
watercolor the walls are decorated at top and bottom
by a frieze of leaves and flowers, whereas the line
drawing expresses only the stereometric consistency
of the decoration, revealing its purely functional nature.
Two top hats, sketched lightly on the chest of drawers
in the foreground, are the only traces of any
human presence.

*The Study of Friedrich Wilhelm III in the Berlin
Palace,* as it is presented in an etching by Ludwig
Schnell (1790–1834) from a painting by Leopold Zielke
(d. 1861), looks like a drawing room. The desk is
overwhelmed by Raphael's large *Sistine Madonna,*
and the waste-paper basket is actually in the form of
a vase. On the right wall there is a monumental stove
crowned by a cup, and a statue on a massive pedestal
between two torchères is reflected in a mirror on the
wall behind it. It is matched by another mirror on the
opposite wall, between the windows, in front of which
is placed an antique amphora holding a blooming
lily. The amphora is on a tiered pedestal which also
includes two smaller vases at its corners. The inevitable
glass-cased clock is found between two candelabra of
female forms to complete the room's solemn décor.

228: Lavr Plachov. *The Study of Alexander I, Winter Palace, Leningrad,* 1830.
RUSSKIJ MUSEJ, LENINGRAD.

The Study of Alexander I, Winter Palace, Leningrad, painted in 1830 by Lavr Plachov (1811–1881), also presents a solemn interior. The floor space is completely occupied by tables covered with green cloth and by mahogany furniture placed against grey walls. Above the tall mirrors of the two corner chimney-pieces there are helmeted heads and symmetry demands that each mantelpiece have a clock. There are no paintings on the walls, but the upper part of the room, in contrast with the static quality of the lower, unfolds in the classical frieze. On the curved ceiling we also see a crowd of moving figures

229: Metternich's Study in the Foreign Ministry. Lithograph after a watercolor by Franz Heinrich. HISTORISCHES MUSEUM DER STADT WIEN, VIENNA.

in black, green, and red, with gilded ornaments. These decorations, of course, were inspired by Greek vase painting. From the ceiling hangs a porcelain lamp.[103] Similarly *Metternich's Study in the Foreign Ministry,* a lithograph reproduced from a watercolor by that noted interior painter, Franz Heinrich (1802–1890),

also resembles a drawing room. The frieze that separates the walls from the ceiling is inspired by the Temple of Antoninus and Faustina and lends a classical air to this otherwise Biedermeier room. It is furnished with varied pieces (note particularly the pot-bellied armchair in the foreground).

In the years 1824-26, the architect Karl Friedrich
Schinkel (1784-1841) was commissioned to renovate
an apartment in the northeastern wing of the Berlin
Palace (*Berliner Schloss*) to be inhabited by the
Crown Prince, later King Friedrich Wilhelm IV
(1795-1861). (The castle itself was destroyed during
World War II.) In this wing were also a late-Gothic
chapel (Erasmuskapelle) and the former writing-room
of Friedrich II, now assigned to be the Crown Prince's
study. From the architectural point of view, Schinkel
left these two rooms untouched. In the 18th century,
the chapel had been divided at the level of the
upper floor by inserting a floor which cut the room's
height in half. This upper part, including the vaults,
Schinkel planned as the Crown Prince's Study,
whereas the corner room with its turret became
Princess Elizabeth's Drawing Room and the rooms
overlooking the Schlossplatz were transformed into a
series of receiving rooms: the Tea Room, the Dining
Room, and the Starred Room (so-called from its
ceiling decorated with stars). In 1817 Schinkel had
executed a Neo-Gothic interior in the palace of Prince
Friedrich, the so-called *Arms Room (Rustkammer)*,
whose appearance is recorded in a painting by Karl
Ferdinand Zimmermann (1796-1820).[104] In this room
the multi-colored glass window, pieced together from
antique glasses, was not situated in the outside wall,
but in a partition, so that in the evening the window,
illuminated by concealed lamps, gave the room a very
romantic light. The suits of armor, the ancient
weapons, the medieval pictures (a partial copy of
Stefan Lochner's polyptych in the Cologne Cathedral
is over the fireplace), the half-figure of Joan of Arc,
the chest decorated with Gothic motifs standing
between two scalloped tapestry chairs, the fireplace,
also decorated with an ogival tracery, the screen with
ogives and pinnacles,—everything behind the two
figures of the Prince and his young wife contributes
to creating an atmosphere that might have enchanted
the readers of Sir Walter Scott. And yet what Schinkel
created here, as Johannes Sievers rightly observes, is an
interpretation of Gothic by an artist of Neoclassic taste
and background.[105] In the case of the Prince's Study,

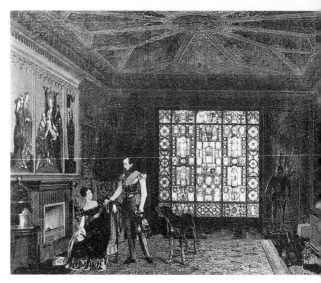

230: K. F. Zimmermann. *Arms Room of Crown Prince Friedrich,
Berlin Palace,* 1817. BURG RHEINSTEIN.

231: J. H. Hintze. *Study of Crown Prince Friedrich, Berlin Palace,* watercolor, 1839. Formerl
in the SCHLOSSBIBLIOTHEK, BERLIN

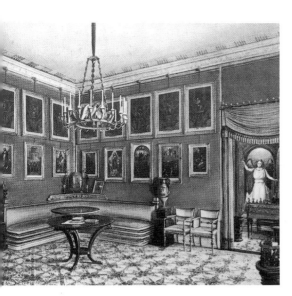

232: E. Biermann. *Sitting Room of Princess Augusta
in the Palace of Prince Wilhelm, Berlin,*
watercolor, 1829. SANSSOUCI, POTSDAM.

as we have pointed out. Schinkel found the Gothic
room ready made. Even so, the decoration he
designed had only a vague and discreet Gothic air.
He designed cupboards with dentilated moulding,
also a torchère with a dentilated top the rest of which
was pure Empire. The rest of the room was furnished
even more simply, almost functionally, as can be seen
from a watercolor, *Study of Crown Prince Friedrich* by
Johann Heinrich Hintze (1800–c.1862).[106] A screen
of little arches, rounded rather than ogival, separated
the study proper from the former apse of the chapel.
In front of the screen were two little cupboards with
ornaments of gilded tin on a red ground which contained the Prince's coin collection. A long, low
cupboard of the same kind ran along the north wall.
The cubical cabinet, of the kind used for storing
drawings and engravings, with an extension that
served as a writing-table, was of pale oak (veneer over
pine). Without even the modest Gothic type ornamentation such as the cupboards had, the cabinet
was a completely functional piece. In the armchairs
and straight chairs (made by the cabinet-maker
Voigt in 1825; like the rest of the furniture Gothic

elements were strongly emphasized) their upholstery
was embroidered with coats-of-arms of a Romantic,
chivalric nature. Nonetheless, even these armchairs
betray their Neoclassic origins in the lions'-paw feet,
although the arms are supported not by sphinxes or
winged lions, but by little lanceolate arches arranged
fanwise around a central rosette. An open Gothic
quatrefoil decorated the chairbacks (made of mahogany
in this case), some of which had arms similar to those
of Neoclassic stools.[107] A designer of Neoclassical
furniture, Schinkel evidently dealt reluctantly with
Gothic, and by reducing the decorative elements to a
minimum, he achieved a functional furniture surprisingly modern in taste. Large and small pictures
occupied the spaces on the walls, while on the tops of
the low cupboards there was the usual profusion of
busts, statuettes, and little knick-knacks and porcelains,
the array so dear to Biedermeier taste.

   The corner room with the turret, intended as the
Drawing Room of Princess Elizabeth (*Fig.* 22) had a
bare, vaulted ceiling and green walls. In Biermann's
watercolor we see a drapery with three swags, very
prominent, but not so complicated as others conceived at that period (there are some very complicated
ones designed by Danhauser, whose drawings are
preserved in the Öesterreichisches Museum für
angewandte Kunst, Vienna), which unified in a bracket-
like fashion the entrance of the turret with the two
windows at either end of the wall. The other object
which draws the eye is in front of the window at
right: a bird cage which also served as flowerstand,
a multiple piece linking fauna and flora which came
into fashion with the Empire and was much admired
with Biedermeier.[108] From the flowerstand fall two
festoons of greenery which almost form an arbor.
(We shall have more to say later about such use of
vegetation in decorating rooms.) Among the pictures
that cover the walls we see some Raphael copies: the
Sistine Madonna, the *Madonna del Gran Duca,* and,
reflected in one of the mirrors that cover the faces of
the dividing walls of the turret, the *Deposition* from
the Borghese Gallery. Writing-table, tea-table, as
well as the *étagère* in the corner to the right, are laden
with objects. Next to the writing-table and the
classical divan designed by Schinkel, we see two
curious statues which are actually set on the floor. If
they had a practical purpose, we do not know it for
although such objects were generally used as door-
stops, their position here in the center of the room
would exclude this possibility.

233: Anonymous. *The Tea Room in the Berlin Palace*, watercolor. SANSSOUCI, POTSDAM.

The *Tea Room* whose appearance has been preserved in a watercolor by an unknown artist, had on its walls a series of *tondi* of Pompeiian inspiration, set in white and gold squares. On the ceiling, the image on an ancient *velarium* opened out. Below ran a frieze of Classical sculptures, the work of Friedrich Tieck (1776–1851). These statues were set on a mahogany dado which went around the lower part of the walls and also served as a shelf for the exhibition of little bronzes, amphorae, and so on. The dado was broken by a splendid fireplace of marble carved with candelabra and garlands, and was also partially hidden by a heavy, gilded sofa crowned with white vases and two large *paterae* one at each end, recalling the decorations of Percier and Fontaine. The sofa was backed by plants, almost as if to suggest the natural surroundings of the gardens where the marble *exedrae,* the forebears of this piece, were set.[109] This

monumental sofa disappeared long before the
destruction of the Berlin Palace. About sixty or
seventy years ago, when the taste for Empire had not
yet been revived, the sofa was removed, considered
a reminder of past bad taste. For that matter the
Crown Prince himself, in a letter to his wife in 1826,
called it a "semicircular monster." The smaller sofas
with their low, curled backs and the turned legs like
the bronze legs of Roman beds, were also inspired by

antiquity, but naturally they were made not for
reclining but for sitting (and quite uncomfortably at
that!). A large chandelier, with tendrils, palmettos
and other ormolu ornaments, crystal drops and
medallions, illuminated this room with its very
Alexandrine classicism, a style which was later to be
popularized by the simpering paintings of Lord
Leighton. This was a somewhat methodical classicism,
that of a German professor.

234: K. F. Schinkel. *Project for a Raphael Room,*
New Pavilion at Charlottenburg.

For Prince Wilhelm, who was later to become
Kaiser Wilhelm I (1797–1888), Schinkel prepared in
1829 a Palace on Unter den Linden, where since 1818
the high command of the Third Army had been
located. A watercolor by an unknown painter depicts
The Sitting Room of Princess Augusta (Fig. 232), also
known as the *Blue Room.* Behind it we see the adjoining
little green room, the "Celestial Room," which was
used as a writing room, guarded by a large angel,
The Angel who Opens the Gate of Heaven by Eduard
Steinbrück. This alcove of the writing room was
separated from the rest of the room by two columns.
(Between them and the wall were set *Zimmerlauben,*
which we shall discuss later.) An enormous divan,
its base pleated like an accordion (the work of the
cabinet-maker Karl Wanschaff), flanked by two large
Berlin vases decorated with miniature landscapes,
occupies one corner of the Sitting Room. Since the
blue wall is crammed with copper etchings of paintings
by Raphael and Titian and of frescoes by Michelangelo, we see very little of it. The design of the
chandelier, surmounted by eagles, and that of the
gallery writing-table in the rear room were also by
Schinkel. In the right corner, in the foreground, we
see part of another gallery writing-table.

In Schinkel's *Project for a Raphael Room, New Pavilion
at Charlottenburg,* there is also something methodical,
almost catalogue-like, in the arrangement of pictures.
This Pavilion, according to the wishes of Friedrich III,
was to be a replica of the Royal Villa of Chiatamone
on the bay of Naples, where the King had lived in
1822.[110] In the Raphael Room, the rectangles of the
prints in their thin frames, hung here horizontally
and there vertically, create a rhythm on the walls
which is amplified in the sections of the long divan
on the left wall, while on the right wall that rhythm
finds its counterpart in two elegant chairs of a sober
classical model, their backs without ornament for
greater comfort. The corner fireplace, surmounted by a
bust between two vases, is also joined with the room's

rhythm, reflecting in its mirror the neat order of the
prints on the walls.

Schinkel's last large commission was to prepare
the palace of Prince Albert, fourth son of Friedrich
Wilhelm III, who in 1830 married Princess Marianne
of the Low Countries, daughter of King William I.
For this purpose, Schinkel renovated a palace on
Berlin's Wilhelmstrasse. The Princess' apartments
were on the ground floor, facing the garden. In
a watercolor *Princess Marianne's Sitting and Work
Room* is shown from the southwest side. Below
the cadenced symmetrical draping of the curtains,
the play between the windows on the garden and the
mirrors creates the unusual and somewhat disturbing
impression of an open space. A striking feature is
the fence-like partition which separates one corner
from the rest of the room. This decorative accessory
was called the *Zimmerlaube* (room-arbor), a fashion
of the Biedermeier period which was employed by
Schinkel in all the apartments which he designed for
feminine royalty. The *Zimmerlaube* consisted of a
row of poles or lances (generally of alder wood,
stained dark and polished) set in a green tin flower-box
base from which ivy or other trailing plants grew,
their tendrils curling around the poles. Generally these
domestic arbors were placed in front of the window
or windows, but if the room had two central columns—
as often happened at that time—the arbors were
set in the spaces between the columns and the side-
walls. In this way a smaller apartment was created
inside the larger, a fanciful corner where the lady of the
house could write. It formed a bower in both senses
of the word (apartment and arbor). As Shelley wrote in
To a Skylark, "Like a high-born maiden / In a palace
tower / Soothing her love-laden / Soul in secret hour
With music sweet as love, which overflows her bower"
so also the *Zimmerlaube*[110a] was a part of the romantic
aura then surrounding woman, who was considered an
angelic creature. It is interesting to note that the
Biedermeier period, more than any other, was im-

235: Princess Marianne's Sitting and
Work Room in Prince Albert's Palace in Berlin,
watercolor. Formerly SCHLOSS KAMENZ COLLECTION.

moderately partial to the figure of the angel—that
impossible being which, as J. B. S. Haldane observed,
would have required an enormous pectoral development on which to base the propellent muscles of its
wings. The *Zimmerlaube* was also part of the age's
paradoxical attitude which first shut out the external
world by means of protective hangings, and then
introduced a domesticated Nature in pots and vases.
The other furnishings of the room, also designed by
Schinkel, include a mahogany sofa, its back decorated
with a massive lyre, and a *guéridon* of carved and
gilded wood with a malachite top.

While the interiors conceived by Schinkel managed
to retain a Neoclassic character despite the introduction of Gothic elements, that character was
gradually lost in the kind of decoration that became
stabilized in the Biedermeier period when, in addition
to the Neoclassic influences, there were also numerous
Gothic and Rococo ones.[111] The Gothic fashion, as
we have seen, began in 18th century England, gained
enormous impetus from the novels and the example of
Walter Scott, who furnished his home, Abbotsford,
with a Gothic manor in mind. Goethe, in a conversation with Eckermann in 1827, spoke out against the
taste for decorating a room in that style: "I cannot
approve one's surrounding oneself with an atmosphere
so alien and antiquated. It is always a kind of masquerade, which in the long run can do no good, but
indeed must have a harmful effect on him who becomes
involved in it. Since there is an element in contrast
with the daily life in which we are placed, and since it
proceeds from a vain and hollow way of thinking,
so in such a room it is merely corroborated." What
the escape into the past and the remote meant in
that first phase of the industrial civilization has been
said by Benjamin (see Introduction). While in architecture the Neo-Gothic was a stillborn style, in interior
decoration, where there was a wider margin for
caprice and combination with other styles, Neo-Gothic

lent an unusual flavor, giving a room's atmosphere
a literary, dream-like character. At times the atmosphere became rather sinister, as was admirably caught
by Poe when he put his grotesque tales in such a
setting. The spirit in which the Gothic style was
approached is well expressed by John Ruskin.
Intoxicated by words which seemed magic to him,
words like "vault," "arch," "spire," "pinnacle,"
"battlement," "barbican," words which seemed
"everlastingly poetical and powerful whenever they
occur," Ruskin asked himself "try to remove from
Scott's romances the word and the idea turret...
suppose, for instance, when young Osbaldistone (in
Rob Roy) in leaving Osbaldistone Hall, instead of
saying 'The old clock struck two from a *turret* adjoining
my bedchamber,' he had said, 'The old clock struck
two from the landing at the top of the stairs,' what
would become of the passage?"

Steeped in poetic and also religious associations
(Gothic was the architecture *par excellence* of the
Faith), endowed with the supreme appeal of the
picturesque (Uvedale Price had spoken of the "splendid
confusion" of Gothic), this taste finally gave interiors
a crowded, padded character, teeming with objects
like a votive chapel, which we shall find again and again
in the following illustrations. The taste was far from
pure, since the tendency was to develop ornamentation
at the expense of the functional nature of the objects,
literally causing them to become unrecognizable
under an abundance of decoration. In the second half
of the 19th century, decoration itself finally lost all
stylistic dignity. This fiendish concept of ornamentation
not only manifested itself in supposed objects of art
but proliferated, mushroom-like, to camouflage
even industrial structures and machines, resulting in
railroad stations with exteriors like medieval fortresses
or Flemish city halls, in turreted bridges following
the dictates of the best "castellated style" (the Tower
Bridge of London is typical) or in covered markets
in the form of Gothic basilicas.

236: J. H. Kretzschmer. *Ernest Augustus of Hanover's Study, Royal Palace, Leinestrasse,* watercolor. SANSSOUCI, POTSDAM.

While silk hangings and gilded wall decorations continued to be used in rooms designed for receptions, from the beginning of the century on wallpapers appear prominently in bedrooms. First, these papers were of a single color (usually blue, green, or flesh-colored, but also chamois-colored, as in the *Yellow Room in the Palace of Friedrich Wilhelm III (Fig. 2)*). Next was added a border of naturalistic floral patterns, as in the *Drawing Room of Prince Wilhelm of Prussia in the Berlin Palace (Fig. 1)*. From about 1830–1840 taste tended toward floral wallpaper or wallpaper with Renaissance or Moorish designs, as in *Ernest Augustus of Hanover's Study, Royal Palace, Leinestrasse*, shown in a watercolor by Johann Hermann Kretschmer (1811–1890). In this study we note the Persian area rug placed over an Axminster carpet of Neo-Rococo pattern, the upholstered chair, and the series of prints in Neo-Rococo frames (mostly portraits) on the walls. The aged sovereign, veteran of the wars fought against the French when he was Duke of Cumberland, is seated, wearing his old uniform of the Hussars of the Guard.

Although in the late 18th century light curtains of calico or muslin were the rule (as we have seen in Kersting's interiors), during the Empire period heavier, colored materials came into fashion. With these the art of the draper could be indulged, following the countless suggestions of La Mésangère, until in the Biedermeier period windows were dressed with an arrangement of drapings and folds that corresponded to those of women's dresses. Already in 1816, on the subject of decorating princely rooms, Goethe remarked that a certain height between windows and ceiling was necessary because, for some time, there had been a great display of draping in the curtains and these covered a part of the tall windows.

Curtains were such a prominent element in decoration that it isn't surprising that Nathaniel Hawthorne should give them a symbolic significance, so that, in *The House of the Seven Gables*, the elimination of the curse which weighed on the old house and which operated from the beginning of the book solemnly takes place in a room where "the sunshine came freely into all the uncurtained windows. . . ." In *The Birthmark*, the apartment where Aylmer shuts up Georgiana to subject her to subtle, impalpable influences which are to eliminate the crimson mark on her face, had walls "hung with gorgeous curtains, which imparted the combination of grandeur and grace that no other species of adornment can achieve; and as they fell from the ceiling to the floor, their rich and ponderous folds, concealing all angles and straight lines, shut in the scene from infinite space."[113]

The high, tile stoves designed after classical models were first colored (the handsomest were made by the firm of Feilner in Berlin); then after about 1830 the completely white stove came into fashion, like the one we see in the study of King Ernest Augustus.

237: F. W. Klose. *Dining Room in the Palace of Friedrich Wilhelm III in Berlin,* watercolor.
CHARLOTTENBURG PALACE, BERLIN.

We have already seen a Raphael Room in the New Pavilion at Charlottenburg, and in the *Yellow Room in the Palace of Friedrich Wilhelm III in Berlin* (*Fig.* 2), we see the walls literally covered with copies, large and small, of Raphael's paintings (in addition to a row of plants by the windows and a row of parrots' cages balancing them, the domestic epitomes of the animal and vegetable worlds). In the *Dining Room in the Palace of Friedrich Wilhelm III*, a watercolor by F. W. Klose, we see no Raphaels: the walls are rather decorated with landscapes and history paintings. But in the *Writing Room in the Palace of Friedrich Wilhelm*

III in Berlin (*Fig.* 21), we find a colossal *Sistine Madonna* on the right wall near the window. Another *Sistine Madonna* and a *Madonna of the Chair* can be seen in the *Green Room in the Berlin Palace* (*Fig.* 239), a watercolor by Eduard Gärtner (1801–1877). All this illustrates the German fashion beginning from about 1820 of decorating princely apartments with Italian religious paintings, especially copies of Raphael. This corresponded not only to an aesthetic ideal, but also to a religious one, since religiosity was then very widespread in court circles. In the *Green Room* the ceiling is painted to imitate a

238: F. W. Klose. *Queen Elizabeth of Prussia's Apartments, in the Charlottenburg Palace,* watercolor.
CHARLOTTENBURG PALACE, BERLIN.

bird-net, a Pompeiian motif that we have already encountered on bed canopies, and we also note the large exedral divan and some chairs in mid-19th century style. After Gärtner settled in Berlin in 1827, he became the chronicler (indeed the Canaletto as they called him) of the monuments of the city, though he was more influenced by the German Krüger than by the Venetian master. He was also in Russia from 1837 to 1839. We see two of his views of the Berlin Palace and its courtyard on the right-hand wall of the *Blue Room in the Palace at Potsdam (Fig. 25),* where the view on the back wall over the piano is

Wilhelm Brücke's *Arsenal and Guard House in Berlin in 1828.* Note the meticulous symmetry with which the pictures are hung on the walls of this room, whose ceiling retains the 18th century decoration applied during a restoration in 1745–51. In *The Etruscan Room in the Palace at Potsdam (Fig.* 240) by F. W. Klose, we see Greek vases and Greek decorations and vase paintings. (We have already indicated the confused nomenclature adopted by the cult of Classical Antiquity, so that what was really Greek was called Etruscan, and what was Pompeiian was attributed to Herculaneum.) In the Neoclassical period the Etruscan

239: E. Gärtner. *Green Room in the Berlin Palace,* watercolor, 1852. CHARLOTTENBURG PALACE, BERLIN.

Room was the equivalent of the 18th century's Chinese Room. Note the upholstery of the sofa and chairs, black friezes on a terracotta ground, an obvious idea which in modern times has also occurred to the person who chose the appropriate binding for the volumes of the Oxford Classics.

Another *Sistine Madonna* hangs on the wall in *Queen Elizabeth of Prussia's Apartments in the Charlottenburg Palace,* seen in a watercolor by Klose (*Fig.* 238). The little copy of Raphael's painting is glimpsed through the right-hand door. The decoration of these two rooms, where Queen Elizabeth of Prussia came to live shortly after the coronation of Friedrich Wilhelm IV in 1840, is in Neo-Rococo style, in con-

formity with the authentic Rococo character of the palace which had been enlarged in 1741–42 by G. V. Knobelsdorff, the same architect who remodeled the palace in Potsdam. Note, however, that the bookcase to the left employs Rococo ornament applied to a pinnacled Gothic structure, and that the swag of the curtain in the rear window also follows a scalloped pattern generally associated with Gothic-inspired décors. Around 1864 Elizabeth Pochhammer (active 1864–1880) made a tempera of the same interior. Various details of the decoration are changed: for example, in the center of the dividing wall there are Chinese vases in front of the console and a flowered carpet covers the floor of both rooms.

240 (opposite page, top): F.W. Klose, *Etruscan Room in the Palace at Potsdam,* watercolor, c. 1840. CHARLOTTENBURG PALACE, BERLIN

241 (opposite page, bottom): Elizabeth Pochhammer. *Queen Elizabeth of Prussia's Apartments in the Charlottenburg Palace,* 1864. COOPER UNION MUSEUM, NEW YORK

242: F. X. Nachtmann. *Queen Theresa of Bavaria's Study, Munich Residenz,* watercolor. SANSSOUCI, POTSDAM.

The confusion of styles which we observe in Queen Elizabeth of Prussia's apartment in Charlottenburg Palace is a phenomenon which became accentuated only after 1830. In the early 19th century the decoration of German palaces was dominated by the Empire style imported from France. Already in 1803 the room of Queen Luise in the Kronprinzenpalais in Berlin was decorated by local artists who drew their inspiration from Percier and Fontaine. From a water-color by Klose[114] we know how influential this Empire importation was, for Klose painted a room hung with blue and white draperies; in the back, separated from the rest of the room by two Ionic columns, the bed is on a raised platform. Before it is a perfume-brazier, while lined up along the right wall are an *athénienne,* a white stove surmounted by a vase, and a divan draped in "antique" style. The ceiling, adorned with stuccoes on a blue ground, has in its center a circle with a recurrent cornucopia pattern, following a geometric scheme similar to those of Aubusson or Savonnerie carpets. The apartments of the Palace at

Potsdam, decorated by Ludwig Friedrich Catel, are also inspired by French models. Empire style spread more rapidly, as is only natural, in the Rhine countries, in the courts of Napoleon's relatives which were directly under French influence. Jacob Desmalter himself supervised the furnishing of the various apartments in the Palace at Mainz. King Jerome of Westphalia engaged a French architect, Grandjean de Montigny, as well as local architects and the Hanoverian Leo von Klenze, who later became the architect of Ludwig I of Bavaria. Some furniture was produced by local cabinet-makers, but much was imported as in the Rote Palais in Cassel (destroyed in the last war) which King Wilhelm II had furnished in Empire style between 1821 and 1826. The architect Thouret furnished the Stuttgart Residenz and the castles of Ludwigsburg and Hohenheim in this style. Empire state apartments were commissioned by the Grand Duke Ferdinando of Tuscany from the architect Salins de Montfort for the Würzburg Residenz. The Empire furniture made in Germany

243: F. X. Nachtmann. *Elizabeth of Bavaria's Bed Chamber, Munich Residenz,* watercolor, c. 1840. SANSSOUCI, POTSDAM.

was distinct from the French, for it echoed Louis XVI and English motifs. The latter were especially predominant in Hanover, because of its connections with the English Court, and in Berlin until the advent of Schinkel who, as we have seen, developed a style of his own. In Munich the arbiter in questions of decoration became Klenze, who designed the furniture for royal and aristocratic palaces. Klenze's white and gold furniture belongs to a standardized Empire style for palace use, and was not very attractive, as can be seen from the documentation that remains of his decorations (1826–1835) of the Munich Residenz (destroyed in the last war). One example of this can be seen in the watercolor by Franz Xaver Nachtmann (1799–1846) of *Queen Theresa of Bavaria's Study, Munich Residenz.* Klenze introduced a certain rounding of line (the curved chair backs which roll at the top) which tempers the rigidity of the Empire style and brings it closer to Biedermeier. The decoration of the walls and ceiling in Queen Theresa's Study is inspired by Raphael's Loggias, but the paintings

illustrate poems by Schiller. (The King's rooms were decorated with frescoes inspired by Greek poetry, the Queen's with frescoes inspired by German poetry.) Also collaborating on this decoration were Ludwig von Schwanthaler, H. Hess, Schnorr von Carolsfeld, Rockl, Georg Hiltensperger, W. Kaulback, and others.

It is believed that another watercolor by Franz Xaver Nachtmann illustrates *Elizabeth of Bavaria's Bedchamber, Munich Residenz.* The Princess Elizabeth ,of Bavaria (1801–1873), who married Friedrich Wilhelm IV of Prussia, was the sister-in-law of Queen Theresa, whose study we have just examined. This Bedchamber is typically Biedermeier, the ceiling decorated by a geometric border in the Moorish style, its wallpaper using Oriental motifs and bordered with a panel of naturalistic foliage on a red ground. The rug is also in Oriental style. Next to the bed stands a table with an eccentric leg, the kind that was used for sick people. The furniture is very simple, and the pictures are for the most part prints. The divan with cornucopia arms dates from about 1830.

244: Anonymous. *Bed Chamber with Blue Walls, Tegernsee Castle,* watercolor. SANSSOUCI, POTSDAM.

Princess Elizabeth's real home was the little castle on the Tegernsee, whose interiors are illustrated in some enchanting views, like that of the *Bedchamber with Blue Walls, Tegernsee* by an unknown watercolorist. The bed's curtains are reflected in the mirror between the two windows. The swags of the curtains are draped over the ends of gilt bows, and each bow is set with a garland. (The model of this arrangement is found in La Mésangère.) The wall decoration simulates a tent, according to the rigidly Empire formula, which is also faithfully followed in the upholstery of the chairs, armchairs, and sofa. The shapes of the furniture, however, with the abundance of curves, indicate the 1830 Biedermeier spirit. Partic-

245: E. N. Neureuther. *Queen Theresa's Dressing Room, Tegernsee Castle,* watercolor. SANSSOUCI, POTSDAM.

ularly enchanting is *Queen Theresa's Dressing Room, Tegernsee,* in a watercolor by Eugen Napoleon Neureuther (1806–1882), thanks to the view of the lake framed by the snowy drapery of the muslin curtains at the windows. On the dresser a bonnet with long ribbons, a lilac-colored dress on a chair, a shawl on the sofa all bear witness—in this bright, airy room cooled by breezes from the lake—to a feminine presence. Placed as he is between the large firescreen (covered by a white *housse,* whose patterns follow the Classic lines of the pediment), and the vase filled with roses, how can that elderly gentleman, whose bust partially hides the black stovepipe, maintain his hauteur?

246 (above): E. N. Neureuther. *Ground-floor Room, Tegernsee Castle,* watercolor. SANSSOUCI, POTSDAM.

There is also an air of purity about the *Ground-floor Room, Tegernsee,* with its windows protected by grills through which the garden and lake are seen. The most important piece is the *secrétaire* between the windows, with the doors of its cabinet decorated with paintings and with its little alabaster columns—a detail of North German origin which was fashionable especially in Russia, Sweden and the United States. The rest of the furniture is ordinary Biedermeier. Note the vivid three-color border of the walls, with its movement of stuffs and plumes. The watercolor of *Elizabeth of Bavaria's Bedchamber, Tegernsee* by Nachtmann shows the future Queen, in her bonnet and dress with the leg o'mutton sleeves so fashionable around 1830, sitting at a simple writing desk on which a portable writing-case is set, with a fan-shaped letter file next to it. Nearby is an enormous waste-paper basket, with a gaily-colored painting of a Chinese family on it. The top of the chest of drawers, of the corner cupboard, the table under the mirror at right, and the seat of one of the chairs are all covered with objects: a clock in the form of a little temple, busts of children, red boxes with silver clasps and woollen letter-cases. Similarly, the walls, wherever there is room, are hidden by pictures (including, to the right of the nearer mirror, a little copy of Guido Reni's *Fortuna*), miniatures, and silhouettes. But the room is dominated and unified by the rhythm of the multiple loops of the white window curtains, which stand out against the background of the green trees in the distance, the green and lilac hangings of the bed, and the Scottish tartan rug. These curtains assume a flower-like quality, becoming bizarre white orchids amidst all this greenery.

On the other hand red was the dominant color of *Elizabeth of Bavaria's Study,* preserved in yet another watercolor by Nachtmann. Some of the furniture is 18th century (the sofa and the armchairs at the left), some is Empire (the mirror on the toilette and the mirrored cupboard), some is Biedermeier (the table with the bulging leg, the armchair near the window at the right, both pieces dating from around 1840). On the right wall, between two large portraits of children, hangs a portrait of Friedrich Wilhelm IV; under it, almost lost in a great sofa with a white *housse,* and perhaps partly covered by the large red blanket with a white flower-pattern that falls over one end of the sofa, the Princess is immersed in her reading. She is lulled, no doubt, by a room where everything is symmetrical: two vases of flowers on the table, two glasses with bunches of violets, two clocks by the central window, one to the left, the other to the right, and so on. She is wearing a lace bonnet and a yellow dress in the style of 1840.

More intimate and simple is *Princess Joanna of Saxony's Study, Royal Palace, Dresden,* seen in a watercolor by an unknown artist. The Princess was the sister of Elizabeth of Bavaria and she later became Queen Amelia. Against the blue, white, and yellow plaid that covers the walls of the little, low-ceilinged room, there are a few pieces of unpretentious furniture and a few paintings (including the two little angels of the *Sistine Madonna,* to the left at the back). A carpet strewn with roses and two little birds in cages must have given an idea of spaciousness to this room in a palace guarded by sentries.

248 (upper): F. X. Nachtmann. *Elizabeth of Bavaria's Bed Chamber, Tegernsee Castle,* watercolor. SANSSOUCI, POTSDAM.

249 (lower): F. X. Nachtmann. *Elizabeth of Bavaria's Study, Tegernsee Castle,* watercolor. SANSSOUCI, POTSDAM.

247 (at left): Anonymous. *Princess Joanna of Saxony's Study, Royal Palace, Dresden.* SANSSOUCI, POTSDAM.

263

250: J. S. Decker. *The Archduchess Sophie's Music Room, Laxenburg Palace,* watercolor. SANSSOUCI, POTSDAM.

The rooms we have just seen, most of them cluttered with furnishings, are in sharp contrast to those of the Imperial Palace of Laxenburg, near Vienna. Here lived another sister of Elizabeth of Bavaria, the Archduchess Sophie of Austria, who was the wife of Archduke Franz II and the mother of Franz Josef. If this simplicity reflected the taste of the Archduchess, she must have had a change of heart later, because the room that bears her name in the Hofburg shows the common tendency to cover the walls with pictures. On the other hand, this simplicity could illustrate a special Austrian taste, for we have already seen bare, or almost bare, walls at the Court of Marie-Louise in Parma. While Biedermeier Vienna produced those knick-knacks of mother-of-pearl, ormolu, and

miniature painting, which certainly do not indicate a very pure taste and in any case are the very opposite of simplicity, it was producing at the same time furniture of an admirable grace and often of an admirable simplicity, in which the influence of Louis XVI and English style could be observed.[115] The *Bedroom of the Archduchess Sophie in the Palace at Laxenburg* (*Fig.* 8), does have a great drapery at the entrance to the alcove, but only one picture, the indispensable holy image, over the bed. (Part of the furniture of this room is now in the Staatliches Mobiliendepot in Vienna). Even more bare is the *Archduchess Sophie's Music Room, Laxenburg Palace,* another watercolor by Decker. Not only is the furniture here without any ormolu decoration, but also the

251: Anonymous. *Interior, Around 1820*, watercolor. SANSSOUCI, POTSDAM.

chandelier with its metallic, graveyard color is of a different nature. Certainly in such a room it was easier to concentrate on the music being played. It's an abstract room, if ever there was one, in a period that was so fanatically figurative. The pattern of the wallpaper seems almost to suggest or to accompany columns of sound.

We close this examination of the interiors of German palaces with the *Interior, Around 1820* by an unknown watercolorist. This is an apartment furnished in Empire style, with huge Aubusson carpets in both this room and in the one which can be glimpsed through the open door. The harmony of the lilac and green colors is skillfully arranged with

a taste typical of the early 19th century. In the rug these colors are combined against a violet background. Against the green walls stand lilac-striped divans, while the bags of the two work-tables are green. Lilac and green are also blended in the window draperies. The two *toilettes*, one of elm root by the window, and one covered with white fabric against the opposite wall, state clearly the function of this low-ceilinged room. Next to it is another in which we see miniature chairs and table, obviously children's furniture. The quantity of pictures on sacred subjects suggest that the lady who lived in this room must have belonged to the same German court circles connected with the other watercolors that we have seen.

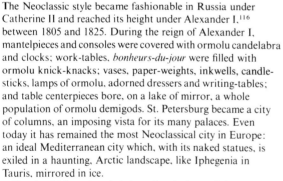

252: A. G. Venetsianov. *Morning Duties of the Mistress,* 1823. RUSSKIJ MUSEJ, LENINGRAD.

253: E. R. Reitern. *Family Group,* 1824. RUSSKIJ MUSEJ, LENINGRAD.

The Neoclassic style became fashionable in Russia under Catherine II and reached its height under Alexander I,[116] between 1805 and 1825. During the reign of Alexander I, mantelpieces and consoles were covered with ormolu candelabra and clocks; work-tables, *bonheurs-du-jour* were filled with ormolu knick-knacks; vases, paper-weights, inkwells, candlesticks, lamps of ormolu, adorned dressers and writing-tables; and table centerpieces bore, on a lake of mirror, a whole population of ormolu demigods. St. Petersburg became a city of columns, an imposing vista for its many palaces. Even today it has remained the most Neoclassical city in Europe: an ideal Mediterranean city which, with its naked statues, is exiled in a haunting, Arctic landscape, like Iphegenia in Tauris, mirrored in ice.

Russian 19th century interiors, that is those of the aristocracy and the upper bourgeoisie, were not very different from the continental interiors which they generally imitated. The furniture was simpler, and above all heavier. A common chair had its back curved, like ears, from solid wood, and armchairs and sofas had robust, curved arms. The circular tables rested either on a heavy central support—a

bulging leg or many-faceted pilaster on a quadrangular b set on lions' paws—or on a peripheral support—massive arches in whose hollow parts were set swans resting on a of the kind just described. The massive glass cupboards, often with monumental wooden grills, provided a kind of furnishing which exploited the value of the compactness c smooth, polished surface.[117]

Furniture of this kind can be seen in the famous *Morni Duties of the Mistress* by Aleksej G. Venetsianov (1780-1 a genre scene by the painter who first introduced into his works Russian peasants as they really were, thus becomir forerunner of popular and national culture in painting as Pushkin and Gogol were in literature.[118] The screen as an element of pictorial composition was a common device us to set off the foreground of a painting, and had become very popular in 18th century France. The busts and the st uette on the cupboard were also conventional elements in the decoration of the period. The subject of the painting, mistress going over the accounts with her dependants, is one of those everyday scenes of life which had already inspired Daniel Nikolaus Chodowiecki.

The surroundings are also very simple in the *Family Group* painted in 1824 by Evgraf Romanovič Reitern (1794–1865). The family is that of Baron Schwertzel and the painter, their relative, is sitting facing us near the grandfather clock. A few pieces of furniture are derived from English models (the chair in the foreground, for instance, and the chest of drawers under the mirror); in addition we see a table covered with a green cloth bordered in the Greek key pattern and an 18th century harp. The low room does not have a well-defined period character, except for the triple row of prints in the study to the rear, a tribute to the fashion for such groupings of pictures.

Even more timeless is the very simple interior painted by Anton Ivanov (b. 1821), *The Cernietsov Brothers in Their Barge*. This is the interior of a barge, a low cabin of wooden planks, in which the two brothers sailed the Volga. One of the artist brothers, in a white shirt and blue trousers, is reading, while the other, in a brown lounging costume and a red nightcap, is drawing the landscape seen from the window. In the compartment to the rear, some arms are hanging on the wall and some watermelons are on a rough counter. The four tables at the windows, on one of which is a box of oils with a riverscape, are rudimentary in form and constitute almost the entire furnishing. Yet this rough interior has a dreamy, pensive charm, as the play of the surrounding waters, illuminated by the sun, is reflected on the low ceiling.

254 (below): A. Ivanov. *The Cerniesov Brothers in their Barge*, 1838. RUSSKIJ MUSEJ, LENINGRAD.

255: A. G. Venetsianov. *Portrait of V. P. Kochubej,* 1830. RUSSKIJ MUSEJ, LENINGRAD.

256: T. P. Tolstoj. *Family Group,* 1830. RUSSKIJ MUSEJ, LENINGRAD.

In contrast, the room illustrated in Venetsianov's *Portrait of V. P. Kochubey* is a typical Neoclassical room. It is a columned hall with a ceiling of painted Classical ornamentation. The two marble busts, a portrait of Alexander I, a few severe pieces of furniture, produce no clutter of objects. In the foreground is a typical Russian chair. This is the portrait of an official person in an official surrounding; here the Empire style effectively expresses that governmental authority with which it is often identified.

Austerity and rigidity are seen again in the *Family Group* by Theodor Petrovič Tolstoj (1783–1873). Against a wall on which a marine painting by Claude-Joseph Vernet is hanging, at a green covered table (similar to the one in Venetsianov's *Morning Duties of the Mistress*), the painter, his throat bare in Byronic style, is sitting with one of his daughters. His wife, in a red dress and plumed hat, and his second daughter are standing nearby. The tall stove is crowned with a vase. The statues of Apollo and Venus, seen in the adjoining room, flank a console which, the painter

tells us in a note, was surmounted by a mirror between the two windows. The sofas are placed directly under these windows and against the wall and their seats seem made from bolts of fabric taken from the shelves of a shop. The angular nudity of the doorframes is reflected in the mirror of the wardrobe in the third room at the back, this also flanked by a statue. These stiffly arranged furnishings give the whole apartment a museum air, and the bonneted woman at the back, sitting at her embroidery frame, looks like the museum's indifferent guard. Certainly this series of rooms does not breathe the same feeling of intimacy we find in similar Dutch painting. The painter tells us that the bust next to the mirrored wardrobe is also his work and represents Morpheus. Indeed, sleep seems to reign in these rooms. According to the memoirs of a contemporary there were many other statues in the apartment (Mercury, Minerva, Sophocles, Homer); there were more pictures on the walls, flowers at the windows, and in the tall, luminous rooms a profound silence prevailed.[119]

257: K. A. Zelentsov. *Interior.* TRETJAKOV NATIONAL GALLERY, MOSCOW.

The *Interior* by Kapiton A. Zelentsov (1790–1845) also shows a series of rooms, but of a far more modest order. Here too, however, there is a plaster cast of the Medici Venus to ennoble the low-ceilinged room, also soberly decorated, in bourgeois fashion, with pictures and plates hanging on the walls. There are plants on the windowsills, and the many casts on the *étagère* in the third room tell us that this is an artist's studio. The young man with a very long pipe who is leaning against the doorjamb seems impatiently awaited beyond the glass by his *Vénus d'Ille,* but with no hint of a tragic epilogue, as in the Mérimée story, and the dog playing with another man adds a note of informal charm.

In the watercolor by an unknown artist of *The Poluiotkov Family* we see another black and white dog, as in the two preceding illustrations, but this is the only thing the three pictures have in common. A group of women dressed in the fashion of about 1840 are sitting, sewing or reading, around a circular Biedermeier table, while the man meditates, or does not meditate, reclining on the very long sofa of rough wood covered by two interminable pallets

covered with striped calico. On the rear wall there are three straight rows of prints: landscapes and vignettes, perhaps English caricatures. On the right wall we see an unframed 17th century portrait and more vignettes. The parrot has climbed to the top rung of his perch, and from that eminence he intervenes in the conversation. The maid is coming from the next room with something to drink. The fireplace, suggesting a country where a large stove is unnecessary, indicates that perhaps the locale is not Russia, but the decoration is Russian and so are the people, whose conversation we can imagine to be rather like that of Chekhov's characters.

The Russian interior seen in the watercolor by Andrej Redkovskij (1831–1909) follows a strictly Biedermeier criterion in the grouping of sofa and chairs around a table (here used for serving tea). The heavy decoration of the sofa is complemented, with a rather comic effect, by the outlines of the chairs which are both dwarfed and gangling—like a group of dachshunds gathered around a bull-dog. Two military statuettes on shelves on either side of a plain mirror stand out against the pale blue wall.

259 (at right): A. Redkovskij. *Russian Interior,* watercolor, 1858. COOPER UNION MUSEUM, NEW YORK.

258: Anonymous. *The Poluiotkov Family*, watercolor. LEMMERMANN COLLECTION, ROME.

260: P. A. Fedotov. *The Fastidious Fiancée,* 1847. TRETJAKOV NATIONAL GALLERY, MOSCOW.

The genre paintings of Pavel Andreevič Fedotov (1815–1852) portray a mean, often grotesque mankind, in settings doubtlessly taken from real life. Although influenced by Hogarth, Fedotov shows no hint of the satire developed by the English master.[120] In Fedotov's décors there is nothing that alludes to the moral of a story, for like the Dutch painters he shows only his pleasure in the beauty of the material. In the *Fastidious Fiancée,* whose subject is supposedly taken from a tale by Krylov but is also thought to have an autobiographical reference (the engagement of the woman he loved to a rich and ugly lawyer), the painter has given great importance to a handsome, Egyptian-figure Empire candelabra and has lovingly painted the rich Russian armchair to the right and the embroidered screen in front of the large Neoclassical stove. Similarly, in *The Aristocrat's Breakfast* the grain in the rosewood table, the reflection of the grill of the screen in the back against the shiny surface of the stove, which is surmounted by the group of Cupid and Psyche, the bulging carafes on the *étagère,* the print of the posters on the chair to the left, the prints of ballerinas on the wall (Taglioni, Fanny Elssler) are all rendered with the same care that the painter takes in depicting the anxious expression of the young man, surprised by a relative who is peering from behind the curtain as the youth reads a book which he hastens to hide.

261: P. A. Fedotov. *The Aristocrat's Breakfast,* 1849. TRETJAKOV NATIONAL GALLERY, MOSCOW.

262: P. Puškarev. *Family Group,* 1846. RUSSKIJ MUSEJ, LENINGRAD.

In the *Family Group* painted by Prokofij Puškarev, we find a room quite similar to German ones of the Biedermeier period. Plaster casts of youths are set in the corners, and we recognize the little boy with his hands joined and his face lifted towards heaven, for we have already encountered him in Princess Elizabeth's Drawing Room in the Berlin Palace (*Fig.* 22). The statue must have been very popular in that period, when the allegorical medallions of Thorvaldsen were also popular, for it reflects the same meek, pious spirit. The vogue for angels was to last for a long time in the 19th century, and its spirit is conveyed by Louisa Kathleen Haldane in her description of her grandmother's apartment (around 1870): "As to the decorations in my grandmother's house: what she

really revelled in were mirrors framed in plush, with wate lilies and kingfishers painted on them. Part of the lightin, the drawing-room consisted of tiny naked gas jets, formi haloes over the heads of two of Thorvaldsen's angels. Th angels must have been fashionable at the time, for I rem them in other houses. I understand that the original ones Denmark are life-size, and are fonts, the kneeling angels holding large shells for christening water. My grandmoth were fastened to the wall at each side of the drawing-roo fireplace, and their haloes would have been big enough f angels to jump through. The curls from the heads of her younger sons were mounted on a stand under glass . . . T were five framed prints of "The Virgin Martyr" hanging

263: A. Korinev. *Russian Interior,* watercolor, 1852. LEMMERMANN COLLECTION, ROME.

different rooms. She is depicted floating on a pond, her halo just clear of the water. In the background, two figures in dark cloaks and sombreros are evidently getting the fright of their lives."[121]

But to get back to Puškarev's picture. Tea has been served and one person is playing the piano while others are smoking: the seated man, for example, with a pipe as long as a golf club, and the young man standing at the window with a cigar. A woman sits knitting in the room at the back, her cup of tea set on a Russian Biedermeier table beside her. With the characteristic full back, the chairs and armchairs in the first room are also Russian. Among the copies of Italian paintings on the right wall there is also a picture by Aleksej Egorov

(1776–1851), *Saint Simeon the Receiver of God* (according to the epithet given the saint by the Orthodox church: *Bogopriimets*).

The *Russian Interior* signed by A. Korinev and dated 1852 came from the Strogonoff collection. The portrait of a lady with a child in her arms in the center of the rear wall could be the one of *Countess Strogonoff holding her child,* painted by Mme. Vigée-Lebrun in St. Petersburg and shown at an exhibition of Russian portraits in that city in 1905, when the work was part of Prince Galitzin's collection. Except for that painting the room is quite simple, with styleless bookshelves, a little mid-19th century glass cabinet with columns, and to the right an armchair of the same period. The pictures are mostly prints, one of them a portrait of Napoleon.

264: M. C. W. Rørbye. *The Surgeon C. Fenger with his Wife and Daughters,* 1829. PRIVATE COLLECTION, COPENHAGEN.

Danish family groups of about 1830 reflect the atmosphere of the Biedermeier period with unsurpassed delicacy, illustrating its domestic joys and its delight in neat furnishings and affectionate gatherings. *The Surgeon C. Fenger with His Wife and Daughter* was painted in 1829 by M. C. W. Rørbye, who also painted the charming little picture of the window with flowers seen earlier (*Fig.* 200). A tall, cylindrical stove surmounted by a head of Mercury, a round mirror, a family portrait surrounded by little still lifes, a table covered with a cloth on which the parrot's cage

is set, an armchair and another chair which can be dated in the 1820's, and an Axminster carpet—this is what we can see of the decoration. The faithful dog is also present, as in so many Biedermeier pictures. In *The Schram Family* by Vilhelm Ferdinand Bendz (1804–1832; he died in Vicenza), a gentleman wearing those tiny spectacles of the time balances his tea and offers a tasty morsel to the dog. The scene is observed by a mature lady in a bonnet with her back to us and by a young girl with a napkin in her hand, leaning on the back of a divan where an older man and a still-

55: V. F. Bendz. *The Schram Family,* c. 1830. PRIVATE COLLECTION, COPENHAGEN.

ung woman are sitting. These two seem to be looking
t the window, following the glance of another young
rl, seated in the window. Standing by the mirror
tween the two windows, a pensive man seems to be
aring at nothing in particular. One can almost
agine the painter assigning the roles: you look that
ay, you look over here, and you look in no particular
rection. There were conventions in these paintings
the intimate moments of the day which one wished
perpetuate, and one of these conventions was to
ve a door open, allowing a further glimpse of the
use. Bendz follows the conventions in this picture
he does in another which portrays *The Waagepetersen*
mily. Here he has also tried to introduce a note of
imation, by having the father and the older child
rn, smiling, towards the baby which the bonneted
other holds in her arms. The dog, with hair like a
rcupine, is crouched under the desk. The furnishing
this study is simple and its walls are not too
ammed with pictures (among which is a portrait of
poleon). Even more simple is the furnishing of the
om in the background, a bedroom with an armchair
a surprisingly modern form and a folding wash-
nd. From all this simplicity emanates an aura of
urgeois well-being, blissfully inhaled like the smoke
the cigars which lie in an open box on the desk,
icating an ample supply.

266: V. F. Bendz. *The Waagepetersen Family,* 1830.
PRIVATE COLLECTION, COPENHAGEN.

267: E. Baerentzen. *The Family Circle,* c. 1830. PRIVATE COLLECTION, COPENHAGEN.

268: V. N. Marstrand. *The Waagepetersen Family.* STATENS MUSEUM FOR KUNST, COPENHAGEN.

he same atmosphere reigns in *The Family Circle,* painted
ound 1830 by Emil Baerentzen (1799–1878). The window,
egantly draped with muslin, looks out on a large courtyard,
tranquil place, surrounded by the rear of the house and the
ach-houses. The women in their bonnets, are doing needle-
ork or spinning, the old gentleman is reading through tiny
ectacles and the little boy, who has made himself a paper
ldier's hat, is asking his mother if it is time for him to eat.
n Aphrodite of the Gardens, in the shadow next to the
ndow, indicates the last gasp of a Classicism which is dying
t in the routine of ordinary bourgeois life.

In this temple of the family, the parents' portraits always
oked down like household gods. We have seen them in the
aagepetersen picture, and we see them again in another
aagepetersen Family, by Vilhelm Nikolai Marstrand (1810–

1873). Here the more youthful portrait of the present lady of
the house is hung a little lower, as if in a family tree. Some of
the people seem the same as those in the Bendz painting: the
lady with the coif and the *ruche* looks like the one who in the
Bendz painting held the baby, now in the arms of the nurse,
and one of the two girls with ruffled collars sitting at the table
with the boys playing skittles must be the one who, in the
other picture, is leaning against her father's knee and smiling
at the baby. The gentle face of the boy looking toward us
contrasts with the grimace of the caricature he is holding in
his hand. The furniture is simple and straightforward, the
broad bell-pull guarantees the servants' promptness and
through the door we see a bed, turned down, under its
columned canopy. These Danish painters gave their now-
vanished world an idyllic quality pleasing to our modern eyes.

269: D. C. Blunck. *Thorvaldsen and his Danish Friends at the Osteria della Gensola*, 1837. THORVALDSEN MUSEUM, COPENH

271: Jakob Alt. *Billiard Room in the Café Löwe, Vienna,* watercolor. HISTORISCHES MUSEUM DER STADT WIEN, VIENNA.

270 (at left): G. B. Bisson, *Caffè dei Servi in Milan,* c. 1835. MARIO PRAZ COLLECTION, ROME.

One can hardly say that the life of taverns and cafés is languishing, but today the customers are a different sort of public. Once artists and writers gathered every day in such places. (This still happened down to the thirties of our own century, at cafés like Florence's Giubbe Rosse, Rome's Aragno, or Paris' Dome. Two of Italy's leading modern poets, Eugenio Montale and Vincenzo Cardarelli used to meet at a café every evening.) Today this tradition has disappeared. But a survey of Biedermeier interiors would not be complete without a glance at these places which were once so much a part of everyday life.[122]

The name of Thorvaldsen is associated with two Roman *osterie,* Raffaele Anglada's at Ripa Grande and the Osteria della Gensola.[123] Artists have left us interior views of both, the first in a celebrated painting by F. Catel (in the Neue Pinakothek, Munich), which actually gives us little of the decoration and presents Thorvaldsen and his friends seated against the view of the Aventine framed in the doorway. The Osteria della Gensola, however, appears in an oil painted by Ditlev Conrad Blunck (1799–1853) in 1837 and entitled *Thorvaldsen and his Danish Friends at the Osteria della Gensola.* Except for the men's dress and the well from which water was drawn, there isn't much difference between this tavern and those in Rome today. Even the metal brackets that support votive lights in front of the Madonna can be found in modern Roman taverns, only supporting electric light bulbs. The cook is fat, as Roman cooks are, and even the regional dress of the Ciociaria women can be seen today in some Roman restaurants with "atmosphere" arranged for the tourist trade. The Osteria della Gensola was in the Trastevere section of the city, near the Ponte Rotto over the Tiber. The artists at the table are (from the left): A. Küchler (who is drawing), M. G. Bindesbøll (speaking with the waiter), Vilhelm Marstrand, Constantin Hansen (in the doorway), J. V. Sonne, D. C. Blunck, Ernst Meyer, and Thorvaldsen.[124]

On the other hand, the character of the period is strongly marked in the view of the *Caffè dei Servi in Milan* by Giuseppe Bernardino Bisson. This café was located in the Corsia dei Servi in Milan, for whose inauguration the poet Tommaso Grossi wrote some verses. The picture discloses a perspective of white columns with gilded capitals around a large room where people in 1835 costume are sitting at the tables or strolling. At the counter in the background, decorated with Pompeiian-style paintings, the waiters are busy preparing the orders. The room is a solemn hall, like the foyer of a theater.

There is also something theater-like about the large *Billiard Room in the Café Löwe, Vienna* by Jakob Alt (1789–1872). Its gallery is supported by caryatids to imitate a row of boxes in a theater, from which observers can enjoy the spectacle of the battles joined on the green tables.[125]

272: P. C. Klaestrup. *Café Knirsch, Copenhagen,* pen and watercolor drawing, c. 1850. ⱷREGAARDMUSEET, COPENHAGEN.

Today Milan's Caffé dei Servi no longer exists and in Copenhagen there is a hotel (the Angleterre) where the *Café Knirsch* once stood. But the Knirsch's appearance has been preserved in a precious work by Peter Chr. Klaestrup (1820–1882), a watercolored pen drawing of about 1850. The picture is doubly precious because the man at the left, with his inseparable cane under his arm and his unmistakable posture, is Kierkegaard. The room itself recalls certain vestibules or lobbies of provincial European hotels.

A private apartment, but one which might also be in a hotel, is the *Room with Hunting Trophies* painted in 1856 by Rudolf von Alt (1812–1905), famous Austrian landscapist and interior painter. The decoration has already embarked on the fatal path that the century is to take: the indiscriminate revival of historic styles. In this case we note particularly Louis XIII, with the typical turned legs and high backs of the stiff chairs. The Biedermeier touch is in the antimacassars which cover the back of the leather side chair and the sofa in the background, next to the

stove of pale green tiles. The metal supports of the lamps are Gothic in flavor as are the scallops of the swags of the curtains with pelmets, but the candlesticks on the chess table, at right, look 18th century. A sabre and a guitar are crossed, trophy-style, on the rear wall, almost as if to suggest a device and a motto like those in the frontispiece of Theodor Körner's poetry, *Leyer und Schwerdt* (Lyre and Sword).

The watercolor view of *St. George's Hall in Windsor Castle* by Joseph Nash (1808–1878) is typical of the halls that are found in all the colleges of the old universities. (Naturally here the arrangement of tables is different from that in the colleges, where there is a high table at the end opposite the entrance, on a platform, with the students' tables occupying the rest of the room.) Portraits are hung on the high panels of the walls and a gallery runs along the rear wall, over the entrance. The castle was restored under George IV and under Queen Victoria, and the great chandeliers which hang from the ceiling are umbrella-like, in the fashion of those in the Brighton Pavilion.

273 (opposite page, top): Joseph Nash. *St. George's Hall in Windsor Castle,* watercolor, 1844. MARIO PRAZ COLLECTION,

274 (opposite page, bottom): Rudolf von Alt. *Room with Hunting Trophies,* watercolor, 1856. MARIO PRAZ COLLECTION,

Some painters delighted in rendering, down to the slightest detail, the effects of light, especially in the evening. A Cassel artist, Johann Erdmann Hummel (1769–1852) specialized in effects of perspective (he was nick-named *Perspektiv-Hummel*) and optical effects (again the local wits invented a whole nomenclature for him: Kaloptrik, Dioptrik, Antoptrik, Hyperoptrik, Kaldioptrik, and Anthyperoptrik . . .). He portrayed the mysterious, magical tricks of reflected light with a sensitivity worthy of the writer E. T. A. Hoffman who was inspired to write a famous story about one of Hummel's paintings *(Die Fermate)*. Hummel's realism is almost magic. Thus, he never tired of painting the great cup of granite in front of the Alte Museum in Berlin, because its polished surface reflected the surrounding objects, always creating a new effect. In his *Chess Game at Count Ingenheim's Home* Hummel has given us a nocturnal atmosphere of great effect, repeating a famous experiment of Raphael's, contrasting artificial light with moonlight.[126]

The Danish painter Vilhelm Bendz also was concerned with effects of light and shadow in his *Meeting Place of the Smokers*, (*Fig.* 276). Here the play is even more complex and harks back to the tradition of Gerard van Hornthorst, Georges de la Tour, and the English artist Joseph Wright of Derby (1734–1797). From the screened sources of illumination spread miraculous haloes of light which cast long shadows. A little two-piece mirror to the left of the window reflects broken outlines and a ghostly pitcher on a distant piece of furniture. The musicians are resting and a wisp of smoke rises from the cellist's mouth. His pipe is of white clay, a baby compared to the sesquipedalian pipes of the others. The man nearest us is cleaning his pipe with a goose quill. The bed at right, the bookshelves, and the table tell us that the occupant also slept in this room.[127]

275: J. E. Hummel. *Chess Game at Count Ingenheim's Home.* KAISER-FRIEDRICH MUSEUM, BERLIN.

The very well-known painting by Constantin
Hansen (1804–1880). *Danish Artists in Rome*, is
not of particular interest as far as furnishings
are concerned. These consist of a plaster figure on a
bracket, a flask crowned with ivy, some Roman views
or figures in local costumes on the wall and a table
and chairs suggesting no particular style. Nevertheless,
the work has a picturesque fascination that made it
very popular and its view of the rooftops of Rome
from the window, those men in their high hats and
chin-whiskers, those long pipes ... all is very much
"of the period." If, however, you observe the faces,
you will see that they all seem grave, pensive, even
dejected. For example, the man seated on the threshhold of the French window is holding his coffee cup
in front of him as if it contained poison. The painter
unwittingly has given us here a gathering of ghosts,
like those seen by Coleridge's Ancient Mariner on
the deck of the accursed ship:
"The mariners all 'gan work the ropes,
Where they were wont to do;
They raised their limbs like lifeless tools—
We were a ghastly crew."

It is as if the people painted by Hansen had
remained there, by that window, under a spell, turned
to stone, to represent forever for posterity, like a
group of Madame Tussaud's waxworks, a historical
scene: *Danish Artists in Rome in the 1830's*. At the
far left we see Hansen himself, who lived in Italy
from 1835 to 1844, next to the architect M. G.
Bindesbøll, who created the Thorvaldsen Museum.
Bindesbøll has just returned from a voyage to Greece
and Constantinople and is depicted here (as well as
in a separate, isolated study of this figure) as he tells
episodes of his journey. The fez is a childish evidence
of his pride in having made such a voyage. The
melancholy man staring at his cup as if reading some
frightful presage in it is Martinus Rørbye. The first
man on the left, leaning on the railing is Vilhelm
Marstrand, who was in Italy from 1836 to 1840. In
the center of the balcony is the painter Albert
Küchler, later known as "Fra Pietro da Copenhagen,"
who was in Rome from 1830, and beside him is Conrad
Blunck, who was in Italy from 1828 to 1838. Sitting
on the table is Jørgen Sonne, creator of the well-
known frieze around the Thorvaldsen Museum, who
lived in Rome from 1831 to 1840.[128]

In the *Musical Evening*, Vilhelm Marstrand did not
attempt light effects as dramatic as those seen above.
In a Neoclassical drawing room, its walls decorated
with pictures which at times do not respect the architectural features of the room (see the three pictures to
the right of the door), we see some musicians and
their audience. At the piano is the famous Danish
composer C. F. Weyse, and through the door at the
back we see the Waagepetersen family. The light is
diffused by two lamps and by the music-stands, as
the large central (Empire) chandelier is only for
decoration. In the right-hand rear corner, we see little
portraits of Haydn, Beethoven and Mozart, and one
imagines that Mozart is the composer of the quartet
being played on this evening.

276: V. F. Bendz. *Meeting Place of the Smokers*, 1828. Ny
CARLSBERG GLYPTOTEK, COPENHAGEN.

277: C. Hansen. *Danish Artists in Rome*, 1837. STATENS MUSEUM FOR KUNST, COPENHAGEN.

278: V. Marstrand. *Musical Evening*, 1834. FREDERIKSBORGMUSSET, COPENHAGEN.

281: C. Motte. *Monthelier in his Studio*. Lithograph after a drawing by François Bellay.

decoration of an artist's studio is rarely calculated to
ect a period. Such rooms are always in part functional and
expects to find easels, plaster casts, canvases and finished
ntings placed in a certain amount of disorder. During the
mantic period, one seldom found an artist's *atelier* without
:ull (we saw one in Tommaso Minardi's garret, *Fig.* 173),
we find another in the house illustrated by Vilhelm Bendz
he Artist's Brothers at Home. It is a simple little room with
pretentious furniture (an English-style 18th century chair),
iily portraits and neat muslin swags at the windows. A
g pipe, the casually draped jacket, students' or soldiers'
, and bottles all provide an intimate atmosphere. However,
he house of Bendz's brothers, the skull was not simply a
orial emblem for H. C. Bendz, who seems to be meditating
r the skull, was an anatomist.

In the studio of Friedrich Moosbrugger (1804–1830)
depicted in *The Artist in his Roman Studio*, the skull (an
animal's) clearly has a burlesque significance, since it is
crowned with laurel and surmounted by a Phrygian cap. This
trophy, and the little wall-cupboard below it, form a pleasant
still life in a room so unpretentious that instead of the central
chandelier there hangs a cluster of empty wineflasks.

Evidently Alexandre Jules Monthelier (1804–1883) had a
higher opinion of himself, since the *Monthelier in his Studio*
shows him in solemn painter's costume, with a large velvet
beret, sitting in front of a seascape. His studio has pretensions
to being a drawing room, with its very orderly gallery of casts,
pictures hung in an equally orderly manner on the walls, and
even a large rug. Monthelier was a rather little known painter
of landscapes and architecture.

(opposite page, top): V. F. Bendz. *The Artist's Brothers at Home*, c. 1830. HIRSCHSPRUNGS COLLECTION, COPENHAGEN.
(opposite page, bottom): F. Moosbrugger. *The Artist in his Roman Studio*, 1828. STAATLICHE KUNSTHALLE, KARLSRUHE.

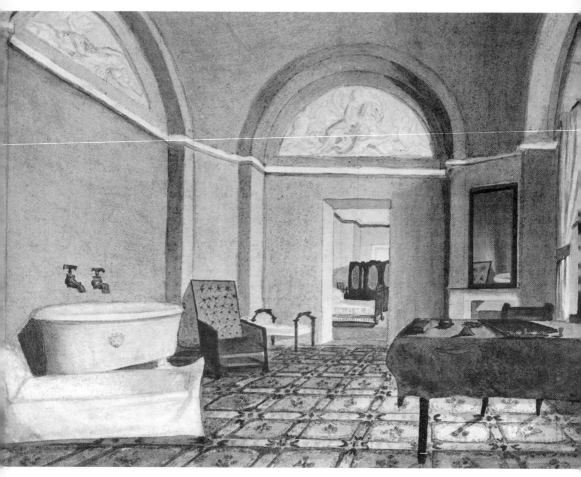

282: Princess "M.B." *Bathroom and Bedroom, Marina,* watercolor, January 1839. DON AGOSTINO CHIGI COLLECTION, ROME.

We have already mentioned the Wittgenstein family album in the Introduction. Ludwig Adolf Friedrich, Fürst zu Sayn-Wittgenstein Berleburg, was born at Kovno, Lithuania in 1799 and died at Cannes in 1866. His first wife was Stephanie, Princess Radziwill (1799–1832) by whom he had two children, Peter and Marie. His second wife was Leonilla Barjatinskij (1816–1918), who bore her husband four children: Antonietta, Friedrich, Ludwig, and Alexander. Antonietta married Orázio Chigi, a relative of the album's present owner.

In general the rooms illustrated in the album display a luxury in no way inferior to that of royal residences. The importance that the Wittgensteins attached to comfort is indicated by their wish to have even the bathrooms recorded by the artist. One such delightful room appears in the watercolor of the *Bathroom and Bedroom, Marina,* which according to its inscription was painted by "La Princesse M. B.," who may have been a relative of Leonilla's. This bathroom, with its classical bas-reliefs in the lunettes, does not seem an unworthy descendant of the Roman

283: Sotira. *Little Living Room in the Razumovskij House,* watercolor, April 1835. DON AGOSTINO CHIGI COLLECTION, ROME.

thermae. The painter Sotira (of whom Thieme-Becker merely says "painter in Vienna around 1830"), painted in 1835 the *Little Living Room in the Razumovskij House* (*Fig.* 283), the *Little Living Room at Pavlino* (*Fig.* 284) and the *Bathroom of the Princess Barjatinskij at Pavlino* (*Fig.* 9). The *Little Living Room in the Razumovskij House* shows a collection of casts of antiquities, including the famous Pompeiian tripod with sphinxes. The casts are displayed in an Empire cabinet surmounted by four enormous busts. Some Russian armchairs are placed against the walls. The

Little Living Room at Pavlino has Gothic-style furniture and an arrangement of vases and other objects behind the slightly curved or exedral divan that recalls Schinkel's arrangement of the Tea Room in the Berlin Palace (*Fig.* 233). The Gothic character is achieved by naïvely camouflaging classical forms under Gothic-style fretwork. Especially curious is the firescreen at the left, which suggests the stained-glass windows of a cathedral. Through the door one glimpses a hothouse with Chinese lanterns. The *Bathroom of the Princess Barjatinskij at Pavlino* (*Fig.* 9) is a pink room with

284: Sotira. *Little Living Room at Pavlino,* watercolor, July 1835. DON AGOSTINO CHIGI COLLECTION, ROME.

two *Zimmerlauben,* which transform it into an enchanting artificial paradise. Among the hydrangeas in the background, the statue of Venus stands above the tub as if over an altar. The oblique shaft of light has been ably exploited by this little-known water-colorist to give an effect of depth and mystery, suggesting almost a sacred place. One is reminded of Foscolo's verse in the ode, *All'amica risanata:*

"E quella a cui di sacro
mirto te veggo cingere
devota il simulacro,
che presiede marmoreo
negli arcani tuoi lari
ove a me sol sacerdotessa appari... "

"And she, whose statue I see you devoutly crowning with holy myrtle, that marble statue which presides in your innermost household, where you officiate sacred rites for me alone..."

285: Hollman. *The Living Room at Pavlino,* watercolor, 1834. DON AGOSTINO CHIGI COLLECTION, ROME.

There are many flowers also in *The Living Room at Pavlino,* seen here in a watercolor by Hollman of 1834. This room has a characteristic conversational arrangement of sofa and armchairs around a table where a pineapple is being served. There are two *Zimmerlauben* in the *Bedroom in Berlin (Fig. 20)* by Eduard Gärtner (1801–1877) which separate the bed from the rest of the room, where the simple furniture is less interesting than the imprint of life on the objects: the toilet accessories on the table between the two windows, the portraits on the other table which serves as writing desk, the doll on the little chair next to it. Despite its solemn ceiling, we feel we have really stepped into this room in the absence of the lady who inhabited it and the personality of the room and something of the personality of its mistress will remain with us.

286: The Library at Ivanovskij, watercolor.
DON AGOSTINO CHIGI COLLECTION, ROME.

287: Boudoir in the House of Maréchal Lobau, Paris, watercolor,
May 1837. DON AGOSTINO CHIGI COLLECTION, ROME.

288: F.-E. Villeret. *Room in the Lobau Palace, Paris,* watercolor,
May 1837. DON AGOSTINO CHIGI COLLECTION, ROME.

289: E. Gärtner. *Interior at Potsdam,* watercolor, 1836. DON AGOSTINO CHIGI COLLECTION, ROME.

n *The Library at Ivanovskij* (a Barjatinskij estate in the district of Kursk) by an unknown watercolorist, our eye s not drawn so much to the bookcase surmounted by the inevitable busts or to the right wall with a row of landscapes urely almost invisible from below, as it is to the little toy house with its garden on the floor to the left. We imagine this ibrary as a seldom-visited room, where such an awkwardly arge toy could be kept when not in use in the nursery, or—an ven more attractive hypothesis—as a room where the child imself could come and "play house," inventing aloud maginary dialogues for his toys in the silence of the lonely ibrary with its aroma of wood and old books and with its arge, luminous windows opening on to the countryside.

The *Boudoir in the House of Maréchal Lobau, Paris,* also by an unknown artist, is a low, mezzanine room, with Neoclassical pilasters, an Empire fireplace and an Empire onheur-du-jour complementing the fireplace on the opposite vall. The writing desk between the windows is of a later eriod. Similarly, the consoles and fireplace in the *Room n the Lobau Palace, Paris,* by François-Etienne Villeret

(1800–1866) are Empire as is the room itself, with its doors painted in classical motifs. The armchairs near the fireplace, however, are Biedermeier. On the mantel are two statuettes of Taglioni and Fanny Elssler, from prints we have already seen in *The Aristocrat's Breakfast* (Fig. 261).

The watercolor by Gärtner, *Interior at Potsdam,* with the white-coiffed woman spinning while a child holds the yarn and a little girl nearby seems intent on some sewing, has the flavor of a little Dutch genre painting. These three figures in iron grey and pale blue are placed in a room with a handsome Neoclassical ceiling. The walls are bare, but to the left stands out the usual Biedermeier "conversation" of sofa, chairs and table (covered by a green cloth decorated with a classical pattern) and an *étagère.*[129] In front of the farther window there is a flowerstand of a rather unusual form. A slender column surmounted by a Winged Victory is flanked by iron curls holding crystal pots. The high hedge of plants between the windows prevents us from seeing the lower part of the stand. This watercolor also uses the familiar Dutch device of allowing us to see other rooms through an open door.

The *Room at Kamenka* (in Podolia, in the Ukraine), painted by Haase, is decorated in Neoclassical taste and furnished with Biedermeier furniture (the sofa and the chairs at the right are Russian) and some vases manufactured in Berlin rather than Imperial Russia. There are some curious details in the decoration, particularly the doilies bordered with cloth flowers (or chenille) under the three vases on the console between the windows, and the veils that were hung to pr pictures, perhaps against the flies which were numerous the Russian summer. From the windows we see a pretty sloping park and a classical colonnade by a little lake. T low *Bedroom and Dressing Room at Kamenka* (*Fig. 19*), a

by Haase, suggests the bed beyond the partition of lances
draped with a pleasant blue stuff. Note that the rear part was
further divided for one can see the top of another row of
lances, perpendicular to the first, in the center of the partition.
The low ceiling and the wooded hill next to this part of the
house give the room an intimate, protected atmosphere.

290: Haase. *Room at Kamenka,* watercolor,
November 1837. DON AGOSTINO
CHIGI COLLECTION, ROME.

The New Living Room at Pavlino has a spectral aspect which would make it the ideal setting for a diabolical story by Barbey d'Aurevilly. The generally crowded décor and the overwhelming proportions of the pictures (especially the one on the rear wall), the suggestion of wilderness given by so much vegetation scattered about (can this palace be like Sleeping Beauty's, where exterior Nature burst in, tangling everything in her climbing vines?), and finally, the nocturnal lighting and the funereal figure kneeling in the center, all contribute to the unreal atmosphere. One must admit that if the picture to the left, a seascape, is inoffensive enough, the outsize historical composition on the rear wall is extremely depressing, with its more than life-size figures, actors in an evidently gloomy scene. Its story is almost certainly that of a tearful Anne Boleyn, taking leave of her little daughter Elizabeth before going to the scaffold, a heart-rending historical event often treated in the 19th century. With the red plush of the sofa and armchairs, the ghostly Gothic chairs, and the massing of plants as in the Good Friday "sepulchres" in Italian churches, the new living room at Pavlino must have elicited cries of admiration from the guests on the day it was inaugurated. We are sure, however, that not many of us would care to live in it today.

The Princess's Study at Pavlino, also by Sotira, is a forest of ogives and pinnacles as well as of flowers. Characteristic of Neo-Gothic taste is the blue velvet that covers the sofa and the chairs, suggesting the favorite color of the ancient kings of France. There is nothing that is not flowered or adorned with fret-work, nothing that is not ogival, pinnacled, lanceolated, flamboyant—even the flowerstands themselves! On the right there is a tall bookstand, reminiscent of a choirstall which, however, bears some korzinki or baskets for sweets. On the pedestal of one of the candelabras, to the left, there are some little opaline bottles, and the candelabra on the table has an ogival screen with figures of saints. The table to the left has a fascia which seems made of glassy paste of several colors, as in certain Sicilian furniture. Under this table a bear, reduced to a mat, does his best to give an ogival profile to his fierce muzzle.

The two outdoor scenes, The Garden at Zausze and The Farm of Macha at Zausze, both by Hess, have already been mentioned in the Introduction (Figs. 14 and 15). July of 1839 must have been a particularly happy season for the Wittgensteins, and that day, the 22nd, when the children played with the nanny-goat in the corner of the woods, near that inviting summer-house surrounded by potted flowers, was a day worth recording. But for that matter, it was probably only one of many such days, all of them serene and happy, enjoyed by those privileged mortals.

The painter (or paintress) of the interior called The Living Room at Zausze is identified only as M*** In it we see muslin curtains supported by arrows, hedges of plants, some Russian chairs and sofa.

291: "M***." The Living Room at Zausze, watercolor, September 1839. DON AGOSTINO CHIGI COLLECTION, ROME.

292: Sotira. The Princess' Study at Pavlino, watercolor, August 1838. DON AGOSTINO CHIGI COLLECTION, ROME.

Sotira painted the splendid Empire Drawing Room at Pavlino, similar to the kind of drawing room that was found more or less everywhere in Europe at that time. The fireplace with Egyptian figures is Empire, and so are the two bookcases, the sofa and the torchère. The curule chairs, however, are a little later. The clock on the fireplace and the statuary groups by the windows (one is the Rape of the Sabines by Giambologna) are rigorously protected by glass bells. In the center of the room stands the statue of the praying boy that was seen in the New Living Room at Pavlino; it is probably the same statue which has changed its location. To perfect the Empire character, this room would need an Aubusson or Savonnerie rug instead of this patterned Bokhara, and would require pictures which—unlike those which cover the walls here — do not post-date the Empire by so many years.

293: Sotira. *The New Living Room at Pavlino,* watercolor, August 1838. DON AGOSTINO CHIGI COLLECTION, ROME.

294: Sotira. *The Drawing Room at Pavlino,* watercolor. DON AGOSTINO CHIGI COLLECTION, ROME.

In Haase's *Room at Warki* (which, like Kamenka, was an estate of the Sayn-Wittgensteins), we see in the center a kind of seat destined to enjoy a great success in the 19th century: the *pouf*, a divan with a central, cylindrical back. On this cylinder was set a plant or a pot of flowers, thus combining the picturesque with the comfortable, the two guiding principles of Biedermeier decoration. This *pouf* is red, and has a bellows-seat, that is to say, a seat with parallel furrows. (This decorative motif was also characteristically Biedermeier, and is, for example, frequently found in furniture made in southern Italy during this period.) The design gives an appearance of solidity, if not of elegance, and the triple underlining is emphatic, like certain underlined signatures. Behind this, there is another kind of sofa also very popular in the 19th century called a *confident* or, in Italy, an *amorino*. A 19th century Italian poet described it: "Two half-moons form the seat, in inverse pose. . ." On our *pouf* lie a work-basket and some ribbons, and there are more ribbons and laces on the little table with turned legs next to the fireplace. The firescreen has an embroidery with an Oriental subject. The seascape to the right of the fireplace has the same subject as the one at the left in the *New Living Room at Pavlino*. An *étagère* for knick-knacks is set between the first and second windows, while a very tall plant is in front of the third. We have already seen the red fabric with a pattern of black tendrils which covers the armchair beside the screen and the *confident* beyond the *pouf*; for it, too, appeared in the *New Living Room at Pavlino*. (The family must have been fond of it.) On a table in front of the second window we see some thick books, probably those albums that Thackeray, in his *Paris Sketch-Book*, says were unfailingly present on the round rosewood table in every middle-class drawing room.

In *The Columned Salon* at Ivanovskij (*Fig. 5*) at the entrance to the veranda a statue of a river nymph stands out white against a pyramid of flowering plants. Chairs and sofa are protected by white slip-covers. It is summer, and the sun streams through the broad windows, illuminating an enchanting conversation piece beyond the columns. While a young couple is playing billiards, a child in a little blue tunic pulls a pair of wooden horses about. His toy whip cracks, the ivory balls click on the green table.

In January 1841, Friedrich Klose painted the *Room in Berlin*, where the Wittgensteins, in their continuous progress through Europe, were then living. In it we see a coffered ceiling with white stucco designs on a blue ground, blue walls divided by white pilasters and a *Zimmerlaube* hiding the high white tile stove, crowned by an antique urn. The display of greenery, however, is the only exuberant note in the room, which in other respects is sober, neat and refreshing. (Perhaps the adjoining one is a bit more cluttered.) In front of the identical mirrors, on two similar consoles, the two gilded clocks under their glass bells continue the symmetry even to the responses of their muffled chimes.

A year later, in January 1842, the Wittgenstein family was in Rome, where the *Drawing Room of the Palazzo Parisani* was painted by Karl Andreevic Beine (or Beyne) (c. 1815–1858), a very fertile painter

295 (upper): Haase. *Room at Warki*, watercolor, April 1840. DON AGOSTINO CHIGI COLLECTION, ROME.

296 (lower): F. W. Klose. *Room in Berlin*, watercolor, January 1841. DON AGOSTINO CHIGI COLLECTION, ROM

97: K. A. Beine. *Drawing Room of the Palazzo Parisani,* watercolor, January 1842. DON AGOSTINO CHIGI COLLECTION, ROME.

of architecture and interiors. This Palazzo Parisani must not be confused, of course, with the palace of that name at Tolentino where the famous treaty was signed,[130] but I have not been able to discover where the Roman palace actually was located. Although this room also has pilasters, and although the furniture here is also Biedermeier, the atmosphere is quite different from the Berlin room. Two purely decorative chandeliers of gilded wood are left hanging here, only to be covered with the traces of flies.(The damage that flies can do to such chandeliers is incredible. I found one once which no amount of cleaning could save.) The light is provided, instead, by the Argand wall-lamp to the left, which within a few years was probably given a gas jet. The female nude, of plaster, seems to be venerating the lamp with her eyes, confusing it perhaps with the sun. In this apartment the Wittgensteins may have found exactly what they wanted, but they did not have the feeling of *home* which animated their Berlin quarters the year before.

By the spring of that same year they were living at Palazzo Carmanico in Naples, where Ciuli portrayed the drawing room (*Fig.* 12), with its pretentiously

frescoed ceiling and its chaotic furnishing. Furnishing became more and more chaotic as the halfway point of the 19th century drew near; the pieces of furniture seem to be in movement, like the toy automobiles of a merry-go-round. Chiavari chairs are paired with Neapolitan armchairs approximating the Empire style. Here there is a cover or a cloak of red velvet, there a shawl. The vases of flowers under glass bells are as stiff as sentries on either side of the window, while the fresh flowers are arranged haphazardly on the tables. The Argand lamps are virtually the only decoration on the walls. The colors clash, but the view of the bay from the window must have been beautiful.

Beine painted the *Room in the Villa Dackhausen at Castellammare* (*Fig.* 11), where the Wittgensteins stayed in July, 1842. The room is very simple, with calico curtains and flower-patterned wallpaper, and to feel more at home the Wittgensteins put a favorite family portrait on the table. Here, too, the view of the bay from the garden was what mattered. The Wittgensteins must have spent many happy hours under the arbor outside this window.

298: Sotira. *The Barjatinskij Sergeevskaia House,* watercolor. DON AGOSTINO CHIGI COLLECTION, ROME.

The *Barjatinskij Sergeevskaia House,* which Sotira painted, had achieved what in the Romantic 19th century was the dream of many: a one hundred per-cent Gothic room. We have seen such rooms in Trieste, Milan, Germany and elsewhere, and while we have always felt that a touch of Gothic was not without charm, the naïveté of a complete reconstruction has always aroused us to either laughter or scorn. This drawing room, all fretwork, vaulting ribs, and lambrequins ought to be inhabited by such extreme characters, sinister or innocent, as those in

Ann Radcliffe's *The Mysteries of Udolpho.* Or else those grim monks and inquisitors should descend from the pictures on the walls to give one counsel and mysterious warnings. Instead, the inhabitants seen in the adjoining room are a mild lady playing the piano and a child drawing his two little brothers in a wagon—human beings guarded by a marble Diana who dispels any sinister sensation of black romance.

In contrast to so much captiously mysterious atmosphere, the bareness of the *Room in a House*

299: Anonymous. *Room in a House near Bonn,* watercolor, September 1842. DON AGOSTINO CHIGI COLLECTION, ROME.

near Bonn, seems refreshing. Indeed, this room can hardly be considered furnished; in fact it looks like a room where the movers are expected any moment. Obviously it is a rented house, and only the minimum necessities were supplied. Thus, we see chairs, sofas, and tables, but no pictures or rugs, or knick-knacks. The painter, aware that the room was of little interest in itself, has furnished it with people.

The *Boudoir of the Princess Barjatinskij in Paris* (*Fig.* 6) represents the height of fashion in decoration of 1842. Little Boulle-style cabinets, a Neo-Rococo

writing-table in the same style, and to the left in the rear, an armchair which, if the date of the watercolor weren't specific, would have led us to date it around 1850. This is a room à la Balzac, already fore-shadowing the taste of the Second Empire. The voluminous chintz curtains, whose glossy surface the painter has captured well, suggest women's skirts which, in those very years, were becoming fuller and covered with flounces. Reflected in the mirrors, these curtains simulate the upper part of a proscenium. Note the fan-shaped brass firescreen.

300 F.-E. Villeret. *Room in the Castel Madrid, Paris,* watercolor, May 1843. DON AGOSTINO CHIGI COLLECTION, ROME.
301 F.-E. Villeret. *Bedroom in the Castel Madrid, Paris,* watercolor, July 3, 1843. DON AGOSTINO CHIGI COLLECTION, ROM

302: F.-E. Villeret. *Empire Living Room, Place Vendôme, Paris,* watercolor,
April 1843. DON AGOSTINO CHIGI COLLECTION, ROME.

The handsome *Empire Living Room, Place Vendôme,
Paris,* painted by Villeret in 1843, retains of its
original decoration the paneling of the walls, the
fireplace, a console, various bronzes, some armchairs,
the firescreen, the central chandelier and other light
fixtures. The most remarkable new piece is the
vis-à-vis or *confident* sofa, which here has three seats
instead of two. (One needn't interpret this as an
allusion to the romantic triangle so common in French
life and fiction of the 19th century. When two-seated,
this sofa was called in France *le confident;* three-
seated, it became *l'indiscret.*) The big books on the
little table in front of the mirror at right are almost
certainly albums, and in the room glimpsed through
the door are a Boulle cabinet and a jardinière.

A cabinet similar to this one and to the one in the
Princess's *Boudoir* in Paris is also found in the *Room
in the Castel Madrid,* in the Bois de Boulogne, Paris,
covered with some of the same objects (a kerosene
lamp and two metal pots for flowers); one may
imagine that the Wittgensteins carried this cabinet
with them from one Paris residence to another. The
armchair, the sofas, and the little table·with a red

cover with black arabesques which we saw in the
Boudoir also turn up in this *Room in Castel Madrid,*
as do the fan-shaped firescreen and another Boulle
piece which in the *Boudoir* was seen at the left, beyond
the writing-table. The gloomy clock on the mantelpiece is a heavier descendant of the kind of clock
fashionable under the Empire. More interesting is the
little picture in a modern Gothic frame on the wall
which separates the two rooms (a less elegant kind
of separation than that obtained with columns, but
very common in more modern times and popular
even today). That little picture, from what we can
make out of it, may well have been a primitive, which
had begun to be collected even at the beginning of the
19th century.[131]

In the *Bedroom in Castel Madrid,* we see a collection
of Biedermeier furniture. Note the Empire *psyché*
behind the screen in the back, the Gothic coffer,
surmounted by an angel, on the little table to the
left of the door, and the large clock hanging from the
chair at right. This watercolor ends the series of
interiors from the Wittgenstein album, an invaluable
document of taste around 1840.

In Holland (as elsewhere) furnishing before 1840 was rarely carried to excess and often it was reduced to the bare necessities.[132] A guest room provided with a *lit d'ange* (a kind of canopied bed), a sofa, a *chaise longue*, a clock, a *psyché* and a satinwood *toilette* was considered luxuriously furnished. Tables laden with knick-knacks, stuffed birds placed on mantelpieces and rich silk hangings of various colors all became common only after 1840. The *Interior of Doctor A. Vrolik's House*, 1837, is governed by a rigid symmetry, though the only object that is centered is the chandelier. The furniture is lined up along the walls, the sofa flanked by a little table and a console. On the little table an inkwell stands between two Chopin lamps[133] supported by bronze figures while on the console we see a clock and two candelabras, all three objects under glass bells. On the other wall, the piano is flanked by two chairs, covered with horsehair. Two women are seated at the piano, but not for reasons of symmetry, for they are playing a duet. The massive circular table, covered by a patterned fabric with a pale green ground, is set on an axis between the piano and the sofa. The furniture flanking the sofa corresponds to the windows of the facing wall, and the sofa itself corresponds to the mirror between the windows. The stripes of the carpet underline the geometrical arrangement. The prints, in simple wooden frames, are hung with symmetrical precision, and rather high, from stiff cords fixed with hooks to a wooden molding under the frieze. Light, serene colors prevail: grey and pink in the carpet, and olive curtains with a lilac swag bordered in gold.

Lightness and serenity also characterize the later *Living Room of Doctor A. Vrolik's House* of 1839. In this room the red damask panels in gilded frames, the ceiling, the paneling and the wall sconces for candles all date from the 18th century. Two years have gone by since the first watercolor was made, and certainly in that time some of the furniture in the house has changed its position, since in the room in the background, reached by some steps, we see again

the heavy pedestal table with rams' heads on the corners of the base. We have already had occasion to observe similar shifts of furniture in the Palace of Naples and in the Wittgensteins' various residences. It is a habit that brings rooms closer to human beings for rooms, too, change with the years. Their appearance alters, they undergo the effects of time and are subject to the whims of a will outside their own. If furniture could talk, sofas and chairs could probably tell of their adventures and misadventures as men and women do. In the rear room, note also the stove which around 1835 definitively replaced the open fire. In the present case this stove is projected, rather inelegantly, toward the center of the room. Around 1840 the stove which circulated hot air was invented, an ancestor of central heating (which, for that matter, had been invented by the Romans). It was filled on one side and the heat circulated through pipes. Its exterior appearance was based on vertical pilasters broken by horizontal box-like heat compartments, a design still found in terracotta stoves sold in Italy today.

In Doctor Vrolik's house no attempt was made to suit the furniture to the 18th century decoration of the room. Though the Neo-Rococo curves of the divan and chairs are the degenerate offspring of an 18th century style, these pieces have a Biedermeier character, quite different from the aristocratic distinction of the room. The little walnut table, inlaid with citron wood, denotes a rather coarse elegance, also a cheap degeneration of Empire style. Divan and chairs are covered in a fabric with a yellow gold pattern on a pale brown ground—a Neo-Rococo pattern reminiscent of the 18th century. To the left of the fireplace we glimpse a card table, then a firescreen on a pole, and behind it the bell-pull. The bronze chandelier in this room, like that in the preceding room, has a form that recalls Empire style. Despite its heterogeneous elements, the room is bright and spacious, aristocratic and bourgeois at the same time, a mixture of distinction and solidity.

A valuable documentation of mid-19th
century taste is furnished by the Album of
Queen Sophia of Holland, first wife of
William III, who reigned from 1849 to 1890.
His two sons (one of whom we shall see
playing in the nursery) died before their
father, who was succeeded by Queen
Wilhelmina, his only child by a second
marriage. The Album was donated to the
Oranje Nassau Museum (which has kindly
allowed its reproduction in this volume) by
the heirs of a certain Beyerman, onetime
aide-de-camp to the older of Queen Sophia's
sons, Crown Prince William (1841–1879).
Beyerman had received it from the Queen's
sister, Princess Maria of Württemberg.

Princess Sophia was King Wilhelm I of
Württemberg's daughter, and in 1839 she
married the man who ten years later became
King of Holland (an unhappy marriage
which ended in complete estrangement).
Princess Sophia's Apartment before her
marriage is shown to us in a watercolor by
an unknown artist. The furniture is of the
Restoration period, as evidenced by the
open fretwork on the tops of the two cabinets
to the right, the two Gothic chairs around
the little table at left, and the two cornucopia
flower vases on the writing desk. From July
1839 to May 1849 the Queen lived in the
Plein Palace in The Hague. Some interiors
of that palace were painted by Hermann
Frederik Carel ten Kate (1822–1891), a
painter who was greatly honored in his day.
But, although he was director of the Royal
Academy of Fine Arts in Amsterdam and
counsellor and court painter to William III,
his paintings, now scattered all over the
world, have not enjoyed the favor of
posterity. The furniture in the *Reception
Room*, of ebony covered with yellow damask,
is in the Neo-Rococo style. The tufted,
two-seated divan at left is typical. Comfort
seems to dominate elegance; and the
enormous corner sofa, sumounted by an
étagère with mirrors and vases, is introduced
with no regard for the structure of the
room (there has been no attempt to disguise
the door that it blocks). Like the vast *pouf*
in the center, under the chandelier, it is
probably comfortable but certainly not
handsome. Similarly the arrangement of the
stove in front of the fireplace, protected by
a firescreen in Empire taste, lacks elegance.
The *étagère* to the right, displaying crystal
and silver, is inlaid with silver as is the little
table on the left. An Axminster carpet covers
the entire floor. The elephantiasis of certain
17th century Dutch cupboards seems to
have been inherited by these very solid
Biedermeier pieces we see here.

In the *Library* there is a fantastic bookcase whose doors bear glass panes in a curved, carved frame. These doors in turn are enclosed within a second sprawling frame, decorated with ponderous festoons of flowers and fruit and terminating in a coat of arms surmounted by a crown. There is something almost surrealistic in its conception. This cabinet looks more like a monumental gateway than a piece of furniture. It is flanked by two *étagères,* also with curved lines, which seem to have been used for holding prints, books and knick-knacks. Here, too, we see the stove placed in front of the fireplace, as well as a table and chair with twisted legs in Louis XIII style, and a Neo-Rococo armchair and occasional chair. The confusion of styles which distinguishes the second half of the century was already under way, and with it, we begin to notice the characteristic disorder. This confusion is also apparent in the *Living Room,* where the furnishings seem to have been placed with a certain contempt for order. The heavy flowerstands are so densely decorated that they look pustulous (another characteristic of decorative art around this period, as was exemplified at the London Exhibition of 1851), and the little baskets for plants are clustered higgledy-piggledy at the window. The spring chairs, which on the continent were sometimes called *confortables,* are covered with enormous lace antimacassars. Two firescreens, one large and one small, are placed in front of the stove, which projects into the room. They were designed in conformity with the practical sense of the period; for the rectangular tops, decorated with mother-of-pearl inlay and with painting, can be tilted so that the two little pieces can also be used as tables. Two tall pedestals in Louis XIV style support vases of Berlin porcelain. On the mantelpiece four kerosene lamps (of the *Moderateurlamp* model), attached to Oriental vases, supply the illumination, which more and more in this period came from table lamps augmented by sconces. The sconces here, on each side of the mirror, hold wax candles. The desks (one in Louis XV style) are covered with books, papers, portraits and knick-knacks. The large portrait of the two boys, one holding the Dutch flag, must be of Sophia's two sons, William (born in 1841) and Alexander (born in 1843). When we remember that both died young (the first at thirty-eight, the second at forty-one) without having married, we feel this painting gives the room that sad air of destiny which accompanies the end of dynasties. In *Queen Sophia's Sitting Room,* we see at the left the desk with curved legs which she had in the Stuttgart room where she lived as a girl. The marble female bust and the two cornucopia vases are also familiar; and we may also recognize, under a chintz *housse,* one of the Gothic chairs from that earlier room and, under another *housse,* the Restoration chair which in both paintings is in front of the desk. One of the portraits, to the left above the desk, is almost certainly of Alexander I of Russia (William II of Holland had married Anna Pavlovna, sister of Alexander I). A Louis XIII chair and a drawing-case complete the decoration.

305 (opposite page, top): H.F.C. ten Kate. *Library, Plein Palace, The Hague,* watercolor, 1849. ORANJE NASSAU MUSEUM, THE HAGUE.

306 (opposite page, center): H.F.C. ten Kate. *Reception Room, Plein Palace, The Hague,* watercolor, 1849. ORANJE NASSAU MUSEUM, THE HAGUE.

307 (opposite page, bottom): H.F.C. ten Kate. *Living Room, Plein Palace, The Hague,* watercolor, 1849. ORANJE NASSAU MUSEUM, THE HAGUE.

308 (this page, upper): Anonymous. *Princess Sophia's Apartment, Stuttgart Residenz,* watercolor, c. 1830. ORANJE NASSAU MUSEUM, THE HAGUE.

309 (this page, lower): H.F.C. ten Kate. *Queen Sophia's Sitting Room, Plein Palace, The Hague,* watercolor, 1849. ORANJE NASSAU MUSEUM, THE HAGUE.

310: Anonymous. *Room in the Palace of the Kneuterdijk,* watercolor, c. 1850. ORANJE NASSAU MUSEUM, THE HAGUE.

In Holland, interest in Gothic revival began relatively late, around 1840. As late as 1839 the Academy building in the Hague was constructed in Classical style; but a short time later, in the same city, a few Gothic revival buildings began to rise. The two opposing parties continued to dispute, and only in 1850 was ten Kate able to announce in the *Spectator* that "the obtuse contempt for the Middle Ages" was gradually disappearing.

King William II, who by preference lived in the palace on the corner of the Kneuterdijk, had it enlarged (the rear part on the Noordeinde) with a series of additions in Gothic style. Here the personal recollections of the Prince came into play, memories of his student days at Oxford when he fell in love with soaring Gothic. The only remains of this series of constructions are the Willemskerk, once a stable, and the Gothic Hall on the Noordeinde, where the King displayed the principal pieces of the art collection he had assembled, sparing no expense. In a recent study of the period we read: "William II with his great, positive qualities, was also surrounded by an aura of Romanticism and the spirit of chivalry. The chivalrous spirit came from the charm of his personal appearance and the memory of the bravery he displayed in the war years (he had taken part in the war

in Spain with Wellington and had distinguished himself at Quatre-Bras at the head of the Belgian and Dutch contingents); the Romanticism lay in the decoration of the palace and the court, in the fantastic uniforms of the court couriers, richly dressed as if they were Hungarian magnates, and in the aspect of Mateling, the court poet, with his guitar and fantastic minstrel's costume. *Style troubadour!...*"[134]

The *Gothic Hall* which William II had built has an arched ceiling with hanging corbels, as in the halls of Hampton Court and of Christchurch at Oxford (second half of the 16th century). In the anonymous watercolor of it, the King is seen in the center of the hall contemplating a picture set against the back of a chair with little twisted columns (Louis XIII style). Rich Empire torchères are seen at the sides and in the corners, while those with arms supporting modern lamps flanking the door at the back are Neo-Rococo.

Queen Sophia's album gives us another interior of the palace on the Noordeinde, *The Nursery,* in which we see some Empire pieces, discarded as out-of-date and considered unworthy of being seen in the grown-ups' apartments. Empire style was decidedly out of fashion. *L'Illustration* of 1843 commented in these terms on a recent creation of the Giroud Manufactory at Ghent: "For a long time, the arts have been

311: Anonymous. *The Nursery in the Palace on the Noordeinde,* watercolor, 1853. ORANJE NASSAU MUSEUM, THE HAGUE.

312: Anonymous. *Gothic Hall of the Palace on the Noordeinde,* watercolor. GEMEENTE ARCHIEF, THE HAGUE

strangers to interior decoration. Ignorant workers
rule as absolute masters. From this chaos has come
the bad taste of the Empire style." The article
went on to add that the chaos was about to be left
behind. In fact, this was the very moment when they
were *entering* chaos. The Neo-Rococo room to which
that comment referred showed, in its richness of
curves, ornamentation and draperies, a desire for
display without any sign of true good taste.

In the *Room in the Palace of the Kneuterdijk* we
again find some objects that formerly decorated the
Plein Palace where the royal couple lived before
William III ascended the throne. The portrait which
was above the piano in the *Library* (*Fig.* 305) is here
paired with that of the children which we saw in the
Queen's *Sitting Room* (*Fig.* 309). The two Louis XIV
pedestals, which in the *Living Room* (*Fig.* 307) bore
Berlin vases here flank the first window at right, but
they bear Chinese vases. Armchairs, chairs, and sofas
—all Neo-Rococo—form a conversational arrangement around a circular table whose legs are typical
of the imitation Louis XIV carried out in this period.
The valances over the curtains, the jardinières, the
chandeliers have all become heavy, and there is a
confused excess of ornamentation.

Queen Sophia's album includes two watercolors by Franz Heinrich (1802–1890), a watercolorist who was born in Bohemia and lived in Vienna, where he studied at the Academy. He traveled in Italy, Switzerland, Holland, Belgium and, in 1852, also in America. Since his interiors reproduced in the album indicate neither the date nor the place, one can only hazard guesses. *The Dining Room* is probably in the Stuttgart Residenz, since in the same album there is another very similar watercolor interior (decorated with vases on pedestals, medallions on the walls, a broad fascia below the ceiling) which bears the inscription: "(Souvenir) Room in the Royal Palace in Stuttgart". The decoration recalls that of Schinkel's *Tea Room in the Palace in Berlin* (Fig. 233), and the chairs are English style, about 1815–1830, with brass mounts. The *Drawing Room* still has some Empire furniture (a little commode at right, next to a tall porcelain stove, a *secrétaire* to the rear at left, both decorated with *gaines* terminating in ormolu female heads), but the sofa behind the table at right, and the chair covered with the same fabric at left are Neo-Rococo. Probably the interior is in a German palace.

Three other interiors shown here are by Pieter Francis Peters (1818–1903) (born at Nijmegen, died in Stuttgart and active after 1841 at Mannheim, after 1845 at Stuttgart). They are all dated 1857, but only one indicates the specific locality: *Drawing Room at Kirchheim*. There are two places with this name in Württemberg, one on the Neckar, the other toward the Swiss border. In any case, the room is certainly in a villa or castle belonging to the Württemberg royal family. The furniture dates from the middle of the century and the armchairs and the sofa are more the work of the upholsterer than of the cabinet-maker. At left there is a firescreen of the kind that converts into a table, one of those pieces of papier-mâché, painted, gilded, and inlaid with mother-of-pearl, which came into fashion in the 1840's. On the walls next to the plethora of pictures, we find brackets for statues and little *étagères* for trifles (left wall). At the central window on the right a plant is hanging from a hook, while at the next window a lantern is hung instead. There is a large cage on the little table with Louis XIV legs which is covered with a scalloped cloth of a Moorish taste. Various picturesque elements are set here and there with no regard for the whole, creating an episodic, confused decoration which, in the course of the century, will give living rooms that bric-a-brac aspect so common in the late 19th century. Here we can still make out an underlying scheme, dating back to the Empire.

The decoration is similar in the other *Drawing Room* (*Fig.* 316), where we apparently find again the same cage and the same hanging vase. Since this room has the same kind of shallow squared alcove, it may also be at Kirchheim. The walls are literally covered from top to bottom with portraits. The hanging plants are more numerous around the larger *Drawing Room* (*Fig.* 317), where we see vases on pedestals, Louis XIII chairs, Neo-Rococo pieces, a *pouf* and even an Empire three-legged *guéridon*. Again there is no unifying idea behind the room's decoration. The covers on the central and side tables show a complete indifference to the elegance of the furniture lines and overstuffed, covered shapes predominate, as in women's clothing of that period.

313 (this page, upper): F. Heinrich. *The Dining Room* (probably in the Stuttgart Residenz), watercolor. ORANJE NASSAU MUSEUM, THE HAGUE

314 (this page, lower): F. Heinrich. *Drawing Room*, (unidentified German palace), watercolor. ORANJE NASSAU MUSEUM, THE HAGUE.

315 (opposite page, top): P. F. Peters. *Drawing Room at Kirchheim*, watercolor, 1857. ORANJE NASSAU MUSEUM, THE HAGUE.

316 (opposite page, center): P. F. Peters. *Drawing Room* (at Kirchheim?), watercolor, 1857. ORANJE NASSAU MUSEUM, THE HAGUE

317 (opposite page, bottom): P. F. Peters. *Drawing Room*, watercolor, 1857. ORANJE NASSAU MUSEUM, THE HAGUE.

Before he signed himself P. F. Peters, this water-colorist used the signature P. Peters J. (junior) because his father—who painted on glass—had the same name. This is the signature appearing on some water-colors of interiors dated 1842. In the *Drawing Room* (*Fig.* 320) we see an Empire style room with pilasters in which a Biedermeier decoration has been installed. The structure of the room has not been greatly respected and little brackets have been fixed to the pilasters on the right while from the central rear pilaster hangs a round case, probably containing miniatures. The two glass cabinets in the background are symmetrically spaced on either side of the *toilette,* but are not centered in front of the wall panels. A vestige of the former Empire decoration seems to remain at left, where we see a console, and a statue and a large vase on high pedestals. The *Bedroom* (*Fig.* 319), also with pilasters, may be in the same palace and certainly was in Germany, perhaps in Mannheim where the painter was working after 1841. This room retains its original Empire decoration: a canopied bed flanked by a little cupboard on the left and another little piece with drawers set on a low table at right, a chest of drawers, a *toilette,* near which has been placed one of those little nests of light tables known in England as *trio* or *quartetto tables.* The stove, placed in front of the fireplace and serving the same function, is a now familiar Biedermeier innovation.

The *Living Room* (*Fig.* 318), must have been the last word in decoration in 1842, with its *pouf* and its kerosene chandelier. The ceiling, fireplace, and chest of drawers surmounted by a large Chinese vase hark back to the 18th century, while the tripod to the right dates from the Empire, and the table to the left has legs in Biedermeier Louis XIV. This room documents the confusion of styles that began at this period.

One of the first appearances of the *pouf* is found in the *Bedroom of Comte Charles de Mornay* by Delacroix. This kind of central sofa which spread through Europe around 1840 may owe its presence in the bedroom of Comte de Mornay (Minister Plenipotentiary in Morocco when the painter traveled there) to its imitation of the Oriental ottoman that Mornay had found in Morocco (however, a drawing of a *Project for the Decoration of a Room* around 1830, or even earlier, at the Musée des Arts Décoratifs already shows this new kind of sofa occupying a place of honor). The rest of the room (which seems like the interior of a tent) is furnished in accord with the taste of the period (1832). There is a note of barbaric-picturesque in the trophies of weapons against the curtain and on the bedpost, and especially in the large panoply on the right, where a horn and a trumpet are added. In addition, the leopard's skin at the foot of the *pouf* is an exotic touch which, at the end of the century, will become all too common.

The *Bedroom* (*Fig.* 321) and two drawing rooms (*Figs.* 349 and 351) painted by Wilhelm Dünckel (1818-1880) were part of the suite of rooms in the *Schloss* in Mannheim which were occupied until 1862 by Stephanie Beauharnais, widow of the Grand Duke Karl de Barden (her portrait, by Winterhalter, can be seen in *Fig.* 351). The *Bedroom* was at the mezzanine level, the other two rooms on the first floor.[134a]

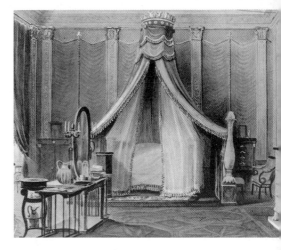

318 *(top):* P. F. Peters. *Living Room,* watercolor, 1842.
MARIO PRAZ COLLECTION, ROME.

319 *(center):* P. F. Peters, *Bedroom,* watercolor, 1842.
MARIO PRAZ COLLECTION, ROME.

320 *(bottom):* P. F. Peters. *Drawing Room,* watercolor, 1842.
MARIO PRAZ COLLECTION, ROME.

322a *(at right): Project for the Decoration of a Room,* waterco
c. 1830. MUSÉE DES ARTS DÉCORATIFS, PA

321 (above): W. Dünckel. *Bedroom,* watercolor,
c. 1850. MARIO PRAZ COLLECTION, ROME.

322 (at right): Eugène Delacroix. *Bedroom of Comte
Charles de Mornay.* LOUVRE, PARIS. (Photo Bulloz)

323: *Portrait of the Commercial Councillor Josef Liebermann,* c. 1842. Formerly MAX LIEBERMANN COLLECTION.

We have already said that one can notice a connection between decoration and female dress, which after all is only a corollary to a well-founded theory advanced by Gerald Heard and by James Laver who see a strict correspondence between style in architecture and style in clothing.[135] For that correspondence is found not only in architecture: the rhythm of a style imposes itself on all the manifestations of a period.[136] The character of the furniture gives us an indication of the character of the people who live in its midst and vice versa: the appearance of the people tells us about the nature of their furniture. Looking at the *Portrait of the Commercial Councillor Josef Liebermann,* painted by an unknown German artist around 1842, how can one help but see a consonance between the heavy, stiff furniture, massive even in its curves and twisted columns, and that dignified, measured man, with his practical expression, not alien, however, to an occasional humorous remark, if the slight contraction of his left eyebrow is not deceiving us? Similarly the arm and the leg of the ponderous sofa glimpsed at the right have a roguish little Rococo movement.

And how can one not see, in *The Keuchen-Werlé Couple with their Grandchild,* 1844, by Peter Schwingen (1815–1863), a solidity that is perfectly in keeping with that of the Biedermeier sofa on which they are sitting? This is the natural shell of such mollusks; it was they who secreted the substance which then

324: Peter Schwingen. *The Keuchen-Werlé Couple with Grandchild,* 1844. Formerly PRIVATE COLLECTION, BARM

became their tegument. The man is brandishing his pipe, the child offers a morsel to the dog. Every day a similar scene must have been repeated, and every day the same noises must have come from the street, whose houses can be glimpsed through the window. Every day the same number of rolls must have been eaten with the same breakfast. This is a culture made of precise, insistent habits, of patience and memory. In this way it achieves a balance, its own kind of classicism: so the comfort of the divan curves at the edge like the acroterion of an antique pediment.

Another couple, *Count August von Normann and his Wife,* by F. S. Stirnbrand (1788–1882), a painting from about 1853, seems the very image of conjugal harmony: the woman touches a key of the piano (the music is painted with such care that one could read it) and the officer bends slightly towards her, resting his arm on the back of the chair where she is seated. And who put that rose on the edge of the

325: F. S. Stirnbrand. *Count August von Normann and his Wife,* c. 1853. STAATSGALERIE, STUTTGART.

piano? Against the wall there are two indoor plants, one with smooth leaves, the other prickly: symbolic of the two aspects of married life? Certainly in Hogarth these details, such as the statuette of Canova's *Perseus* on the bracket at the left, would have a precise reference to the people in the painting. But not here, not in this bourgeois version of the myth of Mars laying down his sword to seek repose in the embrace of Venus after the toils of war; Count August von Normann is resting only after the fatigue of a parade.

There is one literary work which is especially helpful in illuminating the spirit of the mid-19th century, Coventry Patmore's *The Angel in the House,* which appeared in two parts: *The Betrothal* in 1854 and *The Espousals* in 1856: a celebration of Victorian domesticity, an exaltation, in unpretentious, conversational verses, of those ideals of order and moral cleanliness so dear to the 19th century middle class:[137]

"For something that abode endued
With temple-like repose, an air
Of life's kind purposes pursued
With order'd freedom sweet and fair.
A tent pitch'd in a world not right
It seem'd, whose inmates, every one,
On tranquil faces bore the light
Of duties beautifully done,
And humbly, though they had few peers,
Kept their own laws, which seem'd to be
The fair sum of six thousand years'
Traditions of civility.   (The Cathedral Close, 5)

The most frequently quoted verses of this poem by Patmore sum up the atmosphere of many conversation pieces of the middle-class 19th century:

"Geranium, lychnis, rose array'd
The windows, all wide open thrown;
And some one in the Study play'd
The Wedding-March of Mendelssohn."

326: Wilhelm von Harnier. *Self-Portrait with Wife and Children,* 1838. Formerly PRIVATE COLLECTION, ECHZELL (ESSEN).

327: E. Gärtner. *Living Room of the Master Smith, E. F. A. Hauschild, in Stralauer Strasse, Berlin.* MARKISCHES MUSEUM, BERLIN.

In the 19th century people had a veritable passion for plants and flowers in rooms. We have already mentioned this on various occasions, and we have seen not only how natural flowers were used to brighten interiors, but how floral decoration was wide-spread: in stuffs, in embroidery, in wallpapers; *petit-point* flowers, bead flowers, flowers made of shells or of wax took their places beside fresh flowers to give rooms the atmosphere of hothouses. In the same period children were much fussed over, smothered in a sentimentality quite different from the modern attitude of parents towards their offspring. The presence of a child in the house was something like the visitation of a little cherub, and the period, as we have seen, had a weakness for images of angels.

Children appear frequently in 19th century conversation pieces: they are to the adults what the flowers are to the furniture. Wilhelm von Harnier (1800–1838) has included them with their toys in his

Self-Portrait with Wife and Children, an oil painting of 1838. The little peacock, the stable for the wooden horses, the lamb, the toy soldiers, the doll in *pantalettes* create a festive atmosphere, from which, however, the emaciated painter and his sad, pensive wife seem excluded. The picture's liveliness also comes from the window of the house opposite, rendered with such effectiveness that we want to sharpen our eyes and see if, in the shadow behind the raised shutters, someone isn't observing us. In the *Living Room of the Master Smith, E. F. A. Hauschild, in Stralauer Strasse, Berlin,* oil by Eduard Gärtner (1801–1877), there are four little girls, one affectionately leaning against her father's knee while he is eating. And there are flowers, a vase in front of the long mirror which reflects, beyond the grandmother's face, a *secrétaire* similar to the cabinet on the right, and two vases on the latter, flanking a Chopin lamp. The furniture is from around 1830.

328: Peter Fendi. *Evening Prayer*, c. 1840. ÖSTERREICHISCHE GALERIE, VIENNA.

The Viennese Peter Fendi (1796–1842) put children in his pictures with the same generosity with which his contemporaries put flowers in their rooms. He saw them at play, in the garden, in their mother's arms or at her knee to say their prayers. In his interiors children bring such freshness that there is no need of flowers. One of the moments of the day that he was especially fond of depicting was the hour of evening prayer, when the children were closest to the angels. Here in his painting, *Evening Prayer*, led by their mother, the children kneel in front of the holy image before disappearing behind the curtain of the bed. Some Alpine landscapes of Austria on the wall remind us that this country with its Southern religion is, in fact, a Northern country. A little cart resting on its shafts takes up by itself the whole right hand

329: Sebastian Gutzwiller. *Family Concert in Basel,* 1849. ÖFFENTLICHE KUNSTSAMMLUNG, BASEL.

section of the painting, which is divided by a Chinese screen. Another cart, from which a doll has slipped, is found in the *Family Concert in Basel,* 1849, painted by the Swiss Sebastian Gutzwiller (1800-1892). We see a simple room with rustic furniture, an enormous grandfather clock, an 18th century style *trumeau* ennobled by two busts on top of it, a 19th century piano, little shelves built into the wall at the right for books and on the same wall many prints. On the plain little table by the piano there is the still life of the remains of some refreshments, objects as clearly legible as the title of the little booklet hanging on the wall and the notes of the music. But the enchanting touch comes from the group of the little girl teaching the baby the names of the animals from a zoology book open on the stool.

330: Edgar Degas. *Portrait of the Bellelli Family in Florence*, 1859. LOUVRE, PARIS.

The little girls in Degas's famous painting *Portrait of the Bellelli Family in Florence*, 1859, are not much merrier-looking than their mother, whose expression is listless and very sad. With their identical pinafores, the girls look like orphans in an institution. If these children are flowers, they have the graveyard fascination of chrysanthemums. As is usually the case with paintings of the great masters, the artist's interest was only very slightly aroused by the room. This picture, in fact, seems much closer to us than its date would indicate.

The Danish painter Vilhelm Marstrand, whom we have already encountered, is the author of *The Artist's Wife and Children in the "Apartment of Famous Painters"* in the Royal Academy of Fine Arts, 1861–1862. In this painting the boys are pensive, especially the one who has stopped leafing through his picture book and is staring dully into space. The little girl with her back to us is running toward her younger sister, who is holding her doll. Uncharacteristically, this tender scene of children creates a 19th century atmosphere with no help from the decoration.

331: Vilhelm Marstrand. *The Artist's Wife and Children in the "Apartment of Famous Painters,"
in the Royal Academy of Fine Arts,* 1861-62. STATENS MUSEUM FOR KUNST, COPENHAGEN.

332: K. H. Arnold. *Family in the Living Room,* c. 1850. Formerly PRIVATE COLLECTION, NIEDERURF.

For a long time family life in Western countries took place around a table, especially in the 19th century. One of the reasons for this gathering together must have been economic. When the source of light in the evening was a single kerosene lamp, everyone had to collect around it: those who did needlework, those who read, those who smoked. The young married couple withdrew to the shadow of a window to confide their sweet thoughts. It is such a moment that Karl Heinrich Arnold (Kassel, 1793–1874) has captured in his *Family in the Living Room* of about 1850. It is a serene picture, and it is also a slightly sad one, though it is difficult to give a reason for this impression of sadness. The grandmother is reading a story to the child; the grandfather listens, sipping his coffee and smoking his pipe. The young couple at the balcony are looking out at the night. There is nothing explicitly sad in all this. But the painter has given the scene a sense of never-changing habit, of existences slowly being consumed in the same place. He has especially hinted at the fatal cycle of the years, showing us three ages of man: infancy, adulthood,

333: P. C. Skovgaard. *Around the Tea Table at Vejby,* 1843. STATENS MUSEUM FOR KUNST, COPENHAGEN.

and old age, heading toward its final destiny. There is an interesting little detail in the decoration: we observe the shadow cast on the wall by the portrait on the right. This is because it is hung tilting forward. I do not believe this was often the case before the mid-point of the century. But from now on we shall notice it more and more frequently.

The Danish artist Peter Christian Skovgaard (1817–1875) presents another scene of people seated at a table, *Around the Tea Table at Vejby,* 1843. The low room, where the bland Northern sun comes through the window, has an intense intimacy of its own, from which any curiosity concerning manners or decoration is excluded. Except for the curtains of the bed and the symmetry of the paintings and miniatures on the wall, there is nothing to distract our attention from the group of people gathered around the table for a conversation perhaps long anticipated by relatives who live far away from one another. Some of them are elderly, others in the full bloom of youth, but one feels the friendly bond of family congeniality.

334: Moritz von Schwind. *Early Morning,* 1858. HESSISCHES LANDESMUSEUM, DARMSTADT.

More than the decoration, it is the hour and the effect of the light that give *Stimmung* to interiors like these which we now see, by Moritz von Schwind and Adolph von Menzel. *Early Morning* (the German title is *Die Morgenstunde* or *Morgenstübschen*) is perhaps the most popular picture of Moritz von Schwind (1804–1871). The idea of the painting came to the artist in his early youth, and was later strengthened by his life near the Starnbergersee, where he owned a house. The Darmstadt version of this painting dates from 1858.[138] It is one of the few Biedermeier interiors to show a Romantic inspiration, a sense of escape toward an enchanting world of nature. One might almost say that this painting is unique of its kind. The typical Biedermeier room, as we have said, shuts itself off, protects itself from the outside world, bringing indoors some samples of that world on which it has turned its back—usually plants and flowers—as the Egyptians carried into the grave food and utensils of the world of the living they had left behind. But here the girl who has run barefoot to the window (she is said to be the daughter

of the painter) breathes in with delight the mountai͏ air from that immensity which opens out before he͏ The furnishings are modest: an 18th century comm͏ with a curved line, a little Biedermeier worktable, a͏ little bed. It seems almost a maid's room.

The *Room Giving onto the Balcony* by Adolph vo͏ Menzel (1815–1905), painted in 1845, brings the outside world bursting into the interior; as Fritz Laufer has rightly observed of this painting: "The a͏ and the light through the open window of the balc͏ takes possession of the space, to play over the walls and the floors, to stir the curtains, and to make the͏ chairs set in front of the mirror cast shadows. The experience of French Impressionism, the enchantm͏ of a world steeped in light, radiant with light, is he͏ appropriated and absorbed. The *Room Giving onto the Balcony* has rightly been called an 'interior landscape', because in effect, here in the intimacy and privacy of a room, there is achieved what Impressionist painting sought to achieve in the ope͏ air: the transformation of the world, through the enchantment of light, into a sense of vital joy".[139]

335: Adolph von Menzel. *Room Giving onto the Balcony,* 1845. KAISER-FRIEDRICH MUSEUM, BERLIN.

336: C. R. Leslie. *Library at Holland House*, 1838. LADY HOWICK COLLECTION.

We have already observed how in England Regency taste was quite composite and that, while Neo-classical influence prevailed, one still continued to consider Louis XV the style that expressed regal taste, to such a degree that the Waterloo Chamber in Apsley House was furnished for Wellington in the Louis XV style in 1828. Around 1830 an interior continued to have Georgian rather than Victorian characteristics. It was only after Queen Victoria's marriage in 1840 to Albert of Saxe-Coburg, and especially after the great Exhibition of 1851 in London, that the typical Victorian house was established, with its striped or grating-patterned wallpaper (as if the wall were a trellis in a garden), the gilt pelmets, the bright colors, the flowered rugs, the profusion of embroidery, the flowers of wax or shells. If we leaf through the volumes of the catalogue of the London Exhibition of 1851, we see furniture of incredible complication and bad taste, where architecture and sculpture are so predominant that the pieces look more like monuments than furniture. These, however, were bravura pieces of the exhibiting manufacturers. In reality the furniture for ordinary use was much simpler. At first one merely made heavier and coarser the classical models fashionable during the Regency, then followed the inspiration of the Gothic, or French Renaissance, or Rococo or Louis XIV, with that eclecticism which is characteristic of the mid-19th century, until at the end of the century William Morris, through the inspiration of the more sober motifs of the Middle Ages, pointed the way toward *Art Nouveau.*[140]

In the *Library at Holland House* by Charles Robert Leslie (1794–1859), we see, seated at a Louis XV table, Lord and Lady Holland with their secretary John Allen, and their librarian William Dogget on

337: Anonymous. *Victorian Library,* watercolor, c. 1855-60. MARIO PRAZ COLLECTION, ROME.

the right. Holland House in Kensington, built at the beginning of the 17th century, was bought in 1767 by Henry Fox, first Baron Holland (the title came from a place in Lincolnshire called "parts of Holland") and was frequented by well-known figures like Sheridan, Thomas Moore, Thomas Campbell, Macaulay, George Grote, and Dickens. In the left corner of the library we see, resting on the floor, a portrait said to be of Joseph Addison, who had married the widow of one of the Counts of Warwick and Holland and who died at Holland House in 1719. Lord Holland, whom we see seated here, died in 1840. This painting by Leslie was painted in 1838 at Lord Holland's request, who wanted it as a gift for his wife. The modern furniture consists of the armchairs, a chair with twisted legs, a little table to the left, and the Regency colza-oil chandelier. Rows of paintings above the bookcases are hung at an angle to increase

their visibility, which remains, however, quite dubious. The Oriental rug is protected by a colorless canvas.

In the following interior of a *Victorian Library,* which dates from about 1855-60, the Victorian character is very marked. In this large watercolor by an anonymous artist the furnishings combine elements of Gothic style, Louis XIV and Rococo with an exuberance that recalls the furniture displayed at the London Exhibition in 1851. Characteristic is the open-work decoration of the two lateral arches giving onto the bow-window. In these arches are set bronze figures supporting gas lamps. The official catalogue of the 1851 Exhibition, Vol. II, Section III, Class 26, P729 stated that the section devoted to furniture proved the high degree of national prosperity and indicated "not less distinctly the wealth and domestic refinement of those for whose use the greater majority of the articles exhibited are unquestionably intended."

We find much better taste in this interior with *Thomas and Jane Carlyle in the Living Room of their House in Cheyne Row, Chelsea*, where Carlyle lived from 1834 on. In this oil painting by Robert S. Tait we see a neat, warm room, its walls covered with gaily flowered paper, a predominance of red in the curtains, in the rug on the floor and in the table-cov One would never suspect that the man in the violet-and-house robe and the pensive lady in a dark dress, sitting armchair with twisted columns, led in reality a very stor married life. Carlyle was born in 1795 and his wife, Jan

338: R. S. Tait. *Thomas and Jane Carlyle in the Living Room of their House in Cheyne Row, Chelsea.*
MARQUESS OF NORTHAMPTON COLLECTION.

Welsh, in 1801. Here man and wife are still in youthful
maturity. Thus the painting must have been executed some
years before it was exhibited by Tait at the Royal Academy
in 1858. The interior therefore is proto-Victorian, as the
furniture shows. It is still in the Georgian style of about 1830.

339: G.A. Gallier. *Living Room of the Butenev Family in the Palazzo Giustiniani in Rome,* watercolor, 1840-50. LEMMERMANN COLLECTION, ROME.

The documentation of Italian interiors in the latter part of the 19th century in general refers to houses inhabited by foreigners. When Butenev was Russian Minister to the Holy See he lived in Rome in Palazzo Giustiniani. His *Living Room,* shown in a watercolor by Gratien Achille Gallier (1814-1871; worked chiefly in Paris, is known to have been in Rome in 1848), reveals a naïve and pleasing Gothicness, achieved, as often happened in this period, by the ogival treatment of the tops of the chairbacks, pelmets, and other furnishings, including the *Zimmerlaube* at the right: it was a kind of calligraphy. The screen with the figures of armigers against a background that is also ogival is disarming in its innocent illusionism. These elements are for dreaming, for escaping into the past, but the armchairs covered with *housses* provide comfort. The curtains cast throughout the room a reddish light, propitious to the reading of Gothic novels.

The *Loggia of a Villa near Naples* was painted in 1845 by Gabriele Carelli, a Neapolitan who exhibited in London and the Royal Academy between 1866 and 1880. The loggia is a kind of rustic sitting room, with the overweening affirmation of the vegetable world which was never missing in 19th century interiors. Here the plants are in absolute majority, and the armchairs do their best to camouflage themselves by their chintz coverings with a vegetal pattern. That this is above all a sitting room is declared by

340: Gabriele Carelli. *Loggia of a Villa near Naples,* watercolor, 1845. LEMMERMANN COLLECTION, ROME.

e table with its red cover and its display of books:
eepsakes and albums. This watercolor is thought to
epresent the Villa Acton, later Rothschild, and finally
ignatelli Aragona-Cortes. But neither its location,
adicated by the view of Vesuvius visible from the
oggia, nor its architectural details would bear this
ut.[141]

An authentic interior of Villa Acton is found, on
ne other hand, in the work of an unknown and
nodest painter who, shortly after 1830, depicted Lady
etsy Acton writing at a table bearing an Apulian
ase. The frieze of griffins and ornate pilasters, the
nuslin swag, the sphinx tripod and the plant by the
indow are commonplaces of this kind of decoration.

341: Anonymous. *Lady Betsy Acton in her Writing Room of Villa Acton,*
watercolor, c. 1830. SIOLI-LEGNANI COLLECTION, BUSSERO, MILAN.

342: E. Koskilty. *Living Room of Palazzo Policastro in Naples,*
watercolor, 1850. LEMMERMANN COLLECTION, ROME.

A watercolor signed Ed. Koskilty, 1850, depicts the
Living Room of Palazzo Policastro in Naples at the
time when that palace was the seat of the Russian
Embassy to the King of Naples. As in all mid-19th
century living rooms, sofas and armchairs abound,
mostly covered with chintz. At the right, two divans,
upholstered in green velvet and set back to back,
simulate twin beds. The comfortable character is
paramount in this room, with little regard for elegance.
In front of a writing table with 18th century lines and
bronze mounts, there is a light Chiavari chair. Near
the door which allows a glimpse of a series of rooms
is hung a mahogany and bronze barometer, probably
made by Charles Frécot, 89 Rue de la Harpe, Paris.
But the most curious pieces of furniture are the two
bookcases against the left wall, completely similar to
a bookcase in my possession except that mine has

343: Mahogany Bookcase, Sicilian, first half
of the 19th century. PROPERTY OF MARIO PRAZ, ROME.

Gabriele Carelli. *Loggia in the Villa of the Russian Ambassador in Naples,* watercolor, 1859. LEMMERMANN COLLECTION, ROME.

only two doors. This cabinet was meant to contain books, as is indicated by the two bearded heads of philosophers, resembling respectively those of Zeno and Herodotus as illustrated by Pietro Bellori in *Veterum philosophorum, poetarum, rhetorum et oratorum imagines,* 1685. They also recall the two-faced herm of Herodotus and Thucydides in the Museo Nazionale, Naples. At first glance one might think that the two side-projections of this herm had been transferred to the upper part of the cabinet, which has an unusual jutting cornice, but the cabinet-maker meant to imitate the form of a typical Hellenistic monument, the *trilithon,* an architrave crowned with statues which extends beyond the two uprights on which it is set. This unusual piece is Sicilian, of that school of cabinet-makers who followed English and French models and flourished

in Sicily in the first half of the 19th century. They produced pieces of lovely figured mahogany with carved parts but never gilded.

Gabriele Carelli is the artist of the *Loggia in the Villa of the Russian Ambassador in Naples,* 1859, whose wrought-iron railing was brought especially from Russia. The *étagère* for books, at the right, is a Biedermeier piece of practical use; the chintz-covered armchairs and sofas are made for comfort. Their practicality is in contrast with the great ebony cupboard supported by caryatids at the left, a typical Louis XIII piece (c. 1630). In the same style are the table and the straight armchair with twisted columns, which are seen in this room. Both this villa and the other one painted by Carelli (*Fig.* 340) must have been on the Sorrento peninsula, as indicated by the view of Vesuvius and the bay from the loggia.

345: Anonymous. *A Living Room*, watercolor, c. 1860. MARIO PRAZ COLLECTION, ROME.

The appearance of a *Living Room in the Villa Wolkonsky* in Rome has been preserved for us in an anonymous watercolor in the Lemmermann Collection, Rome (*Fig.* 24). In this villa, which was first the German Embassy and is now the British Embassy, Princess Zenaïde Wolkonsky lived between 1830 and 1862, and kept a famous literary and artistic salon there. The villa now has nothing of its former decoration, but the garden is one of the few documents of a Romantic Rome[142], for beyond the tomb of Claudius, builder of the aqueduct that crosses the garden, there is a secluded corner, a path through the greenery with memorial tablets and columns which Zenaïde Wolkonsky placed there in memory of her friends. These tablets and columns bore inscriptions in Russian and in French, like this one for a certain Saščinka: "La neige a gelé la fleur naissante/Ici du moins le vent glacé n'atteindra pas les roses/Que l'amitié cultive pour elle," or this one, for the Princess' sister Lisa Cernisevskij: "Elle essaya des amours de la terre/mais elles n'etaient pas assez pures pour un ange." The spot was called *l'Allée des souvenirs*.

The living room, its walls a dark blue, with red draperies and red predominating in the rug on the floor, in the cover on the table in the background, and on the armchairs of the kind which in England were called balloon-back (balloon back and curved legs remained characteristic of armchai between 1850 and 1870), offers an excellent illustration o taste for intense, dark colors, in just this period between 1850 and 1860.

This taste is also clear in an anonymous watercolor of much more modest living room in the collection of the a which we reproduce above. Here the red almost speaks, suggesting—like the red flannel underclothes that ladies at that time—an ardent, repressed passionate nature. I rooms, the roundness of the bulb and the globe of the ke lamp can easily be given psychoanalytical meanings. Lik the exaggerated curves of the female form imposed by th fashion magazines of the last thirty-five years of the 19th century, these lamps can seem a true if unconscious parc of sex, so deliberately ignored and repressed was it by th conventions of the time.[143]

We do not know who lived in this little middle-class li room, but the person who inhabited the following interio was surrounded by a Romantic aura not inferior to Zen

346: Jean Sorieul. *Bedroom of the Duc de Morny,* watercolor. PIERRE FABIUS COLLECTION, PARIS.

Volkonsky's. This *Bedroom of the Duc de Morny* in his palace on the Champs-Elysées. painted by Jean Sorieul (1824–1871), shows us another flaming interior. The Duc de Morny was the illegitimate son of Hortense Beauharnais and the Comte de Flahaut; he was therefore the half-brother of Napoleon III and was a representative figure of the Second Empire; his name is associated with actresses' dressing-rooms and speculations on the stock market. He could have been one of Balzac's heroes. He was in the army, in business, in politics; he had his mother's fascination, he smoked cigars, and enjoyed the reputation of a great political acumen. His photograph by Nadar, of 1858,[144] shows us a bald gentleman with mutton-chop whiskers, moustache and goatee, with a blasé, supercilious air, rigid in his high collar and double-breasted coat. He launched Deauville and the Grand Prix; he was the Richelieu and the Brummell of the Second Empire, Ambassador to St. Petersburg, President of the Chamber, and an instrument in the *coup d'état* of December, 1851. From St. Petersburg he brought home as his wife a Princess Trubetskoj, who lived on gossip and cigarettes. Suave, ironic, skeptical, and Machiavellian, he played out his role of grey eminence, keeping in the background, *un bandit tombé dans la peau d'un vaudevilliste* as one person defined him. At the time of the Mexican adventure, he made a third of the profits which went to the banker Jecker; stock values rose in Paris when word was spread that Morny was *dans l'affaire.* When, too late, the Empire turned toward a more liberal regime, he suddenly died. A few evenings before his death he had been seen in his box for the opening night of Offenbach's *La belle Hélène.* Warned by his doctors of his approaching end, he sent the Duchess to a ball, then prepared to take his leave of the world. From his bed he watched his papers being burned, shook hands with his father, Comte de Flahaut, received the visit of the Imperial couple: "The lady ascended the stairs straight and proud, enveloped in her black mantillas; the man held the hand rail. slow and fatigued, the collar of his light overcoat turned up. his shoulders bent, and heaving in a convulsive sob." The brothers bade each other farewell, and Napoleon III lost his right arm. This scene took place in this room with its red hangings, with the round portraits of the Imperial family on the wall. amid Louis XVI pieces and 19th century sofa and armchairs.

347: Fernand Pelez. *Living Room,* watercolor, 1852. MARIO PRAZ COLLECTION, ROME.

Among the painters of interiors around the middle of the 19th century. Fernand Pelez. of Spanish origin (his full name was "Pelez de Cordova." b. Paris. 1820; a pupil of Gérôme; d. 1899) deserves perhaps a special position for his very personal manner, softer than that of the ordinary painters of interiors who are often hard to distinguish from one another. No less precise than the others, indeed almost photographic in his precision, Pelez still knew how to create an atmosphere that has something more than middle-class smugness. His interiors, one might say, are narrated with the imagination of a novelist who sees characters in them, who makes them the background of a story. In the first two which we shall now discuss, the human figure is not just a mannikin, and the observer feels that he is being taken into a room where someone looks up at his arrival and will soon rise and come toward the guest. In the first watercolor of a *Living Room,* dated 1852 we see a room with the walls covered with an arabesqued, iridescent wallpaper with a monogram (an "N"

with Rococo flourishes) repeated obsessively. The room almost seems to have walls of majolica, Second Empire *azulejos,* uninterrupted by any pictures, since the few pic are set on pieces of furniture. Here the human figure is a with curly red hair who looks up from an illustrated boo and gazes at us. Red, the favorite color in that period fo covering chairs and sofas, covers the pieces here. The pa has rendered the various shades of this color in the room red of the walls is different from that of the velvet cover one of the tables and the cashmere shawl on the other; a even the red of the peony in the vase and the red of the child's hair are different, though these differences create clash of colors. The arabesqued walls would have please Poe, and one thinks of Poe and of Baudelaire when one at this interior.

The second water color bears a date which can perhaps read as 1862. It is a *Living Room in Second Empire Style* with many stuccos and much gilt, great mirrors, tufted a

348: Fernand Pelez. *Living Room in Second Empire Style,* watercolor, 1862 (?). MARIO PRAZ COLLECTION, ROME.

hairs and divans upholstered in green. The room looks out
n a green park through three French doors. The style is Louis
XVI-Impératrice, which we shall discuss shortly. Sitting
behind the circular table with a green cover is a young girl,
who is raising her eyes from an album to look towards us.
Her plumed *toque* and jacket, in the fashion of around 1860,
are set on an occasional chair in the foreground. On a low
chair by the fireplace there is a tall hat and a pair of gloves.
On the sofa to the right we see some music, a tambourine,
and what looks like a *chasse-mouches* of peacock feathers, as
well as a round cushion in Arab style. The tufted divan near
the window hides the piano. As the painter in the other watercolor created a harmony of various reds, here he aims at the
same result with a variety of greens, contrasting with the
delicate rose color of the Oriental rug.

A third watercolor by Pelez, *Interior of a Bedroom* (*Fig.* 4),
is neither signed nor dated, and one would be inclined to
assign it to a rather late period, especially considering the

toilette at the left whose objects seem foreshortened as if
inspired by photographic angle. Still, if we compare the
furnishing with that of Princess Barjatinskij's Boudoir in
Paris, in the Villeret watercolor dated 1842 (*Fig.* 6), we remain
puzzled. Here too we find chintz and Boulle furniture. And
moreover the circular staircase with the upholstered banister,
in the Pelez watercolor, recalls that of the *Library-Sitting
Room of Princess Mathilde* (*Fig.* 371) which certainly belongs
to the Second Empire period. Also to this period apparently
belong the porcelain plates with the *bleu céladon* ground on
the mantelpiece. In any case, this bedroom, with its walls of
pink and white stripes patterned with bunches of roses,
cluttered with knick-knacks, papers on the table at the right
and flacons on the *toilette* at the left, holy pictures, rosaries
and scapulars over the bed, and the upholstered circular
staircase which repeats the motif of the roses on the walls,
remains more vivid in the memory than many rooms whose
floors our feet have trod.

349: Wilhelm Dünckel. *Interior in Mannheim*, 1860. MARIO PRAZ COLLECTION, ROME.

Never in any period in the history of furniture was there such an abundance of pieces for sitting on as in the late 19th century. Not only were new varieties created, like the *confortable*, the *causeuse*, the *confident*, the *indiscret*, the *fumeuse*, the *crapaud* and the *pouf*, adding to the list which had already been increased in the 18th century, but the old models, after the introduction of the spring, became more ponderous and awkward, covering a greater part of the room's area with their balloon backs. These pieces were upholstered (usually completely) with various stuffs such as silk damask, Genoa velvet, brocade, tapestries from Beauvais or Aubusson, or cloth with velvet or embroidery appliqued. This predominance of stuffs in the decoration created a general gaudiness and a blunting of outlines. The taste of the period for heavy draperies—curtains and portieres—further rounded off the lines. One tried to harmonize the whole around a dominating color, to which the individual notes of the sofas, the armchairs, the hangings, the rugs, the wallpapers and even the ceilings were subordinated.[145]

In Pelez's interiors we have noted various arrangements of red and green. In two interiors painted in 1860 by the Mannheim artist Wilhelm Dünckel (1818-1880), whom we have already encountered, we find a violet shade. These are two rooms in the same apartment. In the first, rug, curtains, armchairs, table-covers are of the same color, against which stand out the blooms of the hothouse plants and the flowered borders of the pale cream-colored wall. One chair is upholstered in a flowered stuff, an armchair by the window with flowered stripes.

alternating with black ones. The stuff that lines the windowsills is also flowered. Here the armchairs have still a wooden outline, but the backs are the characteristic balloon shape. The two Neo-Rococo pieces date from 1840-1850; the Rococo element is especially visible in the frames of the doors. The armchairs and the sofa are of the same period. Similar elements, including the gilded pelmets, are found in the other room, where a *pouf* appears in the center. The *trumeau* against the rear wall and the one in the embrasure of the window are 18th century. Just to the left of the *trumeau* against the rear wall is set a little bronze *torchère* of the Empire period.[146] Observe the Gothic decoration and colored panes in the upper part of the window.

Red sofas and armchairs also clutter the *Room in the Hofburg in Vienna* (presumably the room of the Archduchess Sofie, mother of Franz Josef) with a décor of the period 1850-1860. The furniture is of that Neo-Rococo which was particularly established in Vienna, whereas in France, as we shall see, the influence of the Empress Eugénie led to an attenuation of Neo-Rococo by the more sober lines of Louis XVI style. Family portraits are lined up on the wall above the *étagères*, which are cluttered as usual with porcelains and knick-knacks. But what gives the room a personal note is the twin portrait of Franz Josef and Elisabeth on an easel in front of the writing desk, in the midst of such a frame of plants and flowers that this corner of the room looks like an altar. On the desk an *ormolu* angel and a statuette of a woman playing the lute increase the impression of a family sanctum.

350: Anonymous. *Room in the Hofburg in Vienna,* watercolor. STAATLICHES MOBILIENDEPOT, VIENNA.

351: Wilhelm Dünckel. *Interior in Mannheim,* 1860. MARIO PRAZ COLLECTION, ROME.

352: Bénédic Masson. *Bedroom of the Empress Eugénie at Saint–Cloud,* watercolor, 1855. LEMMERMANN COLLECTION, ROME.

When the Empress Eugénie revived the style Louis XVI and made it fashionable she showed a certain originality, just as she had done in launching the crinoline or bringing the fan back into favor, for indeed under Louis-Philippe every style had been imitated except Louis XVI. Her choice was inspired by a sentimental inclination rather than an aesthetic one: the Empress made a kind of cult of Marie Antoinette, whose personality she hoped to reincarnate, to obliterate her own parvenu origins. So Eugénie became an interior decorator out of emulation of her idol and combined modern comfort with 18th century elegance. She mixed sofas and chairs, overstuffed with navel-like buttons (one might say that the tufted style is a deification of that part of the body which is bourgeois *par excellence,* the belly), with authentic Louis XVI pieces and modern imitations of them made by cabinet-makers so clever that only the experts can distinguish

these precise (*too* precise, which is what gives them away) imitations from authentic 18th century furniture. These cabinet-makers included Henri Fourdinois, Tahan, Grohé, who made copies of Louis XVI furniture also for the English court, Paul Sormani, Jeanselme, Cruchet, and others.[147] When, instead of copying 18th century pieces inch by inch, these cabinet-makers wanted to apply Louis XVI style to new forms, they created hybrid pieces that are easily identifiable. Thus the *psyché* in the Toilette Room of the Empress at Saint-Cloud, made perhaps by Fourdinois, tries in vain to compensate for the heaviness of the outline by applying delicate Pompeiian arabesques of bronze. And thus the monumental jewel cabinet of the Empress[148] suffers from that redundance of ornament and lack of harmony which characterize the vulgar mid-19th century products assembled from all parts of Europe for the great

: J.-B. Fortuné de Fournier. *Bedroom of the Empress Eugénie at Saint–Cloud,* watercolor, 1863. Formerly FABIUS FRÈRES, PARIS.

Exhibition in London in 1851. This is a kind of furniture which even from a distance looks counterfeit, even when it is made with the finest material, with real mahogany, real *ormolu*, and real porcelain. Good taste can redeem poor materials (even in the Biedermeier style, in its first phase, there are pieces of common woods which have a sober, bourgeois distinction), but bad taste can degrade even precious ones. A necklace of real stones will seem suspect when worn by a parvenu, while counterfeit diamonds can be carried off by the distinction of the wearer.

The period of Eugénie's infatuation for Louis XVI runs from 1853 to 1860; the result was the style known as Louis XVI-Impératrice. At Saint-Cloud, where Eugénie stayed often in the first months of her marriage, her room was Marie Antoinette's old music room, with its white panels decorated with gold arabesques. There is a painting of this room by Bénédic Masson (1819-1893) in the Musée des Arts Décoratifs, Paris, and a variant of the same painting, signed B. M., 1855, in the Lemmermann collection, Rome, which we reproduce here. We also reproduce another view of the same room, painted by Jean-Baptiste Fortuné de Fournier (1798-1864) made in 1863, which was formerly at Fabius Frères, Paris. A variant by Fournier exists at the Château de Compiègne.[149] Authentic pieces, like the two sideboards (dining room furniture) by G. Beneman, one against the rear wall, the other between the two windows, are placed among overstuffed chairs, and a bed and little table which are clumsy imitations of Louis XVI. Between 1855, the date of the Masson watercolor, and 1863, the period of Fournier's, we note some changes in the decoration of the room: the spyglass has disappeared, and on the sideboard at the rear a kind of domestic altar has been set up. In the Fournier interior the door is open into the dressing room.

354: Bénédic Masson. *The Drawing Room of the Empress Eugénie at Saint–Cloud,* watercolor, 1855. LEMMERMANN COLLECTION, ROME.

The *Drawing Room of the Empress Eugénie at Saint-Cloud,* like the bedroom, has come down to us in a watercolor by Masson, 1855, and in one by Fournier, 1863. Here, too, authentic pieces are mixed with modern sofas and armchairs, according to a custom which still continues today. The Louis XV writing desk in the center of the room, by Jean François Oeben and Jean Henri Riesener, made between 1760–69, was taken from the Pavillon de Marsan by the Empress,

who had it brought to this room.[150] To the left, between the two windows, there is a commode-*étagère* in Riesener's late style or in the style of Adam Weisweiler, of the last period of Louis XVI. In the Masson watercolor, on this side of the commode we see a Louis XVI jardinière. In the Fournier watercolor the commode is flanked by chairs of the same style, but in front of the solemn and ornate Louis XV writing desk two simple Chiavari chairs have been placed, and nearby

355: J.-B. Fortuné de Fournier. *Drawing Room of the Empress Eugénie at Saint–Cloud,* watercolor, 1863.
Formerly FABIUS FRÈRES, PARIS.

is a 19th century *étagère* for books. In front of the
divan some low armchairs and a little curved table
have been set, and oval flower paintings appear on the
walls. Through the door we see the armchairs
and the *causeuse* which have invaded the adjoining
room. These presumptuous armchairs remind us of the
delirium tremens vision in one of Guy de Maupassant's
anguished short stories, *Qui sait?:* "Suddenly, in the
doorway, I saw an armchair, the big armchair I read

in, which went out, swaying. It went off into the garden.
Other chairs followed it, the armchairs of my living
room, then the low divans which dragged themselves
along like crocodiles on their short legs, then all my
chairs, which bounded like goats, and the footstools
which sprung like rabbits..." Every age has the
nightmares it deserves: the late 19th century (when
de Maupassant wrote his story) could not but have
nightmares of overstuffed furniture.

356: J.-B. Fortuné de Fournier. *Private Sitting Room of the Empress Eugénie at Saint-Cloud*, watercolor. PIERRE FABIUS COLLECTION, PARIS.

357: J.-B. Fortuné de Fournier. *Dressing Room of the Empress Eugénie at Saint–Cloud,* watercolor, 1863. Formerly FABIUS FRÈRES, PARIS.

Of the *Dressing Room of the Empress Eugénie at Sai Cloud* there are two versions by Fournier. One in Compiègne shows the Empress seated at her dressi table. The other, formerly at Fabius Frères, Paris, which we reproduce here, is a variant without the Empress. In the Compiègne version, the *psyché* is the right, in place of the clumsy imitation Louis X washstand which we see here. The table in front of fireplace is different, and there are different knick-knacks on the commode, which is inlaid with vari woods in the style of Riesener and stands between windows against the rear wall. The dressing-table covered with white muslin embroidered in blue, an is what was called a *toilette Pompadour* (already in 1830's the name of Pompadour had been associate with various stuffs: *moiré* Pompadour, *barège* Pom adour, damask Pompadour...) Two *torchères* set front of the *psyché* at the left belong to the more s imitation of Pompeiian models which was practice under the Second Empire.

The *Grand Drawing Room at Saint-Cloud* by Fournier, 1863, formerly at Fabius Frères, Paris (another similar watercolor is in the Musée des Ar Décoratifs, Paris), presents the usual mixture of 18

358: J.-B. Fortuné de Fournier. *Private Sitting Room of Napoleon III
Saint-Cloud*, watercolor. PIERRE FABIUS COLLECTION, PARIS.

century pieces with Neo-Rococo sofas and armchairs.
The grand piano at the right is in Louis XIV style. The
painting on the right wall is a Murillo.

The *Private Sitting Room of the Empress Eugénie
Saint-Cloud* by Fournier with its walls a sickly green,
a large circular ebony table which presides like a
mother hen over the circle of occasional chairs of a
muddy black color, its two large Alpine landscapes
and the smaller genre paintings, the ceiling painted a
natural sky color, gives the impression of a ponderous,
dusty luxuriousness. The curved desk which can be
glimpsed in the next room is that of the *Private Sitting
Room of Napoleon III,* which Fournier shows us in
another watercolor where he has introduced some
figures: the Emperor sitting at that desk, as the Empress
returns to her own sitting room. In this room of the
Emperor, its walls covered with genre paintings then
in fashion, we see several First Empire pieces: sofas,
armchairs, the two *méridiennes* covered with the same
red damask as the walls which flank the fireplace, and
above all, half-hidden by a circle of modest Chiavari
chairs, a magnificent *guéridon* of bronze, mahogany and
marble, with slender legs supported by winged lions.
Here, too, the ceiling is painted to simulate the sky.

359: J.-B. Fortuné de Fournier. *Grand
Drawing Room at Saint–Cloud,* watercolor, 1863.
Formerly FABIUS FRÈRES, PARIS.

360 (at left): J.-B. Fortuné de Four
Council Hall in the
Tuileries, watercolor.
Formerly FABIUS FRÈRES, PARIS.

361 (below): J.-B. Fortuné de Four
Room formerly of Marie
de Medicis in the Château de
Fontainebleau, watercolor, 1863.
Formerly FABIUS FRÈRES, PARIS.

The Louis XVI-Impératrice style had its apotheosis in the grand apartment of the Tuileries, built in 1858 by Hector-Martin Lefuel (1810–1881), with its three drawing rooms—one green, one pink, one blue—entirely covered with panels designed by the architect in a style that recalled especially Jean Charles de la Fosse, and decorated with paintings by artists then in fashion, Edouard Dubufe (1820–1883) official court portrait painter, and Charles-Josuah Chaplin (1825–1891) painter of the elegances of the Second Empire. The album dedicated in 1867 to illustrate these marvels, which were shortly to vanish, bore these words by the architect Rouyer: "One will note the original style of this decoration. The art of today is a prolongation and adaptation of earlier styles, according to the needs and

highly perfected means of execution of the second half of the 19th century." The Louis XVI-Impératrice style was established in all elegant interiors,[151] and its fashion lasted even longer than the Second Empire itself. We here quote some words of Théophile Gautier which characterize the taste of the period: "What could be more charming than a group of women of different and contrasting beauty seated on a *pouf* in the center of a salon in a billow of guipures and lace which froths at their feet like the sea at the feet of Venus?"[152] These words could well describe the famous painting by Franz Xavier Winterhalter: *Eugénie among the Ladies of her Court*.

Of the apartments in the Tuileries, Fournier painted the *Council Hall*, a typical official room, with portraits

(above): J.-B. Fortuné de Fournier.
...one Room in the Château de
...tainebleau, watercolor.
...merly FABIUS FRÈRES, PARIS.

... *(at right):* J.-B. Fortuné de Fournier.
...dy of Napoleon III in
...Tuileries, watercolor.
...merly FABIUS FRÈRES, PARIS.

...ouis Bonaparte, Queen Hortense, and the Empress
...génie, a bust of Napoleon I and a cake-like *pouf* in
...center of the room. He also painted the *Study of*
...poleon, where, as usual in sovereigns' studies, the
...ctical element prevails.

...wo watercolors by Fournier of rooms in the
...âteau de Fontainebleau conclude this series. Some
...fortables and some Chiavari chairs have insinuated
...mselves in the *Room formerly of Marie de Médicis;*
... tables have 19th century covers; on the central one
...re is a First Empire *lampe-bouillotte.* The *Throne*
...om retains First Empire taste in the throne, the
...hères, and the stools: this style had become the
...cial style of the supreme authority of the state, not
...y in France but also abroad.

364: Eugène Lami. *The Grand Staircase in the Château de Ferrières,* watercolor, c. 1865. PRIVATE COLLECTION, ROME.

Eugène Lami (1800–1890) was the chronicler of fashionable life under the July Monarchy and the Second Empire. Gifted with a light and sparkling brush, clever in rendering the atmosphere and the movement of a crowd of people without losing sight of the individual characters, painter of the life of court and theatre, he was elegant and one hundred per cent Parisian. At a reception at the Tuileries under Napoleon III he said: "Les souverains changent, mais les épaules des femmes restent!"[153] At the house of his friends the Delaroches, Lami had often met Baron James de Rothschild, the famous financier, who took a great liking to him. In 1856, seeing that the artist was less taken up with official commissions, which were becoming rarer all the time, Rothschild entrusted to him the construction of the Château de Boulogne, and later, the remodelling of the Château de Ferrières. Thus Lami became a kind of artistic director for the financier, just as he had been for the Duc d'Aumale at

the time of the first restoration of Chantilly. Lami did not have the technical knowledge to handle the architectural part of these undertakings. He limited himself to indicating the general lines for the building and the park, and in more detail he concerned himself with the arrangement of the apartments and their decoration. His stay in England had made him particularly interested in the distribution of light and the type of decoration of the great English country houses. At the Château de Boulogne for example, there are precise reminiscences of Colworth House.

The Château de Ferrières (Seine et Marne) was built in 1857 by J. Paxton, the architect of the Crystal Palace, possibly after a plan by Lami,[154] in Italian Renaissance style with loggias and colonnades and square-cornered towers, at first crowned with spires which were later replaced by cupolas. James de Rothschild put Lami in charge of the transformation and interior decoration of the château and followed

365: Eugène Lami. *Staircase of the Vestibule in the Château de Ferrières,* watercolor, 1866. PRIVATE COLLECTION, ROME.

his advice also in the purchase of the works of art which were to adorn it. Between 1860 and 1866 Lami made some watercolors for the mother of Guy de Rothschild which record for us the interiors of the château.

In the painting of the *Grand Staircase* we see that Lami, on his journey to Venice with the Baroness James de Rothschild, picked up many useful ideas. The coffered ceiling with relief in geometric patterns, with medallions in the center, recalls the ceilings of the Doges' Palace. On the wall of the staircase is a monumental hunting scene by Rubens' contemporary and collaborator, Frans Snyders (1579–1657), or by one of his followers, Paul de Vos, or Adraien van Utrecht. The balustrade is of pale oak and ebony.

The *Great Hall* (*Fig.* 23) is a vast room illuminated from above. Many of the formal rooms open onto this hall. Dividing the height of the outsize room by a gallery, Lami could decorate the upper part with tapestries and save the lower walls for the paintings

by the great masters which formed the Rothschilds' noteworthy collection. In the middle portion of the room, the balcony around the Hall is supported by pairs of columns which are repeated above, reaching up to the ceiling. The lower columns are of blond wood, partially sheathed in gilded ornaments; the upper columns are partly in blond, partly in black wood. The ceiling is supported by gilded corbels, beneath which there runs a frieze of little genii who flank oval medallions in chiaroscuro, containing the initials of the founder of Ferrières, J.R., surmounted by the baron's coronet. At the four corners this frieze is fixed by large polychrome heads in Italian style. This kind of decoration, inspired by the Italian Cinquecento, was later to become popular in Italy in the *Umbertino* period. A monumental fireplace of white marble with *ormolu* ornaments culminates in a large bust of Minerva, the head in white marble, the drapery in black (in the late 19th century combinations of various

366: Eugène Lami. *The Dining Room in the Château de Ferrières,* watercolor, 1860. PRIVATE COLLECTION, ROME.

materials in sculpture were fashionable, especially carved ivory with gold, silver, bronze, wood and even onyx). The low hearth, in English style, shows Lami's intention of uniting English comfort to his grandiose decoration. On the marble plaque set into the mantle, Lami had carved some French verses dated 1570, which read: "Sweet is life, if lived well, / whether in spring or winter, / under white snow or green boughs, / when true friends help us live it; / here then there is room for them all, / for the old as for the young."

As to the furnishing of this *Hall,* we see Louis XIII and Louis XIV forms along with typical 19th century

ones, with some attempt to harmonize them in the solemn surroundings: thus the *pouf* is surmounted by a pilaster with an Atlas bearing a globe topped by the baronial coronet of the Rothschilds.

In conformity with the festive, idle spirit that was to reign in the château, Lami had painted in 1861 in the *fumoir* of horseshoe form on the ground floor, a fresco nine meters long and almost a meter high, with the Carnival in Venice as its subject; above it were Italian verses: "Vario è il vestir, ma il desiderio è un solo: Cercar tutti fuggir tristezza e duolo." ("The dress is various, but the desire is one: All seek to flee sadness

367: Eugène Lami. *The Family Room in the Château de Ferrières,* watercolor, c. 1865. PRIVATE COLLECTION, ROME.

and grief.") The decoration of Ferrières was so admired that one of the château's visitors, Cham, on January 3, 1863, made a drawing in the guest-book, showing the fairies setting their magic wands at Lami's feet, recognizing him as their master.

We now see the other watercolors of interiors at Ferrières by Lami. The *Staircase of the Vestibule* (*Fig.* 365) is of the 18th century French style found in *hôtels particuliers.* The *Dining Room* on the other hand, is modeled on the halls of French châteaux of the 16th century; the chairs are Louis XIII with the characteristic legs and stretchers *à os de mouton;* the mirrors are

18th century Venetian, with frames of cut glass. In the imposing *Family Room* in Louis XIII style, we see a little low 19th century armchair on which a parasol and a bunch of flowers have been placed; and at right a bourgeois rocking chair. In the *Louis XVI Salon* (*Fig.* 10), a white room with Corinthian columns and pilasters, which is meant to be an exact reconstruction, we find only a few extraneous pieces of furniture: an occasional chair and a discreet *pouf;* on the left a lady's writing desk with a Sèvres medallion. The principal piece is really the large round table with its heavy cover, about which members of the family are posed.

The *Sitting Room of Baron Alphonse de Rothschild* is in Louis XV style, with suitable furniture, except for the armchairs. On the left, in the foreground, a *bureau plat* characteristic of the Louis XV style (this type of piece was called *bureau* from the stuff, the Italian "burello," which originally covered the top, later replaced by leather), apparently of dark wood, perhaps ebony. Panels of Gobelin tapestry are inserted in the wood paneling, and the harmony of the warm colors of the wood with the blue of these hangings is a very good imitation of an original Louis XV room. Tapestries also adorn the *Bedroom of the Baron*, which is pleasantly hung in pink, with Louis XV armchairs and a Boulle commode. The balcony with its banister of oak and ebony and an Oriental stuff picturesquely draped between two Chinese vases, is in the bric-a-brac taste which was to prevail in the 1870's. The painting in the alcove is of the type of profile portraits of the Italian 15th century. In the *Bedroom of the Baroness Alphonse de Rothschild* the wall covering, in harmony with the canopy of the bed, is of white bands alternating with bands of red and an arabesque pattern, in rather Victorian taste. The bed is 19th century, as is the sofa in the left foreground. Over the Louis XIII mantelpiece there is a portrait of a lady in 17th century costume, perhaps Dutch.

In concluding our visit to the Château de Ferrières, we quote the passage that Philippe Jullian devotes to the Rothschilds: "As the Romans adorned their capital with the spoils of Greece and Egypt, after the fall of Napoleon a new power adorned itself with the ornaments that the declining powers were forced to abandon. German Princes and Italian churches pawned or sold a part of their treasures to the Seven Brothers of Frankfurt, whose descendants have collections the like of which had not been seen since the days of the Medici. The Second Empire established the type of decoration for the houses that the Rothschilds and their imitators built all over Europe; the best example is offered by the decoration of Ferrières by Eugène Lami. It is the magnificence of a Veronese adapted to a Grand Hotel. Countless Greuzes, Rembrandts and Gainsboroughs cover miles of damask and Genoa velvet; on Riesener tables and in Boulle cabinets are accumulated collections of enamels, gold boxes, miniatures and watches. In their drawing rooms, exactly alike, in Piccadilly or the Faubourg Saint-Honoré, the Rothschilds have translated into reality the dream of Balzac, in a hothouse atmosphere. There is a light Rothschild style: panels of pale wood and *ormolu,* Savonnerie rugs and Fragonards; and there is a dark Rothschild style: tapestries and cupboards, Rembrandts and Cellini bronzes...This passion for objects whose historic origins had to be as important as their artistic qualities distinguishes the Rothschilds from their great contemporaries. In the apartments built by their architects we find Versailles and Chambord again ... Texas millionaires hunt for objects that belonged to the Rothschilds, symbols of a venerable capitalism, just as the Rothschilds hunted for objects that had belonged to Marie-Antoinette."[155]

368: Eugène Lami. *Sitting Room of the Baron Alphonse de Rothschild in the Château de Ferrières,* watercolor, c. 1865. PRIVATE COLLECTION, ROME.

369: Eugène Lami. *Bedroom of the Baron Alphonse de Rothschild in the Château de Ferrières,* watercolor, c. 1865. PRIVATE COLLECTION, ROME.

370: Eugène Lami. *Bedroom of the Baroness Alphonse de Rothschild in the Château de Ferrières,* watercolor, 1865. PRIVATE COLLECTION, ROME.

371: Charles Giraud. *Library-Sitting Room of Princess Mathilde at the Château de Saint-Gratien,*
c. 1865. PIERRE FABIUS COLLECTION, PARIS.

A comparison between an interior of the 1840's and
one of the 1860's is very instructive as to the evolution
of taste. The *Living Room in the Hôtel Crillon,* which
is believed to be the *hôtel* of the Princesse de Polignac,
is seen here in a watercolor by Auguste Caron (b. 1806)
from just a little after 1840. It shows a complex of
tables and armchairs of Biedermeier type installed in
an 18th century room, with tapestry panels on the walls.
These *tentures chinoises* were designed by François
Boucher and executed at Beauvais shortly after 1742.
A century after these pastoral *chinoiseries,* taste has
greatly changed. Men sunk in their *confortables* are
reading the newspaper, a young woman is embroidering
a bell-pull, to add more flowers to those which already
exist in the room in the chintz of the armchairs and
the covers that hide the tables. A large bouquet of
fresh flowers dominates the central table; nearby is a
spyglass. All this remains bourgeois, domestic: the
fabulous, exotic world suggested by the tapestries has
no appeal, it might even not be there for this calm
group of people in an informal gathering, each with
his own little occupation.

In the *Library-Sitting Room of Princess Mathilde
at the Château de Saint-Gratien,* an oil painted by
Charles Giraud (1819-1892) in the 1860's, we are
almost transported into a tropical forest: the greenery
prevents us from seeing the sky ,The great palms in
their monumental pots with their authenticity guaran-
tee to keep green the walls and the ceiling, the flowered
chintzes which hide the doors and are draped on the
circular staircase, imitating the serpentine writhing of
jungle lianes. Red is mixed with the green in the rug,
and it dominates the carpet on the steps which is like a
wound in the trunk of a palm tree. This room, which
was a center of artistic life (the Princess herself was an

amateur painter), seems open to a new form of
exoticism. Livingstone has plunged into the heart of
Africa. Verne has described a journey to the center of
the Earth and has, with his fantasy, descended twenty
thousand leagues under the sea, Rimbaud is about to
write *Le Bateau Ivre;* the Biedermeier world is about
to dissolve. The nature installed in Princess Mathilde's
living room is not the domesticated nature brought
into Biedermeier rooms with flowers and caged birds:
it is like an explosive charge which blows the roof off.
And in the serpentine line of the stairs there is a fore-
shadowing of *Art Nouveau.*

The sitting room of Princess Mathilde was somewhat
avant-garde in its taste. Naturally in the 1850's families
still gathered in their living rooms in comfortable and
clumsy armchairs to read or embroider, as in the
anonymous watercolor of a *Lombard Interior* from
around 1850. Here we see Principessa De Soresina
Vidoni, née Buturlin, looking down at her embroidery,
present—for propriety's sake—at the conversation of
her daughter Maria Carolina with her fiancé Conte
Tommaso Mocenigo Soranzo. The engaged couple are
sitting properly on a two-seated sofa, and another
similar sofa raises its curved back near the *étagère* in
the corner, covered with knick-knacks as are the two
little *étagères* on either side of the mirror. In front of
the fireplace there is a *confident.* On the left wall a
portrait of the daughter with her favorite dog painted
ten years earlier hangs at an angle. Nearby, in a smaller
painting, is an angel's head, perhaps commemorating
a De Soresina child who died in infancy. At the piano
on the left, his sister no doubt occasionally plays for
him some seraphic airs. In Lombardy in those years,
as in much of Europe, this little old-fashioned world
went on, unaware that its sunset was drawing near.

372: Anonymous. *Lombard Interior*, watercolor, c. 1850. CONTESSA M. STUCCHI GIUNTINI COLLECTION, FLORENCE.

373: Auguste Caron. *Living Room in the Hôtel Crillon,* watercolor, c. 1840. PIERRE FABIUS COLLECTION, PARIS.

374: Samuel Butler. *Family Prayers,* 1864. ST. JOHN'S COLLEGE, CAMBRIDGE.

We have on several occasions observed how there exists a kind of room which does not seem to move with the times, which is colorless, or unrepresentative: kitchens, artists' studios, dining rooms of humble people. Still other rooms are in fact representative of a period and of an atmosphere, but they give a generic, reduced, blunted idea of them, like statistics or the "other distinguishing marks" on a passport.

In this category we place the oil painting *Family Prayers,* painted in 1864 by the English critic and novelist Samuel Butler (1835–1902). The scene is a Victorian living room toward the middle of the last century, a very commonplace Victorian living room. A circular table, with a massive leg and a cover of velvet with flowers embroidered around the edge, rises in the middle of the room like a mushroom on the little meadow of the curly rug. The vegetal illusion is also

achieved by the two leafy landscapes in stiff frames which flank a clock on a bracket under a glass bell. Under the landscapes sit two men and three women in a row, the men's faces framed with mutton-chop whiskers, the women's heads surrounded by white haloes which, on closer examination, prove to be lace caps, though at first sight we would have taken the women for saints. In front of this row of faces, her hands on the arms of her chair, is the lady of the house; in perfect symmetry with her at the opposite side of the room is her daughter, also in an armchair; and in the shadow near the window, staring into space, the son. All these people, no less inanimate than the objects around them, are hanging on the words of the central figure, a bald and bespectacled gentleman with thick eyebrows who is sitting at the table, reading from a book. His pronouncements must be as solemn and

375: Anonymous. *Italian Interior,* c. 1880. CONTE GIOVANNI JACINI COLLECTION, MILAN.

funereal as those of a last will and testament. In fact, he is reading verses of the Old Testament, and soon the whole family will sing hymns to the accompaniment of the cabinet piano, which with its sounding board protected by some pleated stuff, forms a background to the gruff and aggressive face of the master of the house. The impression of squalid caricature which we receive from the picture has been repeated by Butler, with quite a different degree of power, in the auto-biographical novel he wrote around 1880, which was posthumously published in 1903: *The Way of All Flesh,* a fierce denunciation of the hypocrisy and cruelty of Victorian family life.[156] The scene of this painting is the living room at Langar, Butler's birthplace, but it could be anywhere in the Anglo-Saxon countries. It is the quintessence of Victorianism, the squalid reverse of the medal, the opposite of the idyllic scenes usually presented by the ordinary painters of Victorian life, just as *The Way of All Flesh,* that ruthless analysis of family symbiosis in the light of positivism, is the exact opposite of those "drawing room or parsonage idylls" which are the poems in Coventry Patmore's *The Angel in the House.*

The *Italian Interior* by an anonymous painter (property of Conte Giovanni Jacini, Milan) is also representative and generic at the same time. From the dress of the lady seated by the window one would date the painting around 1880, but the decoration, except perhaps for the vases and the kerosene lamp on the right, is earlier, from around the middle of the century. It is a kind of living room which could have remained unchanged even down to today, and people visiting it now, though aware of its 19th century character, would retain no very strong impression of it.

376: H. T. Dunn. *Living Room of Dante Gabriel Rossetti in Chelsea,* watercolor, 1882. NATIONAL PORTRAIT GALLERY, LONDON.

Even artists' rooms can leave generic impressions on us, as of rooms that one sees in quantity, of undefined date. The *Artist's Room in the Ritterstrasse,* an oil painting, by Adolph von Menzel could indeed be anywhere for it is but a mere backdrop: the true scene is what is beyond the window. As in the other interior by this painter (*Fig.* 335) the air and light breaking in have destroyed that sense of seclusion, of protection that is characteristic of Biedermeier interiors. Here the view from the window reduces the room to a sort of *camera obscura:* it is no longer secluded, nor is it connected to the outside world with its sweet and savage violence of the sun and air. It is only a means, a room with a view, which is chosen as a dwelling precisely for that view. As to the furniture, the bed and the desk-bookshelf could be found in any student's room in an English college.

There is little imprint of a particular period in the *Living Room of Dante Gabriel Rossetti in Chelsea* painted by Henry Treffry Dunn (active 1870–1890) who became Rossetti's

assistant in 1867 and produced many replicas of his work. Dunn made this and other watercolors after the artist's death in 1882 in the apartment in Cheyne Walk, Chelsea, before it was cleared out. Thus he paints here from memory a scene observed in the house: Rossetti as he reads his verses to Theodore Dunton. Rossetti loved Delft ware and convex mirrors, and we see both in the room; we also see a stuffed owl on the mantelpiece, and on the wall behind it a primitive that might be Lorenzo Veneziano. On the wall in the background are the Rossetti family portraits. The sofa is Regency, in painted wood with gilded decorations, with the typical diagonal lattice. The seats of such sofas were caned. The mirror on the rear has a frame in the style of the James I period. The eclecticism of the 19th century achieved this: taking something from one style and something from another, in the end there was no style at all. Non-style was created from an excess of style, just as all the colors of the rainbow, when mixed together, produce grey.

377: Adolph von Menzel. *Artist's Room in the Ritterstrasse.* DAHLEM MUSEUM, BERLIN.

For the kind of decoration considered elgant in the last part of the century, only the words *bric-a-brac* or *junk* seem appropriate terms. The example was set by artists' studios, and the living room was modeled on them. Already, shortly after 1830, we find the delight in bric-a-brac so developed that, if the *Study of Du Sommerard* by V. Fouquet (*Fig.* 382) were not dated 1837, we would place it in the 1870's.[157] We would say the same of the *Studio of Dantan,* which also belongs to the first half of the century.

Here is the *Studio of the Painter Hans Makart,* in an oil painting of 1885 by Rudolf von Alt. In his day Makart enjoyed in Vienna an unparalleled popularity.[158] He had an influence on fashion and manners, and, if it is unfair to credit him with the invention of the Makart-Bukett of dried grasses, reeds, palm fronds and thistles, which gathered dust in all respectable drawing rooms at the end of the century, one can look at this picture of his studio and see how that kind of bouquet expressed, in a way, the artist's quintessence. The room is treated like a palette smeared with an archipelago of greedy colors, picturesque objects, pseudo-Renaissance bronzes, musical instruments, ivories, old weapons, fragments of Baroque altars, busts, sarcophagi, coats-of-arms, velvets, metal braziers, medieval German lamps of stags' horns ending in sirens' busts, Oriental rugs, animals' skins, African weapons, brackets, screens, and palms, palms, palms. But in Makart's studio all this formed the billowing, foaming surroundings of his enormous, stagy canvases, carnivalesque triumphs whose center was some seductively naked actress: painting of the sort appropriate for a theatre's curtain or for a beerhall, not without a kind of naïve sensuality which perhaps partially redeemed its pastiche nature. A *café-concert* Rubens. But in the thousand living rooms that adopted this style no siren arose from the seaweed, no dryad emerged from the plush lichens. The walls were covered with autographed fans and cases of embroidered velvet for visiting cards destined to turn yellow, the tables with little gilded easels for photographs, also destined to fade, and velvet albums with heavy metal clasps. Oriental rugs were spread on the sofas, climbed up the walls to reach the long Arab rifles, and from the great *cloisonné* vases the palms unfolded their high fans.[159] All this was color. But it also meant dust.

378: Rudolf von Alt. *Studio of the Painter Hans Makart,* 1885. HISTORISCHES MUSEUM DER STADT WIEN, VIENNA.

379: Hans Temple. *Meeting of the Committee for the Erection of a Monument to Hans Makart,* c. 1885. HISTORISCHES MUSEUM DER STADT WIEN, VIENNA.

Makart was struck down at the age of forty-four by a sudden, fatal disease. All Vienna mourned him and covered him with flowers. A little later a committee was formed to erect a monument to him. Hans Temple (b. 1857, d. in the 20th century) has left a painting of a *Meeting of the Committee for the Erection of a Monument to Hans Makart,* which took place in the so-called Makart Room at Nikolaus Dumba's.[160] The room is full of pictures, busts, statuettes and sundries, and for this tropical density it deserved being given Makart's name. In such a room, the simple glasses of water on the table gleam with an uncontaminated chasity.

An etcher of Hanover who was active in Vienna in the 1870's, William Unger (1837–1932), has depicted a similar room for us in his *Self-portrait in His Studio* which recalls an etching by Daubigny of 1861. The etching technique is ideal for densely furnished, redundant rooms, as Rembrandt has shown, and also Piranesi in his Prisons. In this print by Unger even the taste for bric-a-brac achieves a kind of validity of its own, revealing a charm like that of a cavern, encrusted and stratified, with stalactites and patches of moss.

380: Anonymous. *Studio of Dantan,* first half 19th century. MUSÉE DES ARTS DÉCORATIFS, PARIS.

381: William Unger. *Self-Portrait in his Studio,* etching.

382: V. Fouquet. *The Study of Alexandre du Sommerard*, 1836.
MUSÉE DES ARTS DÉCORATIFS, PARIS.

383: Leopold Burger. *Room in the Schloss of Grafenegg, (Austria)*, watercolor, 1887. BARONE MALFATTI COLLECTION, ROME

The Makart-Bukett mentioned above is not lacking
in a corner of the *Room in the Schloss of Grafenegg* in
Austria, of which Leopold Burger (1861-1903) has left
us two views taken from opposite points in the room.
The easel with the draped painting, the panicles of
reeds, the palms, the fans, are like a signature of the
time and its taste. The symmetrical arrangement of
the pictures dates back to the early years of the 19th
century. Under the pictures, to the right of the door,
photographs of relatives and acquaintances substitute
for the earlier miniatures, which however are present
on the opposite wall. The writing desk, a 19th century
pastiche of Renaissance inspiration, has its display of
photographs, with flowers behind them and still further back, a stand with a framed print and some
drapery, whose arrangement recalls a similar one in

385: Leopold Burger. *Room in the Schloss of Grafenegg (Austria),* watercolor, 1887. BARONE MALFATTI COLLECTION, ROME.

386: E. Giraud. *Dining Room of the Princess Mathilde,* c. 1867. MUSÉE DES ARTS DÉCORATIFS, PARIS.

the *Room in the Hofburg in Vienna (Fig.* 350). The *étagère,* the bracket for the plant in its little vase, are favorite decorations. The walls are treated like pages of an album, on which one can stick more or less anything, even plates, stuffed birds and garlands. Every piece of furniture must have one object or more on it, so a ship model is hoisted to the top of the high tile stove, and on the vast, late-Renaissance-style cupboard there is an assortment of blue and white majolicas. Wooden furniture is complemented by wicker pieces, which with the flowers form a garden corner and give a note of informality. The people are Count August Brunner and his daughter. An anonymous *Interior of about 1880,* as well as the *Dining Room of Princess Mathilde* of about 1867 document the same sense of *horror vacui.*

The view, unfortunately partial, of an interior in an
oil by Jules-Emile Saintin (1829-1894) entitled
Distraction is rich in indications of taste. The painting
was shown at the Salon in 1875 and the decoration that
it depicts was certainly *avant-garde*. Saintin, a painter
Parisian to the tip of his toes, had his moment of
celebrity when, on his return from America in 1865,
he turned to genre painting, choosing as his dominant
theme a woman in pose, her expression suggesting
an untold story. His pictures are studies of female
character and studies of rooms, both very conscious,
very deliberate, according to the rather fanatical
documentary method that characterized novels of the
period, especially those of Zola.[161] The exotic, muddled
taste of the living rooms of the 1870's finds its apotheosis in pictures like *Distraction*. Saintin shared the
taste for interiors decorated according to the new
Oriental fashion, and for feminine subjects of a sentimental cast, with his contemporary Alfred Stevens,
whose paintings have titles of the same kind as Saintin's:
*Lost Illusion, Remember, The Painful Certitude, The
Japanese Mask, A Parisian Sphinx*, etc.

In *Distraction* we see a Japanese screen, a Japanese
fan, and a Japanese plate on the wall. The taste for
japonaiserie had begun around 1856; in 1878 it was so
widespread that a critic complained: "It is no longer a
fashion, it's an infatuation, a folly." This was certainly
not the first exotic fancy-dress in the Romantic 19th
century: after the *chinoiseries* of the 18th century, there
had been the Indian-Saracen taste of the Brighton
Pavilion, the Moorish style which began at the time of
the Algerian expedition and continued for the whole
century (we see a little Arab table encrusted with
ivory in the Saintin painting). A stay of five months in
Morocco revealed the Arab world to Delacroix and
was to inspire many of his paintings. Prosper Marilhat
had received such profound impressions from Egypt
that he signed himself "L'Egyptien Prosper Marilhat";
he rendered the majestic aspects of the Orient (also of
Syria and Lebanon) rather than the strange, mysterious
ones that the Romantics doted on. Baudelaire had
identified the beautiful with the bizarre and lived with
a colored woman. Gustave Flaubert, in his study at
Croisset, had collected souvenirs of his journeys in the
East, objects which peopled like bric-a-brac (according
to the Goncourts) his mantelpiece, table, shelves, and
walls. It was precisely Edmond de Goncourt who, with
his two volumes on Japanese Art in the 18th century
(*Utamaro,* 1891, and *Hokusai,* 1896), contributed
considerably to the vogue for Nipponic things, to
which Pierre Loti had also given an added impetus in
1887 with his novel *Madame Chrysanthème*. Perhaps
the most popular work in this vein was to be Puccini's
opera, *Madame Butterfly*.

Europeans approached Japanese art with more
restraint, with more humility than they had shown in
preceding centuries towards Chinese art; since the
19th century had developed the historic sense, there
were not the gross travesties that had occurred with
Chinese art. Japanese fans, screens, porcelains, hilts
of swords, lacquer boxes, those ivory or carved wood
clasps called *netsuké* were avidly sought out to decorate
houses. Chrysanthemums took the place of palms.

387: Jules-Emile Saintin. *Distraction*, exhibited in 1875.

This fashion was not without its comic aspects, as
when Miss Ella Christie planted a perfect replica of a
Japanese garden in Scotland, and imported even a
Japanese gardener,[162] just as in the 18th century, near
the counterfeit ruins of a Gothic chapel in a park,
someone had put a salaried, counterfeit hermit. The last
Japanese living rooms (a luxury of the middle class, as
the Chinese Study had been of the aristocracy) were
dismantled only well into the 20th century: corners
with fans, screens, and lanterns as seen in paintings by
Whistler, J. J. J. Tissot, Saintin, and Alfred Stevens,
living rooms whose taste was already considered passé
when Proust had his demi-mondaine Odette de Crécy
adopt it. And as Chinese style was allied to Rococo, so
the Japanese became confused with the first phase of
Art Nouveau: a double wedding among cousins. The
frame of the mirror in Saintin's *Distraction* is a document of *Art Nouveau* style of a very early date.

Another event which was to revolutionize rooms
even more was the introduction of electricity. In art
this event is commemorated in a painting by the Swede
Hugo Birger (1854-1887), *Interior with Electric
Illumination,* 1885, dedicated by the painter to Madame
Göthilde Fürstenberg, the mistress of the apartment.
In the crystal nest of the old chandelier for wax candles,
the new magic light has taken its place, to banish the
soft penumbra of Biedermeier.

388: Hugo Birger. *Interior with Electric Illumination,* 1885. KONSTMUSEUM, GOTHENBURG.

389: J.J.J. Tissot. *Late Nineteenth Century Interior with Children Playing Hide and Seek,*
exhibited in 1904. Formerly ORMOOD COLLECTION.

The eclecticism of the late 19th century is well
represented by the buildings on the Kärtnerring in
Vienna, built in the '70's and '80's. The one given by
Franz Josef to the famous actress Kathi Schratt
(1855–1940), who was the rage at the Burgtheater
between 1883 and 1900, continues in its interior decoration the taste of the Second Empire for false 18th
century rooms and composite décor, between Rococo
and Empire style, laden with bronzes, knick-knacks,
chinoiserie, cases, cabinets, miniatures in niches, and a
profusion of objects. Here is the *Living Room in the
Apartment of Kathi Schratt* by R. Doblhoff; similar
rooms which bear witness to the bankruptcy of taste
abounded. Indeed this mode continued to represent
the idea of pomp to wealthy people even into times
very close to our own.[163]

390 (upper right):
R. Doblhoff.
Living Room in the
Apartment of Kathi Schratt.
HISTORISCHES MUSEUM
DER STADT WIEN, VIENNA.

391 (lower left):
The Ebony Room in the
Vanderbilt House, 1884.
METROPOLITAN MUSEUM
OF ART, NEW YORK.

392 (lower right):
Interior of the House
of Herbert H. D. Pierce,
Northampton, Massachusetts,
late 19th century.
METROPOLITAN MUSEUM
OF ART, NEW YORK.

None of the great French painters took a special delight in the interior; at most for them it was only one theme among many. Delacroix, for example, painted the *Bedroom of Conte Charles de Mornay* (*Fig.* 322) without even the shadow of that *Stimmung,* that sense of intimacy, which was so widespread among German painters. This and another Delacroix interior, *The Stove,* are still lifes more than interiors. And we have seen what slight importance Degas gave to the interior in painting the Bellelli family (*Fig.* 330).

The only exception among the French painters is Edouard Vuillard (1868–1940), whose art, as André Chastel has justly remarked,[164] seems to have achieved what Edmond Duranty in an essay of 1876 described as the chief character of the painting of "aspects" and of "interiors": "For the man who observes closely there is a whole logic of color and pattern which derives from an aspect, according to the hour, the season, the place in which it is seen. This aspect is not expressed, this logic is not determined by combining Venetian stuffs against Flemish backgrounds. For us the values of the tones in interiors are susceptible to infinite variations. In every interior an atmosphere, a kind of family air, is created among all the furnishings and the objects that fill it. The frequency, the multiplicity and the arrangement of the mirrors with which the apartments are adorned, the number of objects that are hung on the walls, all these things have brought into our dwellings a kind of mystery and, at the same time, a kind of clarity that could no longer be rendered with the means and the harmonies of the Flemish, not even by adding Venetian formulas."[165] This acceptance of the everyday, which had long been practiced by Dutch and Danish painters, was now being achieved in France no longer through a minute description of objects, but through a play of color in which the sublimated sensuality of the elusive and sensitive temperament of Vuillard was expressing itself. One is led to think of still lifes, of certain sonnets of Mallarmé's like "Ses purs ongles" or "Tout orgueil" and of that taste for the familiar interior which informs the objects with a kind of poetic function.[166] Vuillard's intimism, made of a subtle play of delicate nuances, belongs to the same climate as the music of Debussy. *The Reader* is part of a decoration consisting of four panels entitled *Intérieurs,* which Vuillard made in 1896 for Dr. Vaquez. These panels are conceived like tapestries, with a flattening of planes whereby cushions, clothes, rugs, walls, seem made of the same stuff, absorbed in the same woof, the woof of a cloth. The floral patterns reflected in the mirror seem also part of the wall covering, the stylized flowers of the wall paper make a closed garden: this composition which might seem to be inspired by some medieval tapestry actually shows the *Art Nouveau* atmosphere which was the latest thing in those years. The human figure stands out from the background as the saints of the primitives stood out on their gold grounds. Chastel[167] observes: "Nothing better than these decorations tells of a certain pleasure derived from an interior. They express and satisfy that calm, veiled by music, which enchanted the end of the last century. . . There is something (an infinitesimal amount, but still noticeable to a sensitive taste) of the Symbolists' affectation, of the languors of Verlaine, Samain, or of G. Rodenbach, who wrote in that very year of 1896 *Les Vies encloses:* "*L'oeil est un glaque aquarium d'eau somnolente: tranquillité, repos apparent, calmes plis.*"

Vuillard's sensibility, however, did not tarry in this soft, voluptuous savoring of an atmosphere's music to which even Proust succumbed. This chamber music of Vuillard's which, as we have said, makes one think of Debussy, was only the prelude to works in a freer style. If *The Reader* from the series of *Intérieurs* of 1896 and the *Interior* of 1899 could make one think of the Symbolists, in certain still lifes of the early 20th century Vuillard effects that calm metamorphosis of subjects that caused Degas to say: "He takes a dusty bottle of Chablis and makes a bunch of sweetpeas from it." In Chastel's words: "Vuillard is distinguished by the calm, mute, meditative atmosphere in his interiors; he catches the living room, the dining room, the bedroom in the moment when a silence falls and faces relax. The people seem not to have much to say to one another: they smile, close their eyes, pick up a newspaper; the ladies look at their sewing. Vuillard is the painter of silence." Everything seems so ordinary, so everyday, and yet there is a kind of muted magic at work; it may only be that of a mirror, which reads the wall behind the observer's back, doubling the flower vases, and bringing an unexpected corner of the room into the picture. Vuillard, whose formation owes nothing to the Dutch, over the years was to approach their spirit, though from a technical point of view there is no possible comparison between the mineral quality of a Vermeer's paintings and the quality of Vuillard which is grainy and woolly as a stuff. In the portraits painted after World War I he harmonized the attitude of the people to the surroundings and reflected in the pose the spirit of the room; at the same time, he gave the key of the surroundings in the expression of the person. "Je ne fais pas de portraits, je peins des gens chez eux." His *Portrait of Madame Bénard,* 1930, could also be entitled "interior with old lady," for both the lady and the things around her speak the same language, and therefore are presented on the same level of importance, described with an adherence unknown in the painter's youthful works.

393: Edouard Vuillard. *The Reader,* 1896.
MUSÉE DU PETIT PALAIS, PARIS.

394: Edouard Vuillard. *Portrait of Madame Bénard,*
1930. MUSÉE D'ART MODERNE, PARIS.

395: Edouard Vuillard. *Interior,* 1899. ZUMSTEG COLLECTION, ZURICH.

396: M. Bellexy Desfontaines. *Project for a Living Room,* watercolor.
(*Art et Décoration* competition, c. 1905). BIBLIOTHÈQUE DOUCET, PARIS.

397: Baillie Scott-Bedford. *Project for a Private Theatre,* watercolor, BIBLIOTHÈQUE DOUCET, PARIS.

Art Nouveau, at the end of the 19th century, rose from that swampy mess of all styles in which taste had become stuck. This was a style which showed an enormous imbalance between its cultural preparation and its duration: it was like the century-plant which strains for a hundred years and then, all at once, releases its flowering stalk, which promptly withers away and is no more.

What were the roots of Art Nouveau? The resemblances with lanceolate Gothic or with a certain form of Rococo which seem so obvious are not really the answer, which lies in more subtle researches. Was Art Nouveau not already present in certain illuminated pages of William Blake at the end of the 18th century? Must the origin of modern styles be seen in the work of non-architects like Paxton or Eiffel? Paxton, a gardener, along with the architect Decimus Burton, who had already collaborated with him on the great hothouse at Chatsworth, started off rational architecture with that mammoth hothouse which was the Crystal Palace, built for the great Exposition of 1851 in London. With that vertical bridge, the Tower which bears his name, made for another Exposition in Paris in 1889, Eiffel, an engineer, wrote the first letter in the Art Nouveau alphabet, a colossal "A". But there were other precedents: Louis Sullivan in America with the Wainwright Building of 1890-1891; Charles Rennie Mackintosh in Scotland with the School of Art in Glasgow of 1897-1899, and then a whole English current from the Pre-Raphaelites (who rediscovered Blake), to William Morris who reached the masses thanks to a handicrafts movement with the peacock's feather as its emblem. In 1887 Morris and Company began to sell sideboards with uprights that served as candlesticks, inaugurating that verticality that was to become so accentuated in New Style furniture (legs that continue beyond the top of a table or an open cupboard and then terminate in a quadrangular crown). There is then the influence of the painters like Khnopff, Charles Toorop, and the better-known James Ensor, Franz van Hodler, and Edvard Munch, and finally Aubrey Beardsley. And one must bear in mind the influence of Oriental art, especially Japanese.

In effect the symptoms of Art Nouveau can be seen just about everywhere in the second half of the 19th century. Jules Saulnier built in 1871, with visible metallic structure, a factory for the Meunier Chocolate Company near Paris. This building was hailed by Viollet-le-Duc as the fulfillment of certain theoretical ambitions of 19th century architecture.[168] Shortly after 1880, the English architect-decorator A. H. Mackmurdo created designs of semi-naturalistic inspiration

398: E. M. Simas. *Project for a Bathroom,* watercolor. (*Art et Décoration* competition, 1903.) BIBLIOTHÈQUE DOUCET, PARIS.

for textiles and wallpapers which could be taken for the continental Art Nouveau of 1900. In particular, in 1883 he designed the title page for a book on Wren's London churches. This title page combines elements which will later reappear with insistence in Art Nouveau.

All this convergence of movements, sometimes muted, sometimes outspoken, was like the murmuring that, in Stravinskij's Firebird, precedes the lacerating exultation of the fabulous bird's appearance. Suddenly Art Nouveau was born, full-blown, and it took flight in Brussels in 1892, thanks to Victor Horta.

As Henry-Russell Hitchcock observes: "Why Art Nouveau should have been initiated full-fledged by Victor Horta in Brussels in 1892 remains a mystery."[169] Horta cannot have known the work of Sullivan in America, which was very similar to his, because this became known only when foreigners visited the Chicago World's Fair in 1893. Can he have seen illustrations of the wrought-iron decorations of Gaudí's Palau Güell in Barcelona, reproduced in an American magazine, The Decorator and Furnisher? It is more probable that Horta was stimulated by the theories and projects of Viollet-le-Duc, but no more than stimulated, for Horta's construction in iron and masonry has a character all its own. More than with anything else his style has affinity with the English wall papers which he

399: Project for a Smoking Room, watercolor. (*Art et Décoration* competition, 1905.) BIBLIOTHÈQUE DOUCET, PARIS.

had come to know in the year before planning the Tassel house in Brussels, and which he later used in it. This building—especially the entrance hall where from the top of an iron column writhing branches and tendrils, also of iron, extend as if from a treetrunk, and their movement is repeated by the curvilinear decoration painted on the walls, and by the pattern of the mosaic floor—this relatively modest building is the nest of that firebird which for a little more than a decade was to provoke in all of Europe that memorable conflagration variously known as *Art Nouveau, New Style, Jugendstil,* Liberty or *floreal.*

From Belgium where Horta created at least one masterpiece, the Auditorium of the Maison du Peuple, to which slender metal supports and broad crystal spaces give an airy lightness; from Paris, where this new style was adopted by the big department stores like the Samaritaine, by fashionable restaurants like Maxim's, and by the Métro entrances; from Vienna where the Majolika Haus of Otto Wagner has on its façade a majolica tapestry delicately reticulated like a hummingbird's wing, *Art Nouveau* spread rapidly. It reached Eastern Europe and Latin America, where it became provincialized and continued to exist after 1902, when it had begun to disappear in the countries of its origin. In a corner of Spain—in Spain, as is well-known, the phases of taste have a slower course—the style lingered in a form independent of the other continental forms, in a form of gnomes' architecture seen through a magnifying glass by Antonio Gaudi. In England the style went out of fashion around 1900, but lingered to its death in the commercial forms of wardrobes and writing desks decorated with swirls, brass tulips, and inlaid, simplified hearts and roses. This vulgarization finally discredited the style altogether. But England had played a pioneer's role in the spreading of New Style interior decoration, especially through the models furnished by the magazine *The Studio,* which were followed and imitated in France and Germany. Exploiting this situation, the English manufacturers of furniture sold much New Style furniture on the continent, and it is from the name of one of these manufacturers, Liberty, that the style took its name in Italy. Also enormously influential on the continent was C. F. A. Voysey, who from 1880 on designed textiles in New Style. After 1893 he also designed furniture whose characteristics were an accentuated verticality,[170] and accentuated metal clasps in the form of stylized hearts and birds, which stood out against the oak of the furniture, usually left in its natural color. Voysey's was the first successful experiment in achieving simplicity of form in interior decoration. Charles Rennie Mackintosh of Glasgow, whom we have already mentioned as architect, designed the furniture also and concerned himself with the tiniest decorative details of the houses

he built. Particularly memorable pieces of his furniture are the chairs with very tall backs. For these tapering forms and for the equally elongated metallic decorations, the Glasgow group that worked under Mackintosh was called in England "the Spook School." The sober and elegant rooms for which this furniture was designed were generally decorated in white and gold, with white dominant, and little touches of pink, lilac, or silver to underline the effect. The most popular decorative motif was the stylized open rose, inlaid with ivory, in stained glass or printed on the hangings.[171]

The watercolors of projects for *Art Nouveau* decorations which we reproduce here were all but one entries in the competitions set up by the magazine *Art et Décoration.* Typical is the *Project for a Living Room* by Desfontaines (*Fig.* 396), with its paintings of contemporary life in curvilinear frames on the walls and the low cushioned sofas, from the end of which rise up tall supports for electric lights. In the *Project for a Private Theatre* by Baillie Scott-Bedford (*Fig.* 397), symmetrical stylized floral decoration is used in the little arches of the gallery, on the doors of the low white cupboard and on the stained glass at the rear of the stage. The low ceiling, with beams exposed as in an Elizabethan house, was a favorite feature which dated back to Morris and the English Arts and Crafts movement. Another whim of the period was the use of mottos and inscriptions in the decoration of the walls. Such inscriptions can be seen in both these illustrations. In the *Project for a Bathroom* by E. M. Simas (*Fig.* 398), the green of the leaves and the white of the flowers dominant in the tiles of the walls and the stained glass window, the petals scattered on the pavement with a Klimt-like effect, the washstand with its lines partly inspired by Japanese art, all make of this bathroom a very representative interior of the period. The decoration here certainly justifies the name "floral" given to this style: the calla lily and the water-lily were the favorite flowers of the time.[172]

The *Project for a Dining Room* by L. Cauvy won the first prize in the *Art et Décoration* competition in 1905: it must have enjoyed a great popularity because furniture and wall decorations of this type were very wide-spread even in Italy. The modernity of taste of such decoration lies especially in the absence of the clutter of added ornaments (paintings, knick-knacks, objects, hangings, etc.) which characterized 19th century decoration: here the structural lines of a room are bared so as to discourage further additions. The same can be said of the *Project for a Fumoir,* also entered in the 1905 competition, which leaves space only for a vase or two on the shelf over the fireplace and the alcove. This model also arouses familiar sensations in us, vaguely recalling waiting rooms, sleeping cars, and restaurants.

400: L. Cauvy. *Project for a Dining Room,* watercolor. (First prize *Art et Décoration* competition, 1905.) BIBLIOTHÈQUE DOUCET, PARIS.

NOTES TO THE COMMENTARY

1: For a profound study of the house of the Middle Ages see Erik Lundberg, *Herremannens Bostad*, Stockholm (1935).

2: A famous example: the hunt frescoes in the tower of Clement VI in the Palace of the Popes at Avignon. For more details see François Enaud, "L'art de décorer un château au Moyen Age" in *Connaissance des Arts*, No. 96, (Feb. 1960).

3: *Cf.* E. Li Gotti, "Gli affreschi della Stanza della Torre nel Palazzo del Podestà di San Gimignano" in *Rivista d'arte* (1938) pp. 379-391; Giovanni Previtali, "Il possibile Memmo di Filippuccio" in *Paragone*, No. 155 (Nov. 1962) pp. 3-11.

3a: On the custom of bathing before the wedding, recorded in Greece, ancient Persia, Thailand, ancient Peru, Switzerland, Russia and several other countries, see Lord Raglan, *The Temple and the House*, p. 112.

4: An accurate description can be read in H. Kohlhaussen, *Minnekästchen im Mittelalter*, Berlin (1928) fig. 61, No. 830.

5: It is recorded that in 1403 Princess Margaret of Flanders bought 64 lengths of canvas to line two tubs, and a red Malines cloth to make canopies for them.

6: For further details see Lawrence Wright, *Clean and Decent, the Fascinating History of the Bathroom and the Water Closet*, London (1960); also Raimond Van Marle, *Iconographie de l'Art Profane au Moyen Age et à la Renaissance et la Décoration des Demeures*, The Hague (1931) Vol. I: *La Vie Quotidienne*. On the medieval house see K. B. Mummenhof, *Die Profanbaukunst im Oberstift Munster, 1450-1650*; P. A. Faulkner, *Domestic Planning for the 12th and 14th centuries*.

7: As Giovanni Pozzi (M. T. Casella and G. Pozzi, *Francesco Colonna, Biografia e Opere*, Padua (1959) Vol. II, p. 125) observes of the writing of Colonna: "The inanimate object undergoes the opposite treatment of that of the characters of the romance: it becomes animated, a person." In the feast of Eleuterillide "the guests do not exist, only the dishes, the clothes, the recipes, in immobile, unreal surroundings." Francesco Colonna was a sacristan of the church of SS. Giovanni e Paolo, and as Maria Teresa Casella tells us (in Vol. I of the same work, p. 43), he developed an "almost fanatical interest in vessels and stuffs and plates and precious objects of every kind."

8: The creation of pure still lifes in Italy in the 15th century was above all the work of artists working in intarsia. A good example is the intarsiated panels depicting still lifes of books, musical instruments, etc., of the little study of Duke Federigo in the Palazzo Ducale at Urbino. See Charles Sterling, *La nature morte de l'antiquité à nos jours*, Paris (1952).

9: Leo van Puyvelde, *Rubens*, Paris-Brussels (1952) p. 19.

10: See Adolph Donath, *Psychologie des Kunstsammlers*, Berlin (1920) p. 51.

11: See M. Praz, *Studies in Seventeenth Century Imagery*, Rome, Edizioni di Storia e Litteratura (1964) p. 86.

12: For Dutch customs of the period see F. van Thienen, *Das Kostüm der Blütezeit Hollands*, Berlin (1930).

13: Fritz Laufer, *Das Interieur in der europäishen Malerei des 19. Jahrhunderts*, Zurich (1960).

14: Gordon Logie, *The Urban Scene*, London (1954) p. 91.

15: Edouard Huttinger, *La Peinture Hollandaise au XVIIe siècle*, Lausanne (1956) p. 67.

16: This information is derived from an article by W. Martin in *Bulletin van de Nederlandsche Oudheidkundige Bond*, (1914) pp. 246-249.

17: See A. Feulner, *Kunstgeschichte des Möbels*, Berlin (1927) p. 576.

18: For the table with curvilinear legs, see A. Feulner, *op. cit.*, fig. 358; for the chairs, see *Ibid.*, figs. 288 and 291.

19: See Julius von Schlosser, *Kunst- und Wunderkammern*, Leipzig (1908) p. 46 ff.

20: For the story of the great collections of paintings and the migration of masterpieces see Francis Henry Taylor, *The Taste of Angels*, Boston (1948) and my own essay "Addio, cari quadri" in *La Casa della Fama*, Milan-Naples (1952).

On the curious aspect of collecting see "Le Cabinet du curieux" in *Connaissance des Arts* (Dec. 15, 1953) and "L'Extravagant Cabinet de Bonnier" in *Connaissance des Arts* (August, 1959).

21: See S. Speth-Holterhoff, *Les Peintres Flamands de Cabinets d'Amateurs au XVIIe siècle*, Brussels (1958).

22: Fabrizio Clerici, *Allegorie die Sensi di Jan Breugel*, Milan (1946).

23: See my essay on Jan Breugel and Marino in *La Casa della Fama*.

24: Federico Zeri, *La Galleria Pallavicini in Roma*, Florence (1959).

25: See M. Praz, *The Hero in Eclipse in Victorian Fiction*, London (1956) p. 11 ff.

26: *Cf.* H. Clifford Smith, *The Complete History of Buckingham Palace*, London (1931) p. 85 f.

27: *Cf.* Kenneth Clark, *The Gothic Revival*, New York (1929).

28: For further details on 18th century French furnishings the reader is referred to the following works: For a general review: *Le Dix-huitième siècle français*, Edition Connaissance des Arts, Hachette, Paris (1956). More specialized studies: the classic texts of Comte de Salverte *(Ebénistes du XVIIIème siècle)* and André Theunissen *(Meubles et Sièges du XVIIIème siècle)*; Jean Nicolay, *L'Art et la Manière des Maîtres ébénistes français du XVIIIe siècle*, Paris, 2 Vols. (1956 and 1959); Pierre Verlet, *Les Meubles français du XVIIIe siècle*, Paris (1956), in series *L'Oeil du Connaisseur*.

29: This sale has remained famous: see Jacques Wilhelm, "Artistes, Marchands et Amateurs de peinture à Paris au XVIIIe siècle," in *Medécine de France*, No. 102 (1959).

30: Etienne Silhouette decorated with this cheap form of art the walls of his house at Brie-sur-Marne. See E. Nevill Jackson, *Silhouette*, London (1938), and the essay "Silhouettes" in my volume *Fiori freschi*, Florence (1943).

31: *Cf.* Emile Dacier, "L'Athénienne et son inventeur," in *Gazette des Beaux-Arts,* (Aug.-Sept. 1932).

32: *Cf.* Hugh Honour, *Chinoiserie, The Vision of Cathay,* London (1961).

33: It is reproduced as Plate XXI in Denise Ledoux-Lebard, *Les Ebénistes Parisiens (1795-1830),* Paris (1951).

34: For a more ample discussion of Mlle. Gérard, *cf.* M. Praz, *La Casa della Vita,* Milan (1962) pp. 71-75.

35: *Cf.* J. Hartman, *Danske Slotte og Palaer,* Copenhagen (1945) p. 156.

36: He cannot, however, be Sir William Hamilton (as has been suggested), for his face was not plump, as is this man's, but was thin and aquiline. *Cf.* Oliver Warner, *Emma Hamilton and Sir William,* London (1960). The man standing to the right, who has just taken a cameo out of its box and passed it to his neighbour, could be Sir William, however.

37: *Cf.* Alois Riegl, "Möbel und Innendecoration," in *Wiener Congress,* E. Leisching, ed., Vienna (1898) p. 187.

38: The use of the adjective "analogous," derived from the French *analogue,* indicates that the text probably was taken from a French source, for an Italian writer would be more likely to have used words such as "appropriate" or "suitable."

39: *Cf.* Emile Bourgeois, *Le Style Empire, son origine, ses caractères,* Paris (1930).

40: *Cf.* Olivier Lefuel's article on Percier and Fontaine in *Connaissance des Arts* (June 15, 1954).

41: For similar projects of the period, see the 24 fine color reproductions published in F. Contet, *Intérieurs Directoire et Empire,* Paris (1923).

42: Philippe Jullian, *Les Styles,* Paris (1961).

43: The text was translated and revised by Francesco Lazzari, with additions by Giuseppe Borsato. It was published in Venice by Giuseppe Antonelli.

44: *Cf.* exhibition catalogue, *Mostra del Barocco piemontese,* Vol. II., Turin, (June-Oct. 1963).

45: *Cf.* Madame de Basily-Callimaki, *J.-B. Isabey, sa vie, son temps, 1767-1855,* Paris (1909) p. 37.

46: *Cf.* H. R. D'Allemagne, *Histoire du luminaire,* Paris (1891).

47: *Cf.* L. Volkmann, *Bilderschriften der Renaissance,* Leipzig (1923) p. 120.

48: In the collection of La Mésangère *(Meubles et objects de goût)* we also find a bed decorated with hounds and hunting horns.

49: See the design reproduced in Arthur T. Bolton, *The Architecture of Robert and James Adam,* London (1922) Vol. I, p. 97 f. and note 29.

50: From an article on Charles Percier in *Gazette des Beaux-Arts,* I, pp. 148-157. For a discussion of the modern revival of Empire style, see the chapter on this subject in my book *Il Gusto Neoclassico,* Naples (1959).

51: A facsimile edition (without text) was published by John Tiranti & Co., London in 1937.

52: Maria Edgeworth.

53: For a fuller discussion of Hope, *cf.* Sandor Baumgarten, *Le Crépuscule néoclassique,* Paris (1958).

54: From the chapter by Anne M. Buck in *The Regency Period,* an excellent survey of all aspects of regency taste published by *The Connoisseur,* London (1958) p. 137.

55: An equally imaginary Napoleon was introduced into a watercolor by Loeillot dated 1826, *cf.* Jean Hanoteau, ed., *Mémoires de la Reine Hortense,* published by Prince Louis Napoleon, Paris (1927) p. 437.

56: See Egon Hessling, *Empire Möbel,* 2nd edition, Plate XVI, where the desk is shown closed.

57: From the collection of Prince Napo-leon, reproduced in Jean Hanoteau, *op. cit.,* p. 424.

57a: *Cf.* G. and D. Ledoux-Lebard, "L'impératrice Joséphine et le retour du gothique sous l'Empire", in Revue de l'Institut Napoléon, 92 (July 1964), pp. 117-124.

58: The present condition of the room can be seen in *Le XIXe siècle français,* Hachette, Paris (1957) p. 203.

59: Translated from Jean Hanoteau, *op. cit.,* p. 266.

60: *Cf.* H. R. D'Allemagne, *Sports et jeux d'adresse,* Paris (c. 1910) p. 126.

61: *Cf.* Jean Hanoteau, *op. cit.,* p. 286.

62: *Cf. La Casa della Vita,* p. 310 ff.

63: *Cf.* A. N. Savinov, *Aleksej G. Venetsianov,* Moscow, "Iskusstvo" (1955).

64: *Cf.* Jean Hanoteau, *op. cit.,* p. 271, note.

65: *Mémoires de Madame D'Abrantès,* Paris (n.d.) Vol. VI, p. 349.

66: *Cf. Grand Dictionnaire Universel du XIXe siècle français,* Paris (1869).

67: *Cf.* S. Reinach, *Répertoire de le statuaire grecque et romain,* Paris (1906) Vol. I p. xviii.

68: *Cf. La Casa della Vita,* p. 297 ff.

69: This room is the last in this wing of the Palace, a fact which I checked on a personal visit, *cf. La Casa della Vita,* pp. 299, 300.

70: For a discussion of the Duchesse *cf.* Vicomte de Reiset, *Marie-Caroline, Duchesse de Berry,* 1816-1830, Paris (1906).

71: *Cf.* the series of models given by La Mésangère, *Meubles et objets de goût,* published between the end of the 18th century and the 1830's, or the modern edition edited by Paul Cornu. *Cf.* also "Le décorateur qui règne sur l'Empire," in *Connaissance des Arts,* (Oct. 1960). Through the *Journal des dames et des modes* La Mésangère—whose name suggests *les arts ménagers,* although it actually is the name of an ex-ecclesiastic

NOTES TO THE COMMENTARY

—brought the Empire style within everyone's range.

72: Madame de Basily-Callimaki, *op. cit.*, p. 259.

73: Guglielmo de Sanctis, *Tommaso Minardi e il suo tempo*, Rome (1900) p. 32. For the Flemish sources, see I. Faldi, "Il Purismo e Tommaso Minardi", in *Commentari*, Vol. I (1950), pp. 238 ff.

74: Henri Lapuze, *Ingres*, Paris (1911) p. 166.

75: *Cf.* Richard Benz and Arthur Schneider, *Die Kunst der deutschen Romantik*, Munich (1939).

76: *Cf.* Fritz Laufer, *op. cit.*

77: M. Praz, *Il Gusto Neoclassico*, pp. 307-318.

78: This portrait of Mme. Récamier is now in the Musée Carnavalet, Paris.

79: Jean Hanoteau, *op. cit.*, Vol. III p. 120.

80: *Ibid.*, p. 134.

81: Andrea Corsini, *I Bonaparte a Firenze*, Florence (1961) pp. 67-68.

82: *Ibid.*, p. 62.

82a: They might be the "gothic" portraits of Carlotta and Zenaide in the Museo Napoleonico in Rome (see its catalogue, p. 104, n. 19, and p. 105, n. 31).

83: *Cf.* Carlo Pietrangeli, *Villa Paolina*, Rome (1961) pp. 26-27, and also Diego Angeli, *I Bonaparte a Roma*, Milan (1938).

84: This was not the only time in Florence that Lamartine bit off more than he could chew. In the period when he was *chargé d'affaires* in the absence of De la Maison-fort, he not only was excessive in his devotion to duty, awakening Metternich's suspicions by his frequent reports, but also in his pomp, since his table was always open to Frenchmen passing through the city and since he spared no expense to shine in society, displaying, as Pietro Paolo Trompeo has said (*Il lettore vagabondo*, Rome (1942) p. 111): "like a flower in his buttonhole, his liberalism scented with an indefinable religiosity."

85: See M. Praz, "Shelley, Lamartine, Hawthorne and Dostoevskj a Firenze" in *Rivista di letterature moderne*, No. 8, fasc. 1 (1955).

86: *Cf.* Harold Alton, *The Bourbons of Naples*, London (1957) and Idem, *The Last Bourbons of Naples*, London (1961).

87: A copy of this picture, with a variant in the railing outside the window (lozenges with the Bourbon lily are inserted between the rails), belonged to Johan Orth (former Archduke of Austria). It was sold at auction in Germany (Kunstauktionshaus Gebrüder Heilbron) in November, 1912, and erroneously described in the catalogue of the sale as a family group of the Grand Dukes of Tuscany, the Bourbon lilies having been mistaken for the lily of Florence.

88: Years ago a Roman dealer, boasting of its royal provenance, was asking a million and a half lire for this chandelier. It was bought by the dealer, Pietro Accorsi of Turin. One day, showing it to another dealer, Jack Kugel by name, the latter unhappily did not pay attention to the way the crystal globe was held together. Handling it, he dropped it and it was shattered. The crystal globe has been copied, and I believe that this chandelier is now in the magnificent Accorsi villa outside Turin.

89: *Cf.* Marianna Prampolini, *La Duchessa Maria Luigia, Vita familiare alla Corte di Parma, Diari, carteggi inediti, ricami*, Bergamo (1942), and M. Praz, "Maria Luigia" in *Fiori freschi*, pp. 176-183.

90: Quoted in Prampolini, *op. cit.*, p. 111.

91: For an article on the collection of the Museo Glauco Lombardi in Parma (including several Naudins) *cf.* Luciano Bianciardi, "Il Museo di Maria Luigia," in *Le Vie d'Italia* (May, 1962).

92: Reproduced in Margaret Jourdain, *Regency Furniture*, London (1949) fig. 16.

93: The first patent for their use in mattresses and upholstered pieces was granted in 1828 to Samuel Pratt of New

Bond Street, London. *Cf.* John Gloag, *A Short Dictionary of Furniture*, London (1952) p. 446.

94: J. Curling, *James Weathercock, The Life of Thomas Griffiths Wainewright, 1794-1847*, London (1938) pp. 207-217.

95: *Cf.* Hugh Honour, *op. cit.*

96: Osbert Sitwell and Margaret Barton, *Brighton*, London (1935).

97: On the Brighton Pavilion, see also Clifford Musgrave, *Royal Pavilion*, Brighton (1951).

98: John Summerson, *Sir John Soane*, London (1952).

99: *Description of the House and Museum . . . Residence of Sir John Soane*, London (1835) p. 54.

100: *Cf.* M. Willson Disher, *Pharoah's Fool, The Story of Giovanni Belzoni*, London (1957) and also Stanley Mayer, *The Great Belzoni*, New York (1959).

101: On the Soane Museum see also the richly illustrated article by Philippe Jullian, "L'extraordinaire amoncellement du Soane Museum à Londres," *Connaissance des Arts* (Oct. 1962) p. 65.

102: Decker's watercolor is part of a souvenir album given in 1826 to Marie-d'Orleans, daughter of Louis-Philippe. This album is now in the collection of the Print Department of the Metropolitan Museum of Art, New York.

103: A copy of this painting includes the figure of the Czar himself. It is reproduced in Volume IV of N. Schilder's work on Czar Alexander I.

104: Zimmerman's painting found its way to Burg Rheinstein where the Prince commissioned Schinkel to create a summer residence from the ruins of Voigtsburg, near Bingen.

105: *Cf.* Johannes Sievers, *Die Möbel*, Berlin (1950) p. 19.

106: A painting of the same room by Franz Krüger shows Friedrich Wilhelm IV in his study. This painting, once at Sanssouci and later in the Berliner Schloss, is reproduced in color as Plate IV in Paul Weiglin, *Berliner Biedermeier,* Leipzig (1940).

107: For illustrations of these pieces see Sievers, *op. cit.,* figs. 194, 196, and 197.

108: In the Palace at Capodimonte in Naples there is a *table à fleurs* or *jardinière* in whose center rises a cage, surmounted by a gilded bronze statuette of Fortune, and between the legs of the goddess there is a crystal globe supported by dolphins, to be used as an aquarium. (On this type of furniture see Corrado Maltese, "Un disegno di Percier per un mobile un po' complicato," in *Scritti di Storia dell'Arte in onore di Mario Salmi,* Rome, Vol. III (1963) p. 447 ff.)

109: For Schinkel's drawing for this exedra sofa, see Sievers, *op. cit.,* fig. 73.

110: On the Villa of Chiatamone see Johannes Sievers, "Das Vorbild des 'Neuen Pavillon' von Karl Friedrich Schinkel im Schlosspark Charlottenburg" in *Zeitschrift für Kunstgeschichte,* Bd. 23, Heft 3/4 (1960) which reproduces a watercolor of 1841 by G. Gigante, now in Schloss Kamenz (Silesia); this shows the corner room of the Casino of the Villa of Chiatamone with a view of Ischia. The villa no longer exists.

110a: On the Zimmerlaube see Marquise de Custine, *La Russie en 1839,* Vol. II, letter 14, 1843 edition (Paris, Librairie d'Amyot), pp. 67-68.

111: See Herman Schmitz, *Die Gotik im deutschen Kunst- und Geistesleben,* Berlin (1920) and Idem, *Vor Hundert Jahren. Festräume und Wohnzimmer des deutschen Klassizismus und Biedermeier,* Berlin, one volume of illustrated text and one volume with 28 color plates of watercolors in the collection of Friedrich Wilhelm IV formerly at Berliner Schloss, now partly at Sanssouci, partly at Charlottenburg, and partly lost (many of which are reproduced in the present volume).
On the Rococo in the Biedermeier period in Germany see Marianne Zweig, *Zweites Rokoko, Innerräume und Hausrat in Wien um 1830-1860,* Vienna (1924).

113: *Cf.* Barbara Melchiori, "Scenografie di Hawthorne o il dilemma dell'artista," *Studi Americani,* 2, (1956) pp. 67-81.

114: Formerly in Schloss Monbijou, reproduced as Plate XXIV in A. Feulner, *op. cit.*

115: On Viennese Biedermeier see Josef Folnesics, *Innerräume und Hausrat der Empire- und Biedermeierzeit in Österreich-Ungarn,* Vienna (1922).

116: See chapter "Bianco e oro" in M. Praz, *Gusto Neoclassico.*

117: *Cf.* (anonymous) *Bytovaia Mebel russkogo Klassizizma,* Moscow, Gosudarstvennoe Izdatel'stvo Literaturu po Stroitel'stvu i Architekture (1954).

118: *Cf.* A. N. Savinov, *Aleksej G. Venetsianov,* Moscow, "Iskusstvo" (1955), a book completely based on the *"narodnost,"* or national character of the painter.

119: N. Vrangel, *Russkij Musej Imperatora Aleksandra III,* Izdarie Russkago Museia Imperator Aleksandra III, St. Petersburg (1904) Vol. I, pp. 414-415.

120: Hogarth's influence on Fedotov was tempered by that of Sir David Wilkie and Gavarni. *Cf.* Ia. D. Leščinskij, *Paul Andreevič Fedotov,* Leningrad and Moscow, Izdatel'stvu "Iskusstvu" (1946) p. 78 ff.

121: Louisa Kathleen Haldane, *Friends and Kindred, Memoirs,* London (1961) p. 36.

122: For further discussion of this fertile tradition, see Herman Kasten, *Dichter in Café,* Wäln-Munich-Basel (1959); M. Bazzetta de Veminia, *I caffè storici d'Italia da Torino a Napoli,* Milan (1939); Enrico Falgin, *Caffè letterari,* Rome (1963); and the chapter "Les cafés" in H. Clouzot and R. H. Valensi, *Le Paris de la Comédie Humaine,* Paris (1926).

123: *Cf.* Carl V. Petersen, *Italien i Dansk Malerkunst,* Copenhagen (1932) p. 17.

124: This identification is taken from the volume *Rom og Danmark gennen*

tiderne, edited by Louis Bobé, Copenhagen (1935) Vol. II, pp. 220, 224, where there is also further information about the Roman taverns frequented by these artists.

125: On Viennese café life in the Biedermeier period see chapter "Im Wirtshaus bin i wia z' Hans" in Ann Tizia Leitich, *Wiener Biedermeier,* Bielefeld and Leipzig (1941).

126: Two versions of the picture exist, the one reproduced here and another which can be seen in Paul Weiglin's *Berliner Biedermeier,* Bielefeld and Leipzig (1942) Plate XXX. In this alternate version the wallpaper of the room is different from the version reproduced here (there is a pattern of red circles and little squares), the portrait is to the left instead of the right and in its place there is a mirror in which the lamp is reflected, creating a different play of light. On the table where the lamp stands the objects are different in the two pictures, and the chess pieces are in a different arrangement. The position of the people, however, is identical.

127: Luigi Salerno, who in 1954 edited a handsome volume for the Italian State Tobacco monopoly, *Tobacco e fumo nella pittura,* overlooked this picture but included the less relevant *Danish Artists in Rome* by Constantin Hansen.

128: *Cf.* Emil Hannover, *Maleren Constantin Hansen,* Copenhagen (1901) pp. 71-73.

129: The étagère is similar and illustrated in Ferdinand Luthmer and Robert Schmidt, *Empire- und Biedermeiermöbel aus Schlössern und Burgerhäusern,* Stuttgart (1922) Plate 82b, where it is dated "circa 1815."

130: Diego Angeli, in his index to the volume *I Bonaparte a Roma,* Milan (1938) erroneously places the Tolentino palace under Rome.

131: On the first collectors of primitives see Francis Steegmuller, *The Two Lives of James Jackson Jarves,* New Haven (1951).

132: On Dutch interior decoration in the 19th century there exists a volume (unfortunately out of print) by Petra Clarijs, *Een Eeuw nederlandse Woning*, Amsterdam (1941) with precise information concerning the change of taste in the course of the century. For the first part of the century one can also see *Het Tijdperk van de Camera Obscura, Kunst en Leven van 1800-1850*, by H. E. van Gelder, F.W.S. van Thienen, D. F. Lunsingh, L. Wÿsenbeek, The Hague (1940). The title of this book "The Period of the Camera Obscura," was taken from the title of a collection of stories by the Dutch writer Nicolaas Beets (1814-1903) published in 1839 and revised in 1851, Beets' little pieces were of a humorous and moralizing nature whose sound realism was absolutely Biedermeier.

133: Chopin was a maker of lamps *à couronne* supported on black bronze figures. His atelier was at 257 rue Saint-Denis, Paris. The crown supporting the globe of his lamps was hollow and served as a tank for combustible liquid which, through the two tubes supporting the crown, fed the wick. See D'Allemagne, *Histoire du luminaire*, p. 508.

134: *Cf. Het Tijdperk van de Camera Obscura, Kunst en Leven van 1800-1850*, cited in note 132.

134a: *Cf.* Jörg Gamer, "Die Gemächer der Grossherzogin Stephanie im Mannheimer Schloss", in *Mannheimer Hefte* (1968 (2)).

135: Gerald Heard. *Narcissus, an Anatomy of Clothes*, London (1924); James Lever, *Style in Costume*, London (1949).

136: See M. Praz, *Bellezza e bizzarria*, Milan (1960) pp. 42, 67, 91.

137: See M. Praz, "The Epic of the Everyday. Coventry Patmore's 'The Angel in the House'" in *The Hero in Eclipse in Victorian Fiction*, London (1956) pp. 422–423.

138: Another version, formerly at the Schackgalerie in Munich, shows small variations: one does not see the stool near the open window, and the bird cage, basin and pitcher seen in the Darmstadt version are missing.

139: Fritz Laufer, *op. cit.*

140: For the history of English furniture in the 19th century see: Elizabeth Aslin, *Nineteenth Century English Furniture*, London (1962); R. W. Symonds and B. B. Wineray, *Victorian Furniture*, London (1962).

141: On the Villa Acton, designed by the architect Pietro Valente with alterations by Guglielmo Bechi, who decorated the interiors, *cf.* Rinaldo Vendetti, *Architectura neoclassica a Napoli*, Naples (1961) p. 184 ff.

142: Diego Angeli, *Roma romantica*, Milan (1935).

143: See the essay "La donna gotica" in my volume, *Fiori freshi*, on the subject of C. Willett Cunnington, *Feminine Attitudes in the Nineteenth Century*. London (1935).

144: Reproduced in Camille Recht, *Die alte Photographie*, Paris and Leipzig (1931).

145: See the article "Le décor de la vie sous Napoleon III," in *Connaissance des Arts* (October 15, 1954).

146: The base of this *torchère* cannot be seen in the painting but it was certainly formed by three lion paws. Generally the upper part of such *torchères* (the brackets for the candles) was detachable and could also be applied to a candelabra.

147: *Cf.* Hélène Demoraine, "Le Louis XVI qu'aimait Eugénie," in *Connaissance des Arts* (Oct. 1961).

148: Reproduced in color on p. 59 in *Le dix-neuvième siècle français*, Stephane Faniel, general editor, *Collection Connaissance des Arts*, Paris (1959).

149: Reproduced in Hélène Demoraine, *op. cit.*

150: See Pierre Verlet, *Le Mobilier royal français*, Paris (1953) p. 73, where the piece is minutely described.

151: It is true that Jerome Napoleon tried to oppose the Empress' favorite style with a neo-Pompeiian decoration in his house in Avenue Montaigne, which he commissioned from the architect Charles Rossigneux, 1818-1907. This style, however, had no following in decoration, although it enjoyed some vogue in the field of painting. On these vicissitudes of taste see Henri Clouzot, *Le Style Louis-Philippe—Napoleon III*, Paris (1939).

152: Quoted from Henri Clouzot, *op. cit.*

153: See P.-André Lemoisne, *Eugène Lami*, Paris (1912).

154: *Cf.* Lemoisne, *op. cit.* p. 151.

155: Philippe Jullian, *op. cit.*

156: Compare this picture with the episode in chapter XXIII of *The Way of All Flesh*, where Theobald Pontifex thrashes his son for no reason, then assembles the servants for prayers.

157: Alexander du Sommerard (1779–1842) formed the collection which was sold to the state and became the nucleus of the Musée de Cluny, Paris. On du Sommerard see H. Clouzot and R. H. Vanensi, *Le Paris de la Comédie Humaine*, p. 90.

158: See the chapter "Der Zauber in der Gusshausstrasse" in Ann Tizia Leitich, *Verklungenes Wien, vom Biedermeier zur Jahrhundertwende*, Vienna (1942).

159: In Italy, instead of the large paintings of Makart, there were the little pictures of Fortuny. See Silvio Negro "Ricordo di Fortuny" in *Roma non basta una vita*, Venice (1962) especially p. 55.

160: Among the people present at this meeting, in addition to Dumba, are Kaspar Clemens, Zumbusch, Victor Oskar Tilgner (architect), Scharff, and Rudolf von Alt.

161: *Cf.* M. Praz, *La Casa della Vita*, pp. 227–230.

162: Hugh Honour, *op. cit.* p. 218.

163: See on the subject of this "historical eclecticism" at the end of the 19th century the witty chapter with this title in Philippe Jullian, *op. cit.*, p. 134.

164: André Chastel, *Vuillard*, Paris (1946) p. 28.

165: Duranty's essay is contained in E. Duranty, *La Nouvelle Peinture*, Paris (1876), new edition Paris (1946), edited by Marcel Guérin, pp. 44–48.

166: *Cf.* André Chastel, *op. cit.* p. 48.

167: *Ibid.*, p. 58.

168: Viollet-le-Duc praised this building in the second volume of his *Entretiens sur l'architecture*, 2 Vols., Paris (1863, 1872) [translations: *Discourses on Architecture*, 2 Vols., Boston (1875–1881) and *Lectures on Architecture*, 2 Vols., London (1877, 1881)], supplemented with other examples of constructions in iron and masonry; one of them, with an iron frame and brilliantly colored enameled squares, was illustrated by a color plate. The example of this plate proved to be contagious.

169: Henry Russel Hitchcock, *Architecture, Nineteenth and Twentieth Centuries*, The Pelican History of Art (1958) p. 287.

170: Verticality is a recurrent characteristic in the whole of English art. On this see Nikolaus Pevsner, *The Englishness of English Art*, New York (1956).

171: On this and other factories of New Style furniture, see E. Aslin, *op. cit.* p. 74 ff.

172: Claude Monet during World War I celebrated the water lily in his famous swampy frieze in his property at Giverny.

INDEX

INDEX